T0298615

CONTESTED AGRONOMY

The dramatic increases in food prices experienced over the past four years, and their effects on hunger and food insecurity, as well as human-induced climate change and its implications for agriculture, food production, food security and poverty, are key topics within the field of agronomy and agricultural research.

This is a subject that is yet again near the top of the development agenda, and is particularly relevant in the face of population growth, climate-induced environmental change, land degradation and the loss of agricultural biological diversity. Whether the focus is on small-scale or commercial, agro-ecological or input-intensive agricultural systems, agronomic research is one of the keys to a more sustainable and equitable future.

Contested Agronomy: Agricultural Research in a Changing World addresses this issue, exploring the three key developments since the mid-1970s – the emergence of the neoliberal project, and the rise of the participation and environmental agendas – and considering their profound impacts on the practice of agronomic research in the developing world – especially over the past four decades.

Through a series of case studies, the book explores the basis for a much needed 'political agronomy' analysis that highlights the impacts of problem framing and narratives, historical disjunctures, epistemic communities and the increasing pressure to demonstrate 'success' on both agricultural research and the farmers, processors and consumers it is meant to serve.

While a fascinating and thought-provoking read for professionals in agriculture and environmental sciences, it will also appeal to students and researchers wanting to understand more about this essential topic in agronomy, agricultural science and agricultural policy.

James Sumberg completed his postgraduate training in crop improvement in 1978. Since then, he has worked as a plant breeder, agronomist, natural resources specialist and research director, with a particular focus on West Africa. Before joining the Knowledge, Technology and Society Team of the Institute of Development Studies at the University of Sussex, UK as a Research Fellow in 2009, he taught at the University of East Anglia and was Director of Programmes at the New Economics Foundation. His research interests are the dynamics of change within smallholder agriculture in Africa and agricultural research policy.

John Thompson has worked on agricultural science, sustainability and policy issues since 1982, with a particular focus on East Africa. A resource geographer with a BSc from Pennsylvania State University and MA and PhD from Clark University, USA, he was Director of Programmes and Director of the Sustainable Agriculture Programme at the International Institute of Environment and Development, London. He joined the Institute of Development Studies in 2006 as a Research Fellow in Knowledge, Technology and Society, where he serves as Joint Coordinator of the DFID-funded Future Agricultures Consortium and Co-Convenor of the Food and Agriculture Domain of the ESRC-funded Centre for Social Technological and Environmental Pathways to Sustainability (STEPS) Centre.

Pathways to Sustainability

This book series addresses core challenges around linking science and technology and environmental sustainability with poverty reduction and social justice. It is based on the work of the Social, Technological and Environmental Pathways to Sustainability (STEPS) Centre, a major investment of the UK Economic and Social Research Council (ESRC). The STEPS Centre brings together researchers at the Institute of Development Studies (IDS) and Science and Technology Policy Research (SPRU) at the University of Sussex with a set of partner institutions in Africa, Asia and Latin America.

Series Editors:
Melissa Leach, Ian Scoones and Andy Stirling
STEPS Centre at the University of Sussex
Editorial Advisory Board:
Steve Bass, Wiebe E. Bijker, Victor Galaz, Wenzel Geissler, Katherine Homewood, Sheila Jasanoff, Colin McInnes, Suman Sahai, Andrew Scott

Other titles include:

Dynamic Sustainabilities
Technology, Environment, Social Justice
Melissa Leach, Ian Scoones and Andy Stirling

Avian Influenza
Science, Policy and Politics
Edited by Ian Scoones

Rice Biofortification
Lessons for Global Science and Development
Sally Brooks

Epidemics
Science, Governance and Social Justice
Edited by Sarah Dry and Melissa Leach

CONTESTED AGRONOMY

Agricultural Research in a Changing World

Edited by
James Sumberg and John Thompson

Routledge
Taylor & Francis Group

NEW YORK AND LONDON

First published 2012
by Routledge
2 Park Square, Milton Park, Abingdon, Oxon OX14 4RN

Simultaneously published in the USA and Canada
by Routledge
711 Third Avenue, New York, NY 10017

Routledge is an imprint of the Taylor & Francis Group, an informa business

British Library Cataloguing in Publication Data
A catalogue record for this book is available from the British Library

Library of Congress Cataloging in Publication Data
Contested agronomy : agricultural research in a changing world / [edited] by
James Sumberg and John Thompson.
p. cm.
1. Agriculture--Research--Political aspects. 2. Agronomy--Research--Political
aspects. 3. Agriculture--Research--Social aspects. 4. Agronomy--Research--
Social aspects. 5. Agriculture and state. I. Sumberg, J. E. II. Thompson, John,
1959 Feb. 4-
S540.A2C666 2012
630.72--dc23
2011036639

ISBN: 978-0-415-69806-1 (hbk)
ISBN: 978-0-415-50714-1 (pbk)
ISBN: 978-0-203-12844-1 (ebk)

Typeset in Bembo
by Taylor & Francis Books

CONTENTS

ABBREVIATIONS

ACIAR	Australian Centre for International Agricultural Research
ADB	Asian Development Bank
ADE	anthropogenic dark earths
AGRA	Alliance for a Green Revolution in Africa
AHI	African Highlands Initiative
AKST	agricultural knowledge, science and technology
ARDAP	appropriate rural development agricultural programme
ASB	alternatives to slash-and-burn
BMGF	Bill & Melinda Gates Foundation
BRC	Biopesticides Research Consortium
CA	Conservation Agriculture
CAADP	Comprehensive Africa Agricultural Development Programme
CAWT	Conservation Agriculture with trees
CBD	Convention on Biodiversity
CEE	Centre for Environment Education
CF	conservation farming
CGIAR	Consultative Group on International Agricultural Research
CIAT	International Centre for Tropical Agriculture
CIMMYT	International Centre for Maize and Wheat Research
CIRAD	Centre de coopération internationale en recherche agronomique pour le développement
CSA	Centre for Sustainable Agriculture
CWS	Centre for World Solidarity
DAP	diammonium phosphate
DDT	dichlorodiphenyltrichloroethane
DRR	Directorate of Rice Research
EU	European Union

FAO	Food and Agriculture Organization of the UN
FEI	Folk Ecology Initiative
FFS	farmer field school
FIPS	Farm Inputs Promotion Services
G×E	genotype × environment interaction
GFAR	Global Forum for Agricultural Research
GTZ	Deutsche Gesellschaft für Technische Zusammenarbeit
IAASTD	International Assessment of Agricultural Knowledge, Science and Technology for Development
IAE	Institute of Agricultural Engineering
IARI	Indian Agricultural Research Institute
IBI	International Biochar Initiative
ICAR	Indian Council for Agricultural Research
ICRAF	World Agroforestry Centre
ICRISAT	International Crops Research Institute for the Semi-Arid tropics
ICT	information and communication technology
IDRC	International Development Research Centre
IFPRI	International Food Policy Research Institute
IGP	Indo-Gangetic Plains
IHNF	Institute of Human Nutrition and Food, University of the Philippines Los Baños
INRA	Institut national de la recherche agronomique
IPM	integrated pest management
IPR	intellectual property regime
IRRI	International Rice Research Institute
ITPGRFA	International Treaty on Plant Genetic Resources for Food and Agriculture
KAPP	Kenya Agricultural Productivity Project
KARI	Kenya Agricultural Research institute
KEFRI	Kenya Forestry Research institute
N	nitrogen
NERICA	New Rice for Africa
NGO	non-governmental organisation
NPM	Non-Pesticidal Management
OFSP	orange-fleshed sweet potato
P	phosphorus
PLSN	US Federal Plant, Soil and Nutrition Laboratory
PM&E	participatory monitoring and evaluation
PRP	Protracted Relief Programme (DFID)
QPM	quality protein maize
R&D	research and development
RAWE	rural agricultural work experience programme
Rs.	Indian rupi
RWC	Rice–Wheat Consortium

SAP	Structural Adjustment Programme
SCOBICS	sustainable community-based input credit scheme
SERP	Society for the Elimination of Rural Poverty
SOC	soil organic carbon
SOM	soil organic matter
SRI	System of Rice Intensification
SRISTI	Society for Research and initiatives for Sustainable Technologies and Institutions
SSA	sub-Saharan Africa
SWC	soil and water conservation
T&V	training-and-visit extension system
TSBF	Tropical Soil Biology and Fertility Institute
TSP	triple super-phosphate
UNICEF	United Nations Children's Fund
USAID	US Agency for International Development
ZCATF	Zimbabwe Conservation Agriculture Taskforce
ZT	zero tillage

CONTRIBUTORS

Elisabeth Adams is Food and Agriculture Convenor, Knowledge Service Department, Institute of Development Studies, UK

Kojo Amanor is a Professor in the Institute of African Studies, University of Ghana, Legon, Ghana

Jens Andersson is a Senior Lecturer in the Plant Production Systems Group, Wageningen University, the Netherlands

Sally Brooks is a Visiting Fellow at the Science and Technology Policy Research Unit, University of Sussex, UK

Olaf Erenstein is a socio-economist at the International Maize and Wheat Improvement Center, Addis Ababa, Ethiopia

James Fairhead is a Professor of Anthropology, School of Global Studies, University of Sussex, UK

Ken Giller is a Professor in the Plant Production Systems Group, Wageningen University, the Netherlands

Dominic Glover is a Post-Doctoral Fellow in the Technology and Agrarian Development Group, Wageningen University, the Netherlands

Robin Irving works at the Sail and Life Training Society, Victoria, Canada

Sarah Johnson-Beebout is Deputy Division Head and Soil Chemist, Crop and Environmental Sciences Division, International Rice Research Institute, the Philippines

Melissa Leach is a Professorial Fellow and Co-Director of the STEPS Centre, Institute of Development Studies, UK

Harro Maat is a University Lecturer in the Technology and Agrarian Development Group, Wageningen University, the Netherlands

Jacques Pollini works for the University of Hamburg as Scientific Coordinator of the Sustainable Land Management Project, Toliara

G.V. Ramanjaneyulu is Executive Director at the Centre for Sustainable Agriculture, Taranka, India

Joshua Ramisch is an Associate Professor in the School of International Development & Global Studies, University of Ottawa, Canada

O.P. Rupela is an independent consultant and was a Principal Scientist at the International Crops Research Institute for the Semi-Arid Tropics, India

C. Shambu Prasad is a Professor at the Xavier Institute of Management, India

James Sumberg is a Research Fellow at the Institute of Development Studies, UK

T.M. Thiyagarajan is an independent consultant and was Dean, Tamil Nadu Agricultural University, Coimbatore, India

Amod Thakur is a Principal Scientist at the Directorate of Water Management, Bhubaneswar, India

John Thompson is a Research Fellow at the Institute of Development Studies, UK

Philip Woodhouse is a Senior Lecturer in the School of Environment and Development, University of Manchester, UK

ACKNOWLEDGEMENTS

This book is the product of an international workshop organised by the STEPS Centre at the University of Sussex. STEPS stands for Social, Technological and Environmental Pathways to Sustainability, and the Centre acts as a hub for a wide range of international research and engagement collaborations thanks to funding from the Economic and Social Research Council. We are very grateful to our STEPS colleagues and collaborators for their support and inputs to this book.

The STEPS Centre Directors, Melissa Leach, Ian Scoones and Andy Stirling, have been supportive throughout and a helpful source of counsel and encouragement. We also gratefully acknowledge the valuable assistance of Jas Vaghadia and Elisabeth Adams.

1

CONTESTED AGRONOMY

Agricultural research in a changing world

James Sumberg, John Thompson and Philip Woodhouse

Introduction

The 'food crisis' of 2007–08 and record food commodity prices in 2010–11 have renewed interest in questions about agricultural productivity, and reinforce the recent emphasis on agricultural development as a key to economic, social and environmental improvement (e.g. World Bank 2007). This is particularly so in sub-Saharan Africa (SSA), where poor agricultural performance is often seen as a driver of high and persistent levels of rural poverty and food insecurity (Dorward et al 2004; Diao et al 2010; cf. Wiggins 2009) and environmental degradation (Abalu 1998; Mbow et al 2008). The renewed interest in agriculture is underlined by government commitments through the African Union's Comprehensive Africa Agriculture Development Programme (CAADP), the emergence of new funders such as the Bill & Melinda Gates Foundation, high-profile initiatives such as the Alliance for a Green Revolution in Africa (AGRA) (Toenniessen et al 2008), and a rapid rise in commercial investment in African farmland (Cotula et al 2009; Zoomers 2010).

This context brings to the fore the critical role of research in developing and sustaining productive agricultural systems, regardless of whether those systems are described as small-scale or commercial, agro-ecological or input-intensive (World Bank 2007; McIntyre et al 2009; Poulton 2009; Barrett et al 2010). While there is much debate about priorities, methods and the interplay of different knowledges, the need for investment in research is recognised across the political and ideological divides that inform different approaches to agriculture and rural development.

Agronomy is a core element of agricultural research. While there are different currents and traditions within agronomy, it can be most broadly conceived of as a scientific and intellectual endeavour that seeks to understand and affect the biological, ecological, physical, socio-cultural and economic bases of crop production and land management. More narrowly, and particularly within the anglophone tradition, agronomy is usually understood to be the application of plant and soil science to crop production.

Agronomic research is, by and large, an applied and practical undertaking, and research agronomists are only occasionally in the political or media spotlight. Nevertheless, in this chapter we call for a distinctly political analysis of present-day agronomic research in the developing world, and sketch out the terrain that such an analysis should occupy. Our argument is that 'political agronomy' analysis is particularly relevant today because of three key developments since the mid-1970s – (i) the promotion of the neoliberal project; (ii) the emergence of the environmental movement; and (iii) the rise of the participation agenda in agricultural research. We contend that over the past four decades these developments have radically transformed the context within which agronomic research in the developing world takes place. This not only has profound consequences for the practice of agronomic research, but also has opened up new spaces for contestation over the goals and priorities for agricultural research.

The remainder of this chapter is divided into three parts. In the next section, we develop the elements of the argument set out above on the changing context of agronomic research. In the remaining two parts, we trace some of the main contours of a political agronomy approach, and sketch the beginnings of a research agenda to allow for a more systematic and in-depth examination of the clash of epistemologies, priorities and approaches now emerging in the field and their consequences for policy and practice.

Before proceeding, three caveats are required. First, as will become evident in the next section, our identification of a disjuncture since the mid-1970s is not to suggest that agronomic research existed outside the political arena prior to the rise of neoliberal, environmental and participation agendas. Indeed, there is a significant body of scholarship focused on the political economy of agricultural research both before and after the implementation of the neoliberal project (Busch 1981; Hadwiger 1982; Buttel and Busch 1988). Rather, we argue that the 1970s saw the end of a half-century dominated by state-led programmes of agricultural modernisation that had largely defined the economic and institutional (political) relationships between science and agricultural production in industrialised and developing economies alike. We argue that these relationships have changed profoundly in the ensuing four decades, and the present juncture is an opportune moment for systematic analysis of *the politics of contemporary, everyday agronomic research in the developing world* because such an analysis has the potential to influence the emerging trajectories of agricultural development.

Second, this analysis is not driven by a desire to denigrate or dismiss agronomic research or agronomists, whether they are working in the public sector, agro-industry, the Consultative Group on International Agricultural Research (CGIAR) or anywhere else. Rather, our objective is to understand better their responses to the changing opportunities, challenges and incentives they face.

Finally, our focus on the politics of formal agronomic research should not be read either as signalling acceptance of a simple linear model of agricultural technology development, or as denial of the importance of farmer knowledge, experimentation and agency. Our analysis is underpinned by a systems of innovation perspective

(Hall et al 2001) that views formal agronomic research as but one (important) part of a rich, interactive picture in which producers, service providers and others are intimately involved in knowledge generation and innovation processes, and where technology choice decisions are iterative, contingent and socially embedded (Scoones and Thompson 1994, 2009).

The contested agronomy argument

Agronomy and the state

The political economy of agricultural research *per se* is not our main focus here, but it forms an important part of the backdrop to the contested agronomy argument. Until the mid- to late twentieth century, formal agronomic research in both the developed and developing worlds took place largely within state-funded institutions (universities, ministries and research institutes) (Ruttan 1982). In this sense, agronomic research was very much *of the state*, with a role of supporting the state's economic, political and social policy agendas through the generation of practical knowledge and applied technology. It should not be surprising, therefore, that agronomy as an academic discipline developed as a normative, applied and practically oriented field.

Agronomic research as 'state intervention' (Dale 1981) operated at a variety of levels to support policy objectives, including state security, the consolidation of state boundaries, colonial expansion and exploitation, 'cheap food' and agricultural modernisation. For example, agronomic research was critical to the industrialisation project of the Japanese government from the start of the Meiji period in 1868. Following a decade of failed attempts to introduce farm machinery from the USA and UK, the Japanese state sought to expand food supply for the growing industrial workforce by embarking on an entirely different technological trajectory. This was a programme of cereal seed selection and improvement that, by the 1930s, had created the basis for the technology known three decades later as the Green Revolution (cf. Hayami and Ruttan 1985: 231–52).

In the USA, state-supported agricultural research fostered the development of capitalist agriculture dominated by agribusiness (e.g. Hightower 1973; Busch 1981), as exemplified by case studies of the Heinz and Campbell's Soup corporations (Dale 1981; Kloppenburg 1988). While the outputs of this research disproportionately benefited better-capitalised farmers – and made the survival of smaller-scale farms increasingly difficult – the framework of state-funded research enabled researchers to cloak themselves in 'professional neutrality' and 'scientific objectivity' in the service of 'progressive or inevitable' agricultural modernisation.

From the work of Bonneuil (2000) and others, it is clear that science in the form of agronomic research on experimental stations throughout colonial Africa, much of which focused on export or industrial crops destined for Europe, was a critical component of strategic colonial-era projects such as the Gezira Scheme in Sudan, the East African Groundnut Scheme, the Niger Agricultural Project in Nigeria's Middle Belt (Baldwin 1957) and the Office du Niger. With the objective of producing raw materials to fuel European industrial expansion (e.g. groundnuts) and to cut historical inter-European dependencies (e.g. cotton) and European dependence on America (e.g. for vegetable oil; Franke and Chasin 1980), these were political projects in every sense.

Agronomists also played a critical role in the development and promotion of 'mixed farming' as a model for agricultural development in SSA. Initially framed as a response to soil erosion and deforestation, mixed farming soon became an overarching framework for the spatial, social and economic reorganisation of the African countryside, including an explicit goal of creating and supporting a new class of 'peasant farmers' (Sumberg 1998; Wolmer and Scoones 2000). It is true that, while adapting the pieces of the mixed farming model that met their needs and rejecting others, farmers both resisted the state's advances and exercised their agency. Nevertheless, it is impossible to escape the conclusion that agronomists and agronomic research were at the heart of the colonial states' political and social agendas (cf. Bonneuil 2000).

In the period after World War II (in Europe and the USA) and after independence (in Africa and Asia), agronomic research operated within a policy context – including national food security, modernisation, productivity enhancement and increased competitiveness – framed by recent histories of wartime disruption of trade and continuing tensions of the Cold War. This context provided agronomic research with routine, uncontroversial justifications, such as the need to address hunger and the supply of cheap food for a rapidly growing world population, but also with imperatives to serve ideological and strategic geopolitical goals (Thompson and Scoones 2009). Here our central contention is that, because of the historical context in which agronomy developed as a field of academic study and a practical, problem-solving science – one in which national governments unified both funding and priorities of research according to public policy objectives – agronomic research experienced a long period during which scope for contention about priorities, objectives, methods or the meaning of success was narrowly circumscribed by norms of a largely apolitical, professionalised 'scientific' discipline. As outlined in the following section, however, the long-standing unity of purpose between government policy and agronomic objectives, which dominated the politics of agricultural science for much of the past century, has slowly been eroded, both in practice and in policy debates about the priorities for agricultural research and development.

A changing context

Our argument focuses on three related developments that, over time, have radically changed the context within which agronomic research takes place. The neoliberal, environmental and participation agendas emerged as responses to growing criticisms of state-led development as inefficient, environmentally damaging and undemocratic. While each of these has influenced broader discourses in development, their effects on contestation within agronomy have been particularly significant, sometimes in unexpected ways. Although these struggles over the meaning, purpose and priorities of agricultural research have been recognised in some quarters, until now the consequences of these clashes have not been examined systematically.

The neoliberal project

We use the term 'neoliberal project' to refer to the wave of economic liberalisation and reform that emerged in the USA in the late 1970s and early 1980s and, as the overtly hegemonic 'Washington Consensus', was subsequently imposed throughout much of the developing world and post-Cold War Europe (Chang, 2009).

A guiding principle of the neoliberal agenda was that markets are the most efficient way of allocating resources and hence of achieving the greatest public good. Efficient markets required legally enforced property rights and elimination of barriers to trade. The effects on state-funded agricultural research and development in many developing countries came in the 1980s, when deficits in public budgets forced governments to agree Structural Adjustment Programmes (SAPs) with the World Bank and International Monetary Fund. In addition to exchange rate and fiscal reforms, the SAPs followed the Berg Report's (1981) analysis that state provision and/or subsidisation of agri-cultural inputs and services – research, extension services, irrigation, fertilisers, seeds, credit and so on – caused inefficiencies, distortions and corruption, while putting an unsustainable burden on state finances. Consequently, state agencies providing these were targeted for reform or privatisation and any subsidy elements eliminated or radically reduced. State involvement in agricultural marketing (e.g. through marketing boards that set minimum prices) and processing was also curtailed (Bates 1981; cf. Sandbrook 1985).

In one important respect, the neoliberal project directly and significantly affected agronomy research via changes to intellectual property rights. Beginning in the 1960s, the laws in Europe and the USA governing crop variety protection were strengthened, reflecting a more global evolution of the regimes governing intellectual property rights (Tansey and Rajotte 2008). These changes incentivised greater private-sector investment in crop improvement. When combined with the revolution in cell biology and bio-engineering, which were themselves stimulated by the new intellectual property regimes (IPRs), the growing role of private-sector crop breeding set the stage for restructuring and consolidation of the agro-inputs industry (Bijman 2001). The fact that some of the most widely grown genetically modified crop varieties were engineered to be used exclusively with one specific herbicide product illustrates the extent of this consolidation (Wield et al 2010).

The environmental agenda

While there is considerable debate about the roots of the modern environmental movement (Kuzmiak 1991; Barton 2001), in terms of its eventual focus on agriculture, the publication of Rachel Carson's *Silent Spring* in 1962 was a significant landmark that drew public attention to the ecological damage associated with widespread use of the synthetic insecticide dichlorodiphenyltrichloroethane or DDT (Carson 1962). In so doing, Carson set the stage for a broader interrogation of the environmental and health impacts of the chemical-intensive, large-scale farming operations that state-funded research had supported in the pursuit of 'cheap food'.

In the developing world, the Sahel droughts of the late 1960s and early 1970s – and the spectre of the desert marching south to the Guinea coast – cast doubt on the ability of these environments to support conventional models of agricultural intensification. In response, there was renewed research and development interest in alternatives involving indigenous soil and water conservation (Scoones et al 1996), agroforestry (Nair 1991; Kessler and Breman 1991), local crop varieties (Richards 1986) and irrigation (Moris and Thom 1990).

In Asia, concerns were being raised about environmental and related health consequences of the Green Revolution by the 1980s, including water pollution from fertiliser use, waterlogging and soil salinisation, biodiversity loss and human poisoning associated with pesticide use (Loevinsohn 1987; Pimentel and Pimentel 1990; Pingali and Rosengrant 1994). These apprehensions, combined with a growing perception that the Green Revolution had gained limited ground in marginal areas, fuelled interest in a number of related alternatives including agro-ecology (Conway 1985) and 'low external-input' farming (Reijntes et al 1992; Tripp 2005). As with the organic movement in developed countries, these alternatives were frequently shunned by mainstream agronomists, but the promise of a more environmentally friendly agriculture made them attractive to some NGOs and some funders (De Jager et al 2001; Reij and Waters-Bayer 2001; cf. Low 1994).

The rapid spread of Green Revolution crop varieties in Asia, events such as the 1970 epidemic of southern corn leaf blight in the USA (Tatum 1971), and the signing of the 1993 Convention on Biological Diversity drew attention to risks associated with narrowing the crop genetic resource base (Pistorius 1997). Maintenance of agro-biodiversity, particularly in marginal areas where crop genetic diversity was seen to be a key to local adaptation strategies, soon became an important plank of the environmental agenda. The International Treaty on Plant Genetic Resources for Food and Agriculture (ITPGRFA) in 2004 established a system to facilitate access to seed of over 64 major food crops and forages.[1] In what may be seen as a response to the use of IPRs to control access to seeds, the ITPGRFA recognises farmers' role in conservation and development of plant genetic resources in the form of 'farmers' rights', which include the protection of traditional knowledge and the right to participate equitably in benefit-sharing and in national decision-making about plant genetic resources. These arguments about agro-biodiversity lie at the heart of legal and economic relations between people and the crop genetic resources that they develop and use (e.g. Pimbert 1999), and are likely to intensify as agriculture is forced to adapt to climate change (Kotschi 2007).

The participation agenda

The role of the participation agenda in changing the context of agronomic research had two distinct aspects. The first, rooted in populist calls for a shift in the relations between state bureaucracy, elite social groups and the poor, was inspired by works such as Paulo Freire's *Pedagogy of the Oppressed* (2007) and framed in terms of social justice, rights and empowerment (Chambers and Ghildyal 1985; Chambers 1993; Chambers

1997; cf. Cornwall 2003). The second aspect marked a convergence with the neo-liberal agenda to reduce 'inefficient' state power through promotion of administrative decentralisation and the use of market mechanisms to deliver services to the poor (Leal 2007). Here, people become 'stakeholders', and participation has much more to do with efficient development management than with emancipation and justice (Cooke 2003). This ambiguity, coupled with the rapid permeation of participatory rhetoric throughout development policy, led to questions about its emancipatory potential (Gow and Vansant 1983; Weyland 1996; Cooke and Kothari 2001).

For agronomic research, the participation agenda has been highly significant. A view that the Green Revolution had widened the gap between richer and poorer rural people (Pearse 1980), and had provided few benefits for people in 'low-potential' areas, highlighted claims about the irrelevance of research-generated technologies and a rising hostility to anything that smacked of technology transfer or so-called top-down and blueprint approaches to development. This set the stage for a sustained attack on agricultural research and researchers (Richards 1985), and the norms and values of agronomists' 'normal professionalism' as being those of elites, cut off from rural realities, ill-informed and lacking interest in or respect for local people and their indigenous knowledge (Chambers 1986, 1993, 1997). It is important to note, however, the disjuncture between this critique and studies of the economic returns to invest-ment in agricultural research in the developing world and farmers' use of technologies produced by formal research, even in SSA (e.g. Maredia et al 2000; Dalton and Guei 2003; Raitzer and Kelley 2008; Maredia and Raitzer 2010).

These critiques, and the earlier (somewhat disappointing) experience of trying to frame research priorities from farmers' perspectives through farming systems research (Biggs 1995; cf. Collinson 2000), helped fuel a new interest in 'farmer participatory research' (Okali et al 1994), 'participatory technology development' (Haverkort et al 1991), and many other 'farmer-first' approaches (Chambers et al 1989; Scoones and Thompson 1994; Scoones and Thompson 2009). In practice, farmer participatory research laboured under confused objectives (e.g. making research more effective; co-producing knowledge; validating new technologies; empowering the rural poor). Although there have been sustained efforts to develop more inclusive approaches to crop improvement through 'participatory plant breeding' (Almekinders and Elings 2001; Sperling et al 2001), too often 'participatory research' simply reproduced con-ventional on-farm trials prefaced by a 'participatory rural appraisal' exercise (Okali et al 1994; Thompson and Scoones 1994).

In Latin America, there was considerable emphasis on the development of mechanisms that would give farmers more control over the agricultural research that was supposed to be benefiting them (Ashby et al 2000). In SSA, the participation agenda highlighted women's role in agriculture and natural resource management, the need for researchers to take better account of intra-household dynamics (Moock 1986), and the need to empower women vis-à-vis agricultural research (Sperling and Berkowitz 1994). The neoliberal interest in participation was manifest in pressure on agricultural research organisations to become more 'client-oriented'. One hope was that, if agricultural research was able to prove its worth to its 'clients', farmers would be willing to carry more of the financial burden of research, thus opening the way for further state withdrawal and creation of a market for agricultural innovation. In the event, there was little movement in this direction, at least as far as poor farmers and staple food crops were concerned.

More recently, the participation agenda has been associated with the emergence in Latin America, Asia and to a lesser extent in SSA of rural social movements campaigning on issues such as landlessness, corporate control over agricultural technology (e.g. anti-GM) and 'food sovereignty' (Akram-Lodhi 2007; McMichael 2008; Patel 2009; Teubal 2009). These movements' demands on agricultural and rural policy have extended to the orientation and oversight of agronomy and agricultural research. The reach of the rural social movements has been greatly aided by the information, technology and communication revolution, which is creating new opportunities and spaces for debate and organising, including by some seeking to gain recognition as legitimate stakeholders in relation to agronomic research (Shambu Prasad and Sen 2010).

Impacts on agronomic research

The changes in context outlined above have had important direct and indirect impacts on everyday agronomic research. The nature and extent of these impacts have varied tremendously across regions, countries and commodities, depending on agronomic traditions, the policy environment and the size and coherence (and level of dependency on development assistance) of the agricultural research system. Structural Adjustment Programmes – a key instrument of the neoliberal project in the developing world – couched efforts to 'reform' and 'strengthen' public-sector agricultural research in terms of improving efficiency and accountability (to both funders and clients), translating to rationalisation of objectives and programmes, reduced numbers of experimental stations, reduced staffing levels and new incentive structures, and strengthened management (Berg 1981; Byerlee 1998; Byerlee and Alex 1998).

In those developing countries where there has been increasing private-sector investment in agricultural research (Naseem et al 2010), the public sector has been forced to rethink its role, commonly seeking justification in terms of the provision of 'public goods' in the face of market failure. The geographical scale of this language of public goods ranges from 'local' through to CGIAR's ambitions to create 'global public goods' (Anderson 1998; Gardner and Lesser 2003; Lele and Gerrard 2003; Harwood et al 2006).

The new context highlights questions about partnerships and alliances. Increasing prominence of the language of 'public–private partnerships' – as seen for example within the CGIAR – clearly reflects shifting institutional, funding and political landscapes (Spielman et al 2010). There has been heightened emphasis on the creation and management of research partnerships, platforms and networks, and new divisions of labour, resources and recognition. The CGIAR Challenge Programmes, for example, were conceived and presented as new models of partnership and co-production (Woolley et al 2009). Where the interests of agribusiness are opposed by populist social movements, however, such public–private partnerships may be highly contentious, since it may be difficult to demonstrate whether or not partnerships are actually pro-poor; exclusive licensing agreements may emerge that appear to benefit private-sector players disproportionately; and there may be a diversion of international public resources, staff and facilities towards high-value commodities and away from staple crops.

These shifts have important implications, not only for what research areas or questions are prioritised by the public sector, but also for the choice of methods, research sites and partnership arrangements. Associated changes in funding, and the new emphasis on accountability and impact, favour downstream over upstream and short-term over long-term research, and play themselves out through the thousands of everyday decisions made by those who fund, manage and do agronomic research.

In summary, agronomic research is embedded in global processes of transformation framed by ideology, fuelled by the search for advantage, pursued in markets, policy and academic arenas, and that result in new winners and losers. Associated with these changes has been a proliferation of new actors doing, hyping, assessing and debating the nature, scope and results of agronomic research.

New spaces for contestation

The dynamics highlighted above have created new spaces in which agronomic research can be contested. On one hand, unity of purpose between agricultural research and state policy has been undermined by public budget deficits, the arrival of new research actors and funders, calls for greater accountability, participation and client orientation, and the mass availability of information and communication technologies (ICTs). On the other hand, those opposing increasing corporate control of the global food system have sought to open up science and technology policy processes to greater popular participation and to promote alternative forms of agricultural research and development.

Three distinct spaces for contestation can be identified. The first is associated largely with peer-reviewed journals, the traditional channel for the communication of agronomic research findings. In recent years, well respected journals such as *Field Crops Research*, *Agricultural Systems* and *Experimental Agriculture* have seen vigorous and extended exchanges around the value of the System of Rice Intensification (SRI) (Dobermann 2004; Uphoff et al 2008; Latif et al 2009) and Conservation Agriculture (Giller et al 2009; Kassam et al 2009). Other examples include the potential contribution of integrated pest management (Van Huis and Meerman 1997; Orr and Ritchie 2004) and of agro-ecological approaches to crop improvement and management (Altieri 2002; Van Bueren et al 2002; cf. Woodhouse 2010). Unlike many debates among agronomists – typically focusing on the performance of a technology, the choice of experimental methods or the interpretation of statistical analyses – contemporary argument lays bare major epistemological and ontological divisions, not least in relation to the value of different kinds of knowledge and the nature of innovation processes. In this respect, these debates are qualitatively different from those in the 1970s about the Green Revolution in Asia, which saw parallel discussions: one conducted by economists and social scientists in journals not normally associated with agronomic research (Falcon 1970; Cleaver 1972; Ruttan 1977); and a second, more technically focused debate among agronomists (e.g. the relative value of open-pollinated versus hybrid maize varieties; improving crop protection; the potential role of compost in soil fertility management).

A second space has given rise to new contestations around agricultural research in the developing world more broadly. This has seen public critique of agricultural research policy move beyond its established academic arena (see Buttel 2005) with increasing engagement by NGOs and other civil society organisations. Combined with the huge mass-communication potential of the internet and ICTs, this has fundamentally changed the scope and dynamic of debate. The World Wide Web is replete with sites advocating or criticising specific technologies such as Bt cotton, Conservation Agriculture, drought-tolerant maize for Africa, Golden Rice, NERICA (New Rice for Africa) and SRI. These include websites drawing from the journal-based debates cited above; others collating information and experiences from a broader range of sources in order to serve specific communities of interest; and still others that are public relations efforts by research organisations, funders, development organisations and private firms promoting their scientific achievements and innovations. The lack of independent peer review or quality assurance mechanisms for many such internet sites underlines the extent to which the quality of information may be subordinated to broader political goals. Such use of science as a tool of political struggle or corporate promotion means that unsupported evidence and dubious conclusions can be widely propagated, and claims and counterclaims about the impacts, outcomes and potentials of agronomic research, technologies and practices may be partial and ill-informed.

A third set of spaces for contestation arose when agricultural research organisations sought greater engagement with their clients and prospective collaborators and opened themselves up to greater public scrutiny. In many countries, national and sub-national committees were established to help set priorities and monitor progress. These pressures for stakeholder involvement were also evident at the international level, and in 1995 the CGIAR established the CGIAR–NGO Partnership Committee to bring together a diverse set of actors and interests to debate research practice and policy. The Committee experienced deep divisions, which were described as 'irreconcilable' by the time of the CGIAR's Annual General Meeting in 2003 (CGIAR 2003). During the recent CGIAR reorganisation exercise, there was renewed pressure for stakeholder engagement, although the preferred mechanism changed to the Global Forum on Agricultural Research (also see CGIAR 2006).

Impacts on policy processes

The opening up of these new spaces of contestation has complicated agricultural policy processes at a moment when the global food system and the policy-makers who seek to guide it confront many new challenges. Some argue that an 'opening up' to new methods and practices that enhance flexibility, diversity, adaptation and reflexivity is a logical response to the incomplete knowledge available about the nature and dynamics of these challenges (Leach et al 2010). Yet, in the spaces we identified above, prioritisation and framing of these challenges are highly contested and so, too, are the quality, significance and relevance of the results of agronomic research generated in both formal and (increasingly) less traditional research settings. Rather than opening up, there is a tendency – supported by professional, institutional and political pressures – for powerful actors and institutions to 'close down' discussion in favour of particular research agendas and development pathways. A result of this dynamic is the promotion of universal approaches to policy that obscure alternative framings and development pathways (Thompson and Scoones 2009).

Within the new spaces of contestation, the results of agronomic research are often used to support both sides of an argument, for example about the value and environmental implications of GM crops, the technical feasibility of a Green Revolution in Africa, or the potential contribution of 'agro-ecological approaches' to crop production. Along these lines, Scoones (2009) used the recent International Assessment of Agricultural Knowledge, Science and Technology for Development (IAASTD) process (McIntyre et al 2009) to explore the politics of divergent appreciations of agronomic knowledge. Over three years, from 2005 to 2007, the IAASTD evaluated the relevance, quality and effectiveness of agricultural knowledge, science and technology, as well as associated policies and institutional arrangements. It adopted an expert-led scenario approach to explore uncertain scientific, technological and policy futures, drawing on experiences from Intergovernmental Panel on Climate Change and the Millennium Ecosystem Assessment, and solicited suggestions from over 900 stakeholders representing scientific and agriculture-related public, private and civil society organisations around the world. In theory, such an inclusive approach can confer political legitimacy and credibility on a complex assessment process; but in practice it led to logjams and divisions within the agricultural research community, reflecting competing worldviews of agriculture.

The contours of a political agronomy analysis

We see political agronomy analysis focusing principally on the practice of everyday agronomic research. It also highlights the dynamics of epistemic communities within agronomy, and the politics of collaboration, partnership and stakeholder engagement. Finally, it includes a concern for how the legitimacy of research is determined, and how the presentation and interpretation of results supports or counters particular narratives and policy framings, or promotes particular political projects and agendas. We explore these points in more detail below, highlighting the kinds of research questions that would underpin the development of a political agronomy analysis and indicating how the various chapters in the volume relate to this agenda.

Framing and narratives

The importance and politics of problem framing is now widely recognised (Bardwell 1991). Here, framing refers to the particular contextual assumptions, methods, forms of interpretation and values that different groups bring to a problem, shaping how it is bounded and understood. Framing determines to a significant degree how much attention the problem receives, the approach taken to address it, and the eventual solution(s) that are proposed and adopted. Framing sets the stage for narratives or storylines about a given problem: how it has arisen, why it matters, and what can be done about it (Leach et al 2010). A focus on multiple framings and their associated narratives can help advance debate about both innovation in agronomic science and its contribution to agricultural development.

The pertinence of framing to a political agronomy analysis is illustrated by effects of a change in how the objective of a cropping system is framed, for example from 'yield maximisation' to 'yield stability', which focuses attention on different strategies, indicators and experimental methods (Piepho 1998; Van Bueren et al 2002). Another example is the reframing of soil organic matter management as 'carbon sequestration' (Perez et al 2007; Lal 2009), which foregrounds new questions relating to monitoring and markets that were of little interest when soil organic matter management was primarily about soil condition and crop response. Finally, recent work shows how GM crops have been actively framed by some biotechnology companies as 'technology for the poor' (Jansen and Gupta 2009; Glover 2010). While this may have been intended to provide a moral counterweight to the resistance to GM technology still seen in some quarters, it may also shift research agendas toward some areas (e.g. performance under less than optimal conditions; quantification of benefits to poor farmers) and away from other potentially more sensitive questions (e.g. corporate control; environmental impacts).

From a political agronomy perspective, the questions of interest relate to the drivers of processes of framing and reframing; the actors and relationships involved; and the impacts of different framings and narratives on the conception, practice and presentation of agronomic research. Brooks and Johnson-Beebout (Chapter 5) show how the framing and reframing of biofortification of rice within the CGIAR had significant consequences for the research approach, methods and networks. In Chapter 6, Woodhouse argues that the impasse in the development of formal irrigation in SSA is due in part to the fact that agronomists have left agricultural water management either to engineers (who frame the challenge in terms of modernisation of infrastructure), or to environmentalists (who frame it in terms of resource conservation). In neither case have they engaged with the current social dynamics of African agriculture. Along similar lines, Pollini (Chapter 7) uses case-study material from Madagascar to explore the epistemological underpinnings and practical relevance of technological approaches framed as providing alternatives to slash-and-burn cultivation.

Agenda-setting

Closely related to framing is the question of how agronomic research priorities are determined. While a large literature assumes that prioritisation is (or should be) a rational, technical process (Raitzer and Norton 2009), an alternative view sees it as a process in which power and politics are of utmost importance. This latter perspective is useful in analysing why some challenging ideas and innovations are successfully integrated into the agronomic research agenda while others are not. For example, Vanloqueren and Baret (2009) ask, 'Why were GM crops brought quickly within mainstream agricultural research while, in contrast, there has been relatively little funding for research on agroecology?' McGuire (2008) uses notions of path dependency and 'technology lock-in' to explain the persistent focus (since 1977) on F_1 hybrids within the Ethiopian lowland sorghum breeding programme, despite the fact that to date no hybrid varieties have been released. Among many other examples from SSA are the decades of research on fodder legumes and mixed farming, despite limited use by farmers (see Sumberg 1998; Wolmer and Scoones 2000; Sumberg 2002; cf. Starkey 1988).

These examples raise a series of fundamental questions about the direction of agricultural research and who benefits from these investments. What evidence was used to justify the objectives set for particular agronomic research projects or programmes? To what extent are they rooted in analysis of farmers' practice and priorities? Through what processes are these decisions made? How is influence and power brought to bear on these processes, and who gains and who loses as a result?

Political agronomy research along these lines would directly address the interactions amongst and between national and regional actors on the one hand and bilateral and multilateral funders on the other, and how these dynamics affect decision-making. As in Fairhead et al's discussion of the emergence of interest in anthropogenic dark earth soils and biochar in SSA (Chapter 4), political agronomy research would also explore historical and regional differences and disjunctures in the setting of research agendas. Andersson and Giller, in their analysis of the dynamics around the promotion of Conservation Agriculture in Zimbabwe (Chapter 2), also focus on the importance of historical disjunctures in agronomic knowledge. The story of Conservation Agriculture in Zimbabwe and Shambu Prasad et al's discussion of the role of 'dissenting agronomists' in the development and promotion of SRI and non-pesticidal management in India (Chapter 10) both illustrate the value of a focus on the influence of epistemic communities within agronomic research.

Partnership

A strong narrative in agricultural science maintains that collaborative research is nearly always desirable. This narrative is couched in terms such as learning, multidisciplinarity, institution-strengthening, capacity-building, coalition-building and comparative advantage. It both supports, and is in turn strengthened by, donor investments in research networks and innovation platforms (Plucknett and Smith 1984; Greenland et al 1987). Indeed, it is not uncommon for funders to insist that research programmes and projects be designed and implemented collaboratively. Collaboration and partnership are also central to the language of innovation systems that has increasingly permeated agricultural research over the past decade (Hall et al 2001; Sumberg 2005).

Collaborative research ranges in scale and complexity, from individuals in different departments or disciplines collaborating on a project within an institute to multifarious linkages across a wide array of institutions, universities, NGOs and firms, such as the CGIAR's Challenge Programmes (Spielman et al 2010) and its new Consortium Research Programs (CGIAR 2011). Partners may bring different ideas and skills, access to financial resources, or the local knowledge, language skills and legitimacy that facilitate access to field sites and target populations. The division of labour created by these partnerships should, in principle, allow each party to go some way in achieving its mandated or self-declared purposes. However, the workings of partnerships and networks relating to agricultural research, in terms of capacity-strengthening, new innovations and delivery of public goods, have as yet received scant critical attention (Plucknett and Smith 1984; de Lattre-Gasquet and Merlet 1996; Goldberger 2008; cf. Shrum and Campion 2000).

A political agronomy analysis would explore the motivations and incentives driving research partnerships. Whose agendas do these arrangements serve? Do they play a role in establishing and legitimating certain normative framings, and hence delegitimising others? Who benefits from partnership, and how? Can collaboration and partnering be empowering, transformative experiences, in what situations, and for whom? To what degree are collaborative arrangements delivering innovation that meets the needs of poor producers? Maat and Glover (Chapter 8) use the example of SRI to reflect on the 'partnership' that is arguably at the centre of all agricultural development – that between agronomic research and extension. Specifically, they focus on different approaches to field activities characterised as 'experiments' and 'demonstrations', and argue that they result in radically different configurations of the relationship between science and farming practice. In Chapter 9, Ramisch explores some of these questions around partnership through the experience of a participatory soil fertility management project in Kenya. Brooks and Johnson-Beebout (Chapter 5) also reflect on the dynamics of partnership within the CGIAR HarvestPlus Challenge Programme.

Validation and use

In earlier sections of this chapter, we argued that changes in the context within which agronomic research takes place have made it a more pluralist and contested arena. As a result, some of agronomy's defining assumptions about the objectives, methods, practices and meanings that define it as a discipline are being transformed.

At issue here is how the knowledge that is generated through agronomic research is produced, validated, communicated and used. The attacks on the normal professionalism of agricultural research referred to earlier, and the subsequent interest in new, more participatory modes of research, posed major challenges to the agronomic research establishment. Unable to articulate a coherent response that identified the potential and limitations of different kinds of participation in different research situations, many researchers were swept along by the participation imperative (Sumberg et al 2003). This could be seen as agronomists escaping from the shackles of a normal science that was no longer fit for purpose. However, a political agronomy perspective demands critical assessment of whether the use of alternative methods was linked to clearly articulated research goals, and in turn, whether they enabled progress towards those goals.

Increasing pressure to demonstrate impact has fostered new and innovative politics around impact claims and their validation, exemplified by recent efforts to identify, document and disseminate 'success stories' about agriculture and agricultural development in Africa (e.g. Spielman and Pandya-Lorch 2009). More critical analysis includes that by Orr et al (2008) on the institutional dynamics behind success claims for NERICA rice; and by Orr (2003) and Orr and Ritchie (2004) on the success story that has been constructed around IPM in Malawi. In these cases and others, scientists' claims about the characteristics and potential of the technologies were amplified through the media by the organisations they worked for and funders who supported them, leading to increased public profile, international accolades and, crucially, continued funding. The importance of claiming impact and celebrating success is only likely to increase in a time of resource scarcity.

A political agronomy analysis must explore how the changing context is affecting views of the relative value of different research and analytical methods, data sources and dissemination channels. It would also focus on the range of factors associated with the use (or otherwise) of the results of agronomic research. Here, Erenstein's analysis of the history and spread of Conservation Agriculture on the Indo-Gangetic Plain (Chapter 3) is particularly valuable: he argues that, despite its promise, differential and above all partial use of Conservation Agriculture can be explained by a combination of political economy factors and the complexity of the technology itself. As illustrated by Sumberg et al's discussion of success stories about agricultural research on SSA (Chapter 11), analysis of the making and use of claims about the impact of agronomic research should offer rich insights into the new world of contested agronomy.

Conclusion

In this chapter, we identified three developments since the mid-1970s – the neoliberal project, and the rise of the environmental and participation movements – that have opened new spaces for contestation within and around agronomic research. We argued that analysis of the impact of these changes on agronomic research in the developing world is of particular importance in the light of recent global food crises and renewed interest in the links between agricultural development, food security and poverty alleviation (Foresight 2011). It is also timely, given the increasing pressure being applied to agricultural research at all levels, to demonstrate impact and value for money.

We have outlined the main thrusts of political agronomy analysis and some of the issues and questions that such an analysis could most beneficially address. Focusing on the practice of everyday agronomic research, we suggested that larger political agronomy questions may be illuminated by analysis of contestation around framing and narratives, agenda setting, partnerships, and the validation and use of the results of agronomic research.

We fully expect the dynamics of change and contestation within and around agronomic research in the developing world will continue to manifest themselves in the coming decades. An important element of political agronomy analysis will be to map these dynamics, the factors affecting them, and their effects on agronomic research and agricultural change. The contributions to this volume represent a first step in establishing the foundations of the new political agronomy.

Note

1 www.planttreaty.org/content/texts-treaty-official-versions

References

Abalu, G. (1998) 'Agricultural productivity and natural resource use in southern Africa', *Food Policy*, 23(6): 477–90.

Akram-Lodhi, A.H. (2007) 'Land reform, rural social relations and the peasantry', *Journal of Agrarian Change*, 7(4): 554–62.

Almekinders, C.J.M. and Elings, A. (2001) 'Collaboration of farmers and breeders: participatory crop improvement in perspective', *Euphytica*, 122(3): 425–38.

Altieri, M.A. (2002) 'Agroecology: the science of natural resource management for poor farmers in marginal environments', *Agriculture, Ecosystems & Environment*, 93: 1–24.

Anderson, J.R. (1998) 'Selected policy issues in international agricultural research: on striving for international public goods in an era of donor fatigue', *World Development*, 26(6): 1149–62.

Ashby, J.A., Braun, A.R., Gracia, T., Guerrero, M.P., Hernandez, L.A., Quiros, C.A. and Roa, J.A. (2000) *Investing in Farmers as Researchers: Experiences with Local Agricultural Research Committees in Latin America*. Cali: CIAT.

Baldwin, K.D.S. (1957) *The Niger Agricultural Project: An Experiment in African Development*. Oxford: Blackwell.

Bardwell, L.V. (1991) 'Problem-framing: a perspective on environmental problem-solving', *Environmental Management*, 15(5): 603–12.

Barrett, C., Carter, M.R. and Timmer, C.P. (2010) 'A century-long perspective on agricultural development', *American Journal of Agricultural Economics*, 92(2): 447–68.

Barton, G. (2001) 'Empire forestry and the origins of environmentalism', *Journal of Historical Geography*, 27(4): 529–52.

Bates, R.H. (1981) *Markets and States in Tropical Africa: The Political Basis of Agricultural Policies*. Berkeley, CA: University of California Press.

Berg, E. (1981) *Accelerated Development in Sub-Saharan Africa: An Agenda for Action*. Washington, DC: World Bank.

Biggs, S.D. (1995) 'Farming systems research and rural poverty: relationships between context and content', *Agricultural Systems*, 47(2): 161–74.

Bijman, J. (2001) 'Restructuring the life science companies', *Biotechnology and Development Monitor*, 44/45: 26–30.

Bonneuil, C. (2000) 'Development as experiment: science and state building in late colonial and postcolonial Africa, 1930–70', *Osiris*, 15: 258–81.

Busch, L. (ed.) (1981) *Science and Agricultural Development*. Totowa, NJ: Allanheld, Osmun & Co.

Buttel, F.H. (2005) 'Ever since Hightower: the politics of agricultural research activism in the molecular age', *Agriculture and Human Values*, 22(3): 275–83.

Buttel, F.H. and Busch, L. (1988) 'The public agricultural research system at the crossroads', *Agricultural History*, 62(2): 303–24.

Byerlee, D. (1998) 'The search for a new paradigm for the development of national agricultural research systems', *World Development*, 26(6): 1049–55.

Byerlee, D. and Alex, G.E. (1998) *Strengthening National Agricultural Research Systems: Policy Issues and Good Practice*. Washington, DC: World Bank.

Carson, R. (1962) *Silent Spring*. Boston, MA: Houghton Mifflin.

Chambers, R. (1986) *Normal Professionalism, New Paradigms and Development*. Brighton: IDS.

——(1993) *Challenging the Professions: Frontiers for Rural Development*. London: IT Publications.

——(1997) *Whose Reality Counts: Putting the Last First*. London: Intermediate Technology Publications.

Chambers, R. and Ghildyal, B.P. (1985) 'Agricultural research for resource-poor farmers: the farmer-first-and-last model', *Agricultural Administration*, 20(1): 1–30.

Chambers, R., Pacey, A. and Thrupp, L.A. (1989) *Farmer First: Farmer Innovation and Agricultural Research*. London: IT Publications.

Chang, H.-J. (2009) 'Rethinking public policy in agriculture: lessons from history, distant and recent', *Journal of Peasant Studies*, 36(3): 477–515.

CGIAR (2003) *Consultative Group on International Agricultural Research Annual General Meeting and Stakeholder Meeting, October 29–30, 2003, Nairobi, Kenya: Summary Record of Proceedings*. Washington, DC: Consultative Group on International Agricultural Research

——(2006) *A Strategic Framework for Engagement Between the CGIAR and Civil Society Organisations (CSOs) – The CGIAR Perspective*. Washington, DC: Consultative Group on International Agricultural Research Secretariat.

——(2011) *A Strategy and Results Framework for the CGIAR*. For submission to the CGIAR Funders Forum (February 20, 2011). Washington, DC: Consultative Group on International Agricultural Research.

Cleaver, H. (1972) 'The contradictions of the Green Revolution', *American Economic Review*, 62(2): 177–86.

Collinson, M.P. (ed.) (2000) *A History of Farming Systems Research*. Wallingford: CABI.

Conway, G. (1985) 'Agroecosystem analysis', *Agricultural Administration*, 20: 31–55.

Cooke, B. (2003) 'A new continuity with colonial administration: participation in development management', *Third World Quarterly*, 24(1): 47–61.

Cooke, B. and Kothari, U. (eds) (2001) *Participation: The New Tyranny?* London: Zed Books.

Cornwall, A. (2003) 'Whose voices? Whose choices? Reflections on gender and participatory development', *World Development*, 31(8): 1325–42.

Cotula, L., Vermeulen, S., Leonard, R. and Keeley, J. (2009) *Land Grab or Development Opportunity? Agricultural Investment and International Land Deals in Africa*. London: IIED, FAO and IFAD.

Dale, C. (1981) 'Agricultural research as state intervention', in: Bush, L. (ed.) *Science and Agricultural Development*. Totowa, NJ: Allanheld, Osmun & Co.

Dalton, T.J. and Guei, R.G. (2003) 'Productivity gains from rice genetic enhancements in West Africa: countries and ecologies', *World Development*, 31(2): 359–74.

De Jager, A., Onduru, D., van Wijk, M.S., Vlaming, J. and Gachini, G.N. (2001) 'Assessing sustainability of low-external-input farm management systems with the nutrient monitoring approach: a case study in Kenya', *Agricultural Systems*, 69(1–2): 99–118.

Diao, X., Hazell, P. and Thurlow, J. (2010) 'The role of agriculture in African development', *World Development*, 38(10): 1375–83.

Dobermann, A. (2004) 'A critical assessment of the system of rice intensification (SRI)', *Agricultural Systems*, 79(3): 261–81.

Dorward, A., Kydd, J., Morrison, J. and Urey, I. (2004) 'A policy agenda for pro-poor agricultural growth', *World Development*, 32(1): 73–89.

Falcon, W.P. (1970) 'The Green Revolution: generations of problem', *American Journal of Agricultural Economics*, 52(5): 698–710.

Foresight (2011) *The Future of Food and Farming: Challenges and Choices for Global Sustainability. Final Project Report*. London: Government Office for Science.

Franke, R. and Chasin, B. (1980) *Seeds of Famine: Ecological Destitution and the Development Dilemma in the West African Sahel*. Montclair, NY: Allanheld, Osmun/Universe Books.

Freire, P. (2007) *Pedagogy of the Oppressed*. New York: Continuum.

Gardner, B. and Lesser, W. (2003) 'International agricultural research as a global public good', *American Journal of Agricultural Economics*, 85(3): 692–97.

GFAR (2010) *The GFAR RoadMap: Transforming Agricultural Research for Development (AR4D) Systems for Global Impact*, Rome: Global Forum for Agricultural Research.

Giller, K.E., Witter, E., Corbeels, M. and Tittonell, P. (2009) 'Conservation agriculture and smallholder farming in Africa: the heretics' view', *Field Crops Research*, 114(1): 23–34.

Glover, D. (2010) 'The corporate shaping of GM crops as a technology for the poor', *Journal of Peasant Studies*, 37(1): 67–90.

Goldberger, J.R. (2008) 'Non-governmental organizations, strategic bridge building, and the "scientization" of organic agriculture in Kenya', *Agriculture and Human Values*, 25(2): 271–89.

Gow, D. and Vansant, J. (1983) ' Beyond the rhetoric of rural development participation: how can it be done?', *World Development*, 11(5): 427–46.

Greenland, D.J., Craswell, E.T. and Dagg, M. (1987) 'International networks and their potential contribution to crop and soil management research', *Outlook on Agriculture*, 16(1): 42–50.

Hadwiger, D.F. (1982) *The Politics of Agricultural Research*. Lincoln, NE: University of Nebraska Press.

Hall, A., Bockett, G., Taylor, S., Sivamohan, M.V.K. and Clark, N. (2001) 'Why research partnerships really matter: innovation theory, institutional arrangements and implications for developing new technology for the poor', *World Development*, 29(5): 783–97.

Harwood, R.R., Place, F., Kassam, A.H. and Gregersen, H.M. (2006) 'International public goods through integrated natural resources management research in CGIAR partnerships', *Experimental Agriculture*, 42(4): 375–97.

Haverkort, B., van der Kamp, J. and Waters-Bayer, A. (1991) *Joining Farmers' Experiments: Experiences in Participatory Technology Development*. London: Intermediate Technology Publications.

Hayami, Y. and Ruttan, V.W. (1985) *Toward a Theory of Induced Institutional Innovation*. Baltimore, MD: Johns Hopkins University Press.

Hightower, J. (1973) *Hard Tomatoes, Hard Times: A Report of the Agribusiness Accountability Project on the Failure of America's Land Grant College Complex*. Cambridge, MA: Schenkman Publishing Co.

HLPE (2011) *Price Volatility and Food Security. A Report by the High Level Panel of Experts on Food Security and Nutrition of the Committee on World Food Security*. Rome: Food and Agriculture Organization.

Ingram, J., Ericksen, P. and Liverman, D. (eds) (2010). *Food Security and Global Environmental Change*. London: Earthscan Publications.

Jansen, K. and Gupta, A. (2009) 'Anticipating the future: "Biotechnology for the poor" as unrealized promise?', *Futures*, 41(7): 436–45.

Kassam, A., Friedrich, T., Shaxson, F. and Pretty, J. (2009) 'The spread of Conservation Agriculture: justification, sustainability and uptake', *International Journal of Agricultural Sustainability*, 7(4): 292–320.

Kessler, J. and Breman, H. (1991) 'The potential of agroforestry to increase primary production in the Sahelian and Sudanian zones of West Africa', *Agroforestry Systems*, 13: 41–62.

Kloppenburg, J.R. (1988) *First the Seed: The Political Economy of Plant Biotechnology, 1492–2000*. Cambridge and New York: Cambridge University Press.

Kotschi, J. (2007) 'Agricultural biodiversity is essential for adapting to climate change', *Gaia – Ecological Perspectives for Science and Society*, 16(2): 98–101.

Kuzmiak, D.T. (1991) 'The American environmental movement', *Geographical Journal*, 157: 265–78.

Lal, R. (2009) 'Sequestering atmospheric carbon dioxide', *Critical Reviews in Plant Sciences*, 28: 90–96.

Latif, M.A., Ali, M.Y., Islam, M.R., Badshah, M.A. and Hasan, M.S. (2009) 'Evaluation of management principles and performance of the System of Rice Intensification (SRI) in Bangladesh', *Field Crops Research*, 114(2): 255–62.

de Lattre-Gasquet, M. and Merlet, J.F. (1996) 'Agricultural research networks in sub-Saharan Africa: an analysis of the situation and its consequences', *Knowledge, Technology & Policy*, 9(1): 36–48.

Leach, M., Scoones, I. and Stirling, I. (2010) *Dynamic Sustainabilities: Technology, Environment, Social Justice*. London: Earthscan.

Leal, P.A. (2007) 'Participation: the ascendancy of a buzzword in the neo-liberal era', *Development in Practice*, 17(4): 539–548.

Lele, U. and Gerrard, C. (2003) 'Global public goods, global programs, and global policies: some initial findings from a World Bank evaluation', *American Journal of Agricultural Economics*, 85(3): 686–91.

Loevinsohn, M.E. (1987) 'Insecticide use and increased mortality in rural Central Luzan, Philippines', *Lancet*, 8546: 1359–62.

Low, A.R.C. (1994) 'Environmental and economic dilemmas for farm-households in Africa: when low-input sustainable agriculture translates to high-cost unsustainable livelihoods', *Environmental Conservation*, 21(3): 220–24.

Maredia, M.K., Byerlee, D. and Pee, P. (2000) 'Impacts of food crop improvement research: evidence from sub-Saharan Africa', *Food Policy*, 25(5): 531–59.

Maredia, M.K. and Raitzer, D.A. (2010) 'Estimating overall returns to international agricultural research in Africa through benefit-cost analysis: a "best-evidence" approach', *Agricultural Economics*, 41(1): 81–100.

Mbow, C., Mertz, O., Diouf, A., Rasmussen, K. and Reenberg, A. (2008) 'The history of environmental change and adaptation in eastern Saloum-Senegal – driving forces and perceptions', *Global and Planetary Change*, 64(3–4): 210–21.

McGuire, S.J. (2008) 'Path-dependency in plant breeding: challenges facing participatory reforms in the Ethiopian Sorghum Improvement Program', *Agricultural Systems*, 96(1–3): 139–49.

McIntyre, B.D., Herren, H.R., Wakhungu, J. and Watson, R.T. (eds) (2009) *Agriculture at a Crossroads: IAASTD Global Report*. Washington, DC: Island Press.

McMichael, P. (2008) 'Peasants make their own history, but not just as they please', *Journal of Agrarian Change*, 8(2/3): 205–28.

Moock, J. (ed.) (1986) *Understanding Africa's Rural Households and Farming Systems*. Boulder, CO: Westview Press.

Moris, J. and Thom, D. (eds) (1990) *Irrigation Development in Africa: Lessons of Experience*, Boulder, CO: Westview Press.

Nair, P.K.R. (1991) 'State-of-the-art of agroforestry systems', *Forest Ecology and Management*, 45(1/4): 5–29.

Naseem, A., Spielman, D.J. and Omamo, S.W. (2010) 'Private-sector investment in R&D: a review of policy options to promote its growth in developing-country agriculture', *Agribusiness*, 26(1): 143–73.

Okali, C., Sumberg, J. and Farrington, J. (1994) *Farmer Participatory Research: Rhetoric and Reality*. London: IT Publications.

Orr, A. (2003) 'Integrated pest management for resource-poor African farmers: is the Emperor naked?', *World Development*, 31(5): 831–45.

Orr, A. and Ritchie, J.M. (2004) 'Learning from failure: smallholder farming systems and IPM in Malawi', *Agricultural Systems*, 79(1): 31–54.

Orr, S., Sumberg, J., Erenstein, O. and Oswald, A. (2008) 'Funding international agricultural research and the need to be noticed: a case study of NERICA rice', *Outlook on Agriculture*, 37(3): 159–68.

Patel, R. (2009) 'Food sovereignty', *Journal of Peasant Studies*, 36(3): 663–73.

Pearse, A. (1980) *Seeds of Plenty, Seeds of Want: Social and Economic Implications of the Green Revolution*. Oxford: Clarendon Press.

Perez, C., Roncoli, C., Neely, C. and Steiner, J.L. (2007) 'Can carbon sequestration markets benefit low-income producers in semi-arid Africa? Potentials and challenges', *Agricultural Systems* 94(1): 2–12.

Piepho, H.P. (1998) 'Methods for comparing the yield stability of cropping systems – a review', *Journal of Agronomy and Crop Science*, 180(4): 193–213.

Pimbert, M. (1999) *Sustaining the Multiple Functions of Agricultural Biodiversity. Gatekeeper 88*. London: IIED.

Pimentel, D. and Pimentel, M. (1990) 'Comment: Adverse environmental consequences of the Green Revolution', *Population and Development Review*, 16: 329–32.

Pingali, P. and Rosengrant, M. (1994) *Confronting the Environmental Consequences of the Green Revolution in Asia. EPTD Discussion Paper No. 2*. Washington, DC: IFPRI.

Pistorius, R. (1997) *Scientists, Plants and Politics: A History of the Plant Genetic Resources Movement*. Rome: International Plant Genetics Resources Institute.

Plucknett, D.L. and Smith, N.J.H. (1984) 'Networking in international agricultural research', *Science*, 225(4666): 989–93.

Poulton, C. (2009) 'Agricultural research', in: Kirsten, J.F. et al (eds) *Institutional Economics Perspectives on African Agricultural Development*. Washington, DC: International Food Policy Research Institute.

Raitzer, D. and Norton, G.W. (2009) *Prioritizing Agricultural Research for Development: Experiences and Lessons*. Wallingford: CABI Publishing.

Raitzer, D.A. and Kelley, T.G. (2008) 'Benefit–cost meta-analysis of investment in the International Agricultural Research Centers of the CGIAR', *Agricultural Systems*, 96(1–3): 108–23.

Reij, C. and Waters-Bayer, A. (eds) (2001) *Farmer Innovation in Africa: A Source of Inspiration for Agricultural Development*. London: Earthscan.

Reijntes, C., Haverkort, B. and Waters-Bayer, A. (1992) *Farming for the Future. An Introduction to Low-External-Input and Sustainable Agriculture*. Leusden, the Netherlands: ILEIA.

Richards, P. (1985) *Indigenous Agricultural Revolution: Ecology and Food Production in West Africa*. London: Hutchinson & Co.

——(1986) *Coping With Hunger: Hazard and Experiment in an African Rice Farming System*. London: Allen & Unwin.

Ruttan, V. (1977) 'The Green Revolution: seven generalizations', *International Development Review*, 19: 16–23.

——(1982) *Agricultural Research Policy*. Minneapolis, MN: University of Minnesota Press.

Sandbrook, R. (1985) *The Politics of Africa's Economic Stagnation*. Cambridge: Cambridge University Press.

Scoones, I. (2009) 'The politics of global assessments: the case of the International Assessment of Agricultural Knowledge, Science and Technology for Development (IAASTD)', *Journal of Peasant Studies*, 36(3): 547–71.

Scoones, I. and Thompson, J. (eds) (1994) *Beyond Farmer First: rural people's knowledge, agricultural research and extension practice*. London: Intermediate Technology Publications.

——(2009) *Farmer First Revisited: Innovation for Agricultural Research and Development*. London: Practical Action Publishing.

Scoones, I., Toulmin, C. and Reij, C. (1996) *Sustaining the Soil: Indigenous Soil and Water Conservation in Africa*. London: Earthscan.

Shambu Prasad, C. and Sen, D. (2010) 'The new commons in agriculture: lessons fron the margins and SRI in India', paper presented at ISDA meeting, 28 June–1 July 2010, Montpellier, France. http://hal.archives-ouvertes.fr/docs/00/52/13/98/PDF/Shambu_The_new_common.pdf

Shrum, W. and Campion, P. (2000) 'Are scientists in developing countries isolated?', *Science Technology and Society*, 5(1): 1–34.

Sperling, L. and Berkowitz, P. (1994) *Partners in Selection: Bean Breeders and Women Bean Experts in Rwanda*. Washington, DC: CGIAR.

Sperling, L., Ashby, J.A., Smith, M.E., Weltzien, E. and McGuire, S. (2001) 'A framework for analyzing participatory plant breeding approaches and results', *Euphytica*, 122(3): 439–50.

Spielman, D.J. and Pandya-Lorch, R. (eds) (2009) *Millions Fed: Proven Successes in Agricultural Development*. Washington, DC: IFPRI.

Spielman, D.J., Hartwich, F. and Grebmer, K. (2010) 'Public–private partnerships and developing-country agriculture: evidence from the international agricultural research system', *Public Administration and Development*, 30(4): 261–76.

Starkey, P. (1988) *Perfected Yet Rejected: Animal-drawn Wheeled Toolcarriers*. Braunschweig, Germany: GTZ & Eschborh and Vieweg.

Sumberg, J. (1998) 'Mixed farming in Africa: the search for order, the search for sustainability', *Land Use Policy*, 15(4): 293–317.

——(2002) 'The logic of fodder legumes in Africa', *Food Policy*, 27(3): 285–300.

——(2005) 'Systems of innovation theory and the changing architecture of agricultural research in Africa', *Food Policy*, 30(1): 21–41.

Sumberg, J., Okali, C. and Reece, D. (2003) 'Agricultural research in the face of diversity, local knowledge and the participation imperative: theoretical considerations', *Agricultural Systems*, 76(2): 739–53.

Tansey, G. and Rajotte, T. (eds) 2008. *The Future Control of Food: A Guide to International Negotiations and Rules on Intellectual Property, Biodiversity and Food Security*. London: Earthscan.

Tatum, L.A. (1971) 'The Southern Corn Leaf Blight epidemic', *Science*, 171(3976): 1113–16.

Teubal, M. (2009) 'Agrarian reform and social movements in the age of globalization: Latin America at the dawn of the twenty-first century', *Latin American Perspectives*, 36(4): 9–20.

Thompson, J. and Scoones, I. (1994) 'Challenging the populist perspective: rural people's knowledge, agricultural research and extension practice', *Agriculture and Human Values*, 11(2–3): 58–76.

——(2009) 'Addressing the dynamics of agri-food systems: an emerging agenda for social science research', *Environmental Science & Policy*, 12(4): 386–97.

Toenniessen, G., Adesina, A. and DeVries, J. (2008) 'Building an Alliance for a Green Revolution in Africa', *Annals of the New York Academy of Sciences*, 1136: 233–42.

Tripp, R. (2005) *Self-Sufficient Agriculture: Labour and Knowledge on Small-Scale Farming*. London: Earthscan.

Uphoff, N., Kassam, A. and Stoop, W. (2008) 'A critical assessment of a desk study comparing crop production systems: the example of the "system of rice intensification" versus "best management practice"', *Field Crops Research*, 108(1): 109–14.

Van Bueren, E.T.L., Struik, P.C. and Jacobsen, E. (2002) 'Ecological concepts in organic farming and their consequences for an organic crop ideotype', *Netherlands Journal of Agricultural Science*, 50(1): 1–26.

Van Huis, A. and Meerman, F. (1997) 'Can we make IPM work for resource-poor farmers in sub-Saharan Africa?', *International Journal of Pest Management*, 43(4): 313–20.

Vanloqueren, G. and Baret, P.V. (2009) 'How agricultural research systems shape a technological regime that develops genetic engineering but locks out agroecological innovations', *Research Policy*, 38(6): 971–83.

Weyland, K. (1996) 'Neopopulism and neoliberalism in Latin America: unexpected affinities', *Studies in Comparative International Development*, 31(3): 3–31.

Wield, D.V., Chataway, J. and Bolo, M. (2010) 'Issues in the political economy of agricultural biotechnology', *Journal of Agrarian Change*, 10(3): 342–66.

Wiggins, S. (2009) 'Can the smallholder model deliver poverty reduction and food security for a rapidly growing population in Africa?' in: *Expert Meeting in How to Feed the World in 2050*. Rome: Economic and Social Development Department, FAO.

Wolmer, W. and Scoones, I. (2000) 'The science of "civilized" agriculture: the mixed farming discourse in Zimbabwe', *African Affairs*, 99(397): 575–600.

Woodhouse, P. (2010) 'Beyond industrial agriculture? Some questions about farm size, productivity and sustainability', *Journal of Agrarian Change*, 10(3): 437–53.

Woolley, J., Cook, S.E., Molden, D. and Harrington, L. (2009) 'Water, food and development: the CGIAR Challenge Program on Water and Food', *Water International*, 34(1): 4–12.

World Bank (2007) *Agriculture for Development: World Development Report 2008*. Washington, DC: World Bank.

Zoomers, A. (2010) 'Globalisation and the foreignisation of space: seven processes driving the current global land grab', *Journal of Peasant Studies*, 37(2): 429–47.

2

ON HERETICS AND GOD'S BLANKET SALESMEN

Contested claims for Conservation Agriculture and the politics of its promotion in African smallholder farming

Jens A. Andersson and Ken E. Giller

Erosion > natural soil formation = NOT sustainable.

Tillage is incompatible with sustainable agriculture!

Further promotion of tillage-based agriculture in Africa is irresponsible.

... research questions are NOT WHEN and WHERE Conservation Agriculture is applicable, but 'HOW' it can be best made work and upscaled.

(Friedrich and Kassam 2011)

Introduction

Conservation Agriculture (CA) has captured the imagination of an impressive array of organisations, including the FAO, DFID, the EU, international research and development organisations (CIMMYT, CIRAD, ICRAF and ICRISAT) and numerous NGOs. Defined by FAO (2008a) as having three essential components – zero or minimal soil disturbance; a permanent soil cover provided by a growing crop or a mulch of organic residues; and crop rotation[1] – CA is now promoted widely to smallholder farmers in sub-Saharan Africa.[2] Next to international agricultural research and policy institutes, the faith-based organisations, international donors and NGOs have been at the forefront in such promotional efforts. Often building on the Judeo-Christian notion of environmental stewardship, which follows from the belief that it is the responsibility of man to look after the Earth (Passmore 1974), some of these organisations equate CA with 'farming God's way'.[3]

This chapter investigates the development of this conglomerate of faith-based, science-based and policy organisations as a distinct epistemic community. Following Haas (1992), an epistemic community is understood as a network of professionals with recognised expertise in a particular domain, who help decision-makers to define problems, identify policy solutions and assess policy outcomes.[4] An epistemic community thus pushes a particular policy enterprise, excluding or silencing alternative policy options and expertise. This chapter shows how CA became a policy success sanctioned by religion, despite earlier agronomic research suggesting the value of other options, evidence of dis-adoption, and contestation over the suitability of particular CA technologies. The focus is on this epistemic community's particular institutional manifestation and its related agronomic narrative.

As illustrated by the opening quotes, the agronomic narrative around CA stresses sustainability and the universal applicability of its three main principles. Sometimes adopting an idiosyncratic definition of sustainability[5] – which disregards the fact that soil erosion is also a natural process – this narrative portrays the plough as the major cause of soil degradation (Marongwe et al 2011; Thierfelder and Wall undated) and as 'an enemy of sustainability'.[6] Adopting CA principles thus becomes a universal prerequisite for sustainable agriculture or, in the narrative of its Christian proponents, the only way to farm that is faithful to God. In such a narrative, the socio-economic and agro-ecological environments cease to be structuring forces of agronomic practice. Instead, practising CA becomes a righteous act, an act of faith, where agronomic practices also have religious meanings, such as mulch cover being understood as 'God's blanket' (Oldreive 2009: 52).

Thus we may understand the apparent tension between the blanket, or perhaps more aptly, 'God's blanket' recommendations for CA and the recent trend toward more adaptive, on-farm and farmer-led agronomic research. The focus here is largely on Zimbabwe, where both agronomic research on CA technologies targeting African smallholder farmers and faith-based promotion of CA to African smallholders have their origins.

We first explore the history of research on conservation tillage in Zimbabwe, and show how the current drive to promote CA is largely disconnected from earlier on-station and on-farm experimentation. We argue: (1) that this disconnect relates to growing attention to CA in international policy discourse in the late 1990s and early 2000s (Benites and Steiner 1998; Vaneph and Benites 2001) and a shift in donor support from government-linked agricultural research to the (faith-based) NGO sector following Zimbabwe's political and economic crisis in the early 2000s; and (2) that these two developments gave rise to a distinct epistemic community of faith-based NGOs, international agricultural research institutes and policy organisations (such as the FAO). Subsequently, CA was turned into a successful policy model for smallholder farming in southern Africa, following positive reports on smallholder CA farming in Zambia. This was done by bringing together different technologies promoted by various research and development organisations into a standardised CA package. In many areas, practising a form of CA based on planting basins became a requirement if resource-poor smallholder farmers were to receive inputs. The widespread extension of this planting basin-based CA package was the impetus for current attempts to mainstream CA in the sub-region through national agricultural policy. Although there are now different CA packages, the suitability and applicability of CA in highly diverse smallholder farming systems remains contested. It is suggested that actual adoption of CA will be patchy at best as it is suited to the circumstances of only a limited number of farmers and farming systems.

Experimentation with CA technology in Zimbabwe

Reduced tillage practices were developed following the dust bowl in North America in the 1930s. These practices were seen as a means to reduce soil erosion and thus conserve the soil. Agronomic research has subsequently developed practices involving what have become the three principles of CA: reduced or zero-tillage; permanent soil cover; and crop rotation. In mechanised agriculture where herbicides are used, CA practices offer huge advantages for farmers with sufficient capital (Bolliger et al 2006). Apart from being effective in controlling soil erosion and increasing soil moisture, direct planting into the residue of a previous crop can reduce energy costs (for ploughing), increase the area that can be managed by a given labour force, and reduce or eliminate the fallow time between crops. In some areas, reduced fallow time allows for an extra crop being grown within a year. It is thus a means of intensification that increases the efficiency of land, energy, water and nutrient use and prevents soil erosion. Such practices have been adopted on a massive scale on large-scale farms in North and South America, Australia, South Asia and southern Africa.

The spread of CA has not been restricted to very large, mechanised farms. Researchers have developed animal-drawn zero-till planters suitable for use by Brazilian 'smallholders' on farms typically less than 50 ha in size (Bolliger et al 2006).

Although the American dust bowl also inspired a preoccupation with soil con-servation among colonial officers in southern Africa (Beinart 1984; Bolding 2004: 60), here reduced tillage systems were introduced primarily in response to escalating fuel, machinery and maintenance costs (Smith 1988). Such cost considerations were probably most acute in Southern Rhodesia (now Zimbabwe) following the economic sanctions imposed on the white minority regime after 1965. Testing of various reduced tillage techniques, including ripping[7] and conservation tillage, took place at Henderson Research Station, the Institute of Agricultural Engineering (IAE), and the Cotton Research Institute (Figure 2.1). Findings were evaluated in terms of their effects on maize and cotton yields, and were geared towards the large-scale commercial farming sector (Smith 1988). Results indicated that conservation tillage practices could have a marked influence on soil properties, moisture conservation and yield, but 'that seasonal climatic variations have more direct influence on crop yields than any tillage treatment' (Smith 1988: 207). The erosion-reducing effects of conservation tillage practices were considered to be most relevant for smallholder farming in the Communal Areas, but were not systematically tested under smallholder conditions.

Following Zimbabwe's independence in 1980, agricultural research was re-oriented towards the smallholder sector (Taonezvi 1994). Often supported by international donors, government research institutes now focused on conservation tillage techniques that were more suitable for smallholder farmers (Mupangwa et al 2006; Twomlow et al 2006). Practices such as no-till tied ridging (Norton 1987; Elwell and Norton 1988; McClymont and Winkfield 1989) and no-till with tied furrows (see note 7) now began to be systematically investigated and recommended to smallholders (Nyamudeza and Nyakatawa 1995). Because mulch is not a requirement for either

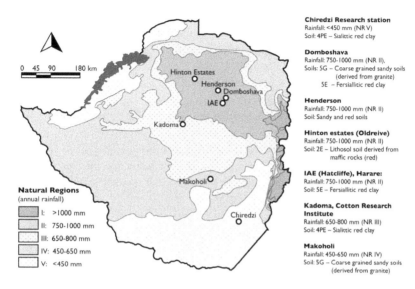

0 45 90   180 km

Natural Regions
(annual rainfall)

I: >1000 mm
II: 750-1000 mm
III: 650-800 mm
IV: 450-650 mm
V: <450 mm

Chiredzi Research station
Rainfall: <450 mm (NR V)
Soil: 4PE – Sialitic red clay

Domboshava
Rainfall: 750-1000 mm (NR II),
Soils: 5G – Coarse grained sandy soils
      (derived from granite)
    5E – Fersiallitic red clay

Henderson
Rainfall: 750-1000 mm (NR II)
Soil: Sandy and red soils

Hinton estates (Oldreive)
Rainfall: 750-1000 mm (NR II)
Soil: 2E – Lithosol soil derived from
    maffic rocks (red)

IAE (Hatcliffe), Harare:
Rainfall: 750-1000 mm (NR II)
Soil: 5E – Fersiallitic red clay

**Kadoma, Cotton Research
Institute**
Rainfall: 650-800 mm (NR III)
Soil: 4PE – Sialitic red clay

Makoholi
Rainfall: 450-650 mm (NR IV)
Soil: 5G – Coarse grained sandy soils
    (derived from granite)

FIGURE 2.1 Agro-ecological circumstances (rainfall and soil characteristics) at different
research stations in Zimbabwe (Vincent and Thomas 1961), soil classification
taken from Nyamapfene (1991).

practice, they were seen as better adapted to the smallholder sector, where crop
residues are scarce as they are normally fed to livestock during the dry season.

The Contill project

In 1988, the governmental research and extension service (Agritex) and the German
Technical Agency (GTZ) initiated a collaborative research project on conservation
tillage (Contill) on the granite-derived sandy soils at Domboshava and Makoholi
research stations (Figure 2.1). Aiming to test and develop sustainable conservation
tillage practices for smallholders farming on similar soils, four conservation tillage
practices were compared with conventional mouldboard tillage: (1) no-till tied ridging;
(2) mulch ripping; (3) clean ripping into bare ground; and (4) hand hoeing into bare
soil before the onset of the rains (Munyati 1997). To complement the on-station
trials looking at yield, soil loss and run-off, the project introduced adaptive on-farm
research in 1990, seeking to test socio-economic, technical and environmental feasibility in farmers' situations (Hagmann 1993; Nyagumbo 1999). Although the on-farm
trials suggested that 'from a soil and water conservation point of view, [both] mulch
ripping and no-till tied ridging [showed] high potential', only the latter technique
was taken for testing and further development with farmers as 'stover mulch is normally fed to cattle' (Chuma and Hagmann 1995: 48). Yet, as crop emergence proved
a problem in no-till tied ridging, it was recommended that farmers delay planting
until the ridges were fully moist, a practice that may reduce yields (Munyati 1997: 31).
Other techniques, such as clean ripping and hand hoeing in bare ground, were considered unsustainable as 'surface run-off and erosion rates ... were still above tolerable

levels', albeit lower than with conventional tillage. In addition, at the drier Makoholi site 'hand-hoeing appeared to reduce yields' (Chuma and Hagmann 1995: 54, 56), while at Domboshava 'high weed infestation prevent these systems from being sustainable' (Munyati 1997: 32; see also Vogel 1994).

The results from the on-station trials at Domboshava and Makoholi (Tables 2.1 and 2.2) show that both ripping and no-till tied ridging were effective at keeping soil loss and runoff below what was considered the tolerable rate of 5 t ha^{-1} year^{-1} (Elwell 1980). However, only mulch ripping was found to be a 'truly [ecologically] sustainable tillage technique' as it 'was able to maintain high organic matter levels, reduce soil erosion to a minimum and to achieve the highest water use efficiency … [T]he organic matter status of the soil could not be sustained at the desired level' with no-till tied ridging (Chuma and Hagmann 1995: 54).

Yields showed more diverse trends in comparison with conventional tillage. At Domboshava planting on ridges produced significantly better yields than all other treatments in seasons with above average rainfall (Munyati 1997: 29), but at Makoholi mulch ripping generally outperformed no-till tied ridging. Yet, in contrast to the on-station trials, no-till tied ridging performed generally better than conventional ploughing in the on-farm trials, albeit that there was much variability from farmer to farmer. Treatment effects appeared 'to be extremely site, soil and farmer specific' (Chuma and Hagmann 1995).

Conservation tillage trials were also established at the Institute of Agricultural Engineering in 1991. Among the tillage treatments tested were conventional ploughing, mulch ripping and no-till tied ridging, as in the Contill project. Results over five seasons revealed no clear trends or significant differences between different tillage treatments in terms of crop yields, but average yields tended to be larger in no-till treatments (Nehanda 1999). As the Contill and Institute of Agricultural Engineering experiments were conducted on contrasting soils (Figure 2.1), they provide insights into the effects of tillage on soil organic matter. The physical protection afforded by (1) the binding of organic matter to clay particles (the textural effect); and (2) aggregation (the structural effect) in clay soils means that the negative effect of tillage on soil organic matter can be significant in clay-rich soils (Chivenge et al 2007). By comparison, in sandy soils – which predominate in Zimbabwe's Communal Areas – there is little physical protection and thus tillage does not have a strong effect on organic matter. Sandy and clay soils thus require different management in order to maintain soil organic carbon (see also Grant 1995).

Conservation tillage experimentation: what determines success?

This brief history of experimentation with conservation tillage in Zimbabwe reveals three marked institutional changes. First, initial interest in conservation tillage was motivated primarily by escalating costs – for fuel and imported farm machinery – rather than conservation concerns. The experimentation served the large-scale farming sector. Second, following independence, agricultural research was re-oriented towards the smallholder sector, and experimentation on conservation tillage followed suit (Prestt

TABLE 2.1 Grain yield, surface runoff and soil loss for different tillage treatments, Domboshava, 1988/89–1994/95 (sources: Munyati 1997; Nehanda 1999)

Season	Rainfall (mm)	Yield (t ha^{-1})			Surface runoff (mm)			Soil loss (t ha^{-1} year^{-1})		
		Conventional tillage	No-till tied ridging	Mulch ripping	Conventional tillage	No-till tied ridging	Mulch ripping	Conventional tillage	No-till tied ridging	Mulch ripping
1988/89	905	3.8	5.0	3.8	62.9	2.3	86.2	1.7	0.2	2.0
1989/90	1180	2.8	4.6	2.1	274.3	116.5	109.1	9.5	2.2	2.6
1990/91	739	3.1	4.6	4.0	15.0	1.4	4.8	1.1	0.3	0.6
1991/92	438	1.2	0.8	0.3	9.4	0.1	1.0	1.0	0.1	0.3
1992/93	797	5.1	6.6	4.3	105.0	13.0	15.2	11.8	0.9	1.1
1993/94	610	4.6	6.0	5.7	13.0	0.7	1.7	1.5	0.2	0.6
1994/95	480	2.4	2.4	3.5	99.5	5.9	4.4	10.3	0.7	0.6
Average	736	3.3	4.3	3.4	82.7	20.0	31.8	5.3	0.7	1.1
SD	258	1.4	2.0	1.7	93.7	42.8	45.7	5.0	0.7	0.9

TABLE 2.2 Grain yield, surface runoff and soil loss for different tillage treatments, Makoholi, 1988/89–1994/95 (sources: Nehanda 1999; rainfall, Chuma and Hagmann 1995)

Season	Rainfall (mm)	Yield (t ha⁻¹)			Surface runoff (mm)			Soil loss (t ha⁻¹year⁻¹)		
		Conventional tillage	No-till tied ridging	Mulch ripping	Conventional tillage	No-till tied ridging	Mulch ripping	Conventional tillage	No-till tied ridging	Mulch ripping
1988/89	425	2.8	2.1	3.2	7	0.3	5	0.7	0.0	0.5
1989/90	742	6.6	3.0	7.1	93	26	28	1.3	0.1	1.0
1990/91	342	1.9	1.5	3.0	41	0.2	2	5.8	0.1	0.6
1991/92	174	0	0	0	1	0.1	1	0.7	0.1	0.3
1992/93	679	5.8	4.8	7.0	92	34	35	11.8	2.7	3.7
1993/94	472	2.4	3.0	2.6	95	16	5	40.2	3.0	0.2
1994/95	no data	0.9	1.1	2.2	49	4	4	6.8	0.1	0.1
Average	472	2.9	2.2	3.6	54.0	11.5	11.4	9.6	0.9	0.9
SD	212	2.4	1.6	2.6	40.5	14.0	13.9	14.1	1.3	1.3

1986; Norton 1988; Shumba et al 1992). With this re-orientation, soil conservation and coping with climate variability became more prominent in the narrative around conservation tillage (e.g. Chikowo 2011). Soil conservation was a well established theme even during the colonial period in Zimbabwe, as smallholder farmers were historically concentrated on degradation-prone soils with highly variable rainfall (Andersson 2007). Third, as the development and promotion of conservation tillage practices for the smallholder sector intensified in the 1990s, research increasingly shifted from formal trials on research stations to adaptive on-farm experimentation with farmers. This latter approach sought not only to adjust emerging technology to the socio-economic circumstances of resource-poor farmers in agro-ecologically marginal areas, but also to 'empower' farmers (Hagmann et al 1995; cf. Okali et al 1994). Experimentation with farmers in the Contill project not only revealed contradictory yield results from on-farm and on-station trials, but the performance of different tillage techniques proved to be highly variable depending on soil, site and farmer-specific conditions. Hence researchers concluded that, given the diversity in agro-ecological and socio-economic conditions, 'different techniques and systems should be promoted as options' (Nyagumbo 1999: 114) as 'it is impossible to develop blanket recommendations' (Chuma and Hagmann 1995: 56).

The results further suggest that the most appropriate technologies from a technical point of view, such as mulch ripping, may not suit the circumstances of the majority of resource-poor smallholders who lack both sufficient mulch and the animal draught power required to pull rippers.

Faith-based CA: the emergence of planting basins and God's blanket

Unlike the conservation tillage technologies discussed above, the current drive to extend CA to African smallholder farmers is not well rooted in scientific experimentation. Rather, it has its origins in a different epistemological tradition, building on the experience of one large-scale commercial farmer in Zimbabwe, Brian Oldreive, who developed a minimum-tillage technology in the early 1980s (Oldreive 2009, 1993).

Oldreive was a tobacco grower, but as a newly converted Christian he considered tobacco cultivation unethical and switched to maize. Following two years of drought and poor harvests, the banks made the next loan conditional on Oldreive returning to tobacco. However, he refused, and as a result had to sell his farm. He then went to manage a farm in northern Zimbabwe where yields were declining. His experimentation with conservation tillage in the early 1980s was motivated by both costs and conservationist concerns:

> On this [large-scale, mechanized] farm the common practice was to plough very deeply after having burnt off all the stover from the previous crop. This caused the soil structure to break down and large clods, the size of footballs, were being ploughed up, which then had to be broken down with two harrowings and two rollings, which was very expensive. The soil structure had

collapsed resulting in water running off the surface and the topsoil washing away. *Our costs were rising steeply, while our yields were going down ...*

(Oldreive 2009: 7; emphasis added)

Although Oldreive knew about zero-tillage and the American dust bowl, his inspiration came from elsewhere:

I would go into the virgin bush for times of prayer, and one day God began to reveal me His ways in nature (Romans 1: 19–22). There I saw that there is no mechanism in nature in which the soil is inverted and there is a thick blanket of fallen leaves and grass which covers the surface of the soil. I realized that these two factors in nature prevented the soil from being washed away.

(Oldreive 2009: 7)

As his mechanised no-till experiments with mulch gave positive results, he increased the no-till area and reversed the downward trend in production. Oldreive won several agricultural prizes, and approached the research community for advice on conservation tillage. Apparently, he was told it would not work in the region where he farmed (Oldreive 2009: 7). He nevertheless continued, and saw it as his Christian duty to extend the principles of conservation tillage to smallholder farmers, convinced that 'the same principles may be applied to any scale of operation' (Oldreive 1993: xi). Without mechanisation or draught power, farmers could simply dig planting basins in the period before the onset of the season when there was little demand for labour. Whereas his handbook on conservation farming initially targeted farmers in the higher-rainfall areas (Natural Regions II and III) (Winkfield 1993: v), the training and extension programmes Oldreive set up – such as the 'Hinton Estate Outreach Programme' and 'Operation Joseph' (Twomlow et al 2008b: 3) – extended the principles of conservation farming throughout Zimbabwe through demonstration plots, training and extension leaflets. Without scientific testing under various agro-ecological circumstances, Oldreive's faith-based approach to CA, also known as Conservation Farming (CF; see Box 2.1), focused on planting basins or shallow planting furrows in conjunction with mulch ('God's blanket'), seeds, fertiliser and a cereal–legume rotation (Twomlow et al 2008b). Its promoters claim that CF is scale-neutral and suitable across different agro-ecological circumstances, yet dependent on good management (Oldreive 1993; see also IIRR/ACT 2005: ix) (Figure 2.2).

Box 2.1 Definitions and descriptions

'**Conservation Agriculture (CA)** is a broader term that encompasses activities such as minimum tillage and zero tillage, tractor powered, animal powered and manual methods, integrated pest management, integrated soil and water management, and includes CF. ... it is any tillage sequence that minimises or reduces the loss of soil and water; operationally a tillage or tillage and planting combination which leaves 30% or more mulch or crop cover on the surface, equivalent to more than 3 t ha^{-1} of crop residues' (ZCATF 2008: 3).

'**Conservation Farming (CF)** refers to the particular technology of using planting basins and mulch cover which was developed by Brian Oldreive. This is a modification of the traditional pit systems once common in southern Africa and is a variation on the *Zaï* pit system from West Africa, which may also be considered as a CF technology' (ZCATF 2008: 3).

Precision Conservation Agriculture (PCA) was initially used by ICRISAT to refer to the hand-hoe, basins-based CA package as promoted through relief and recovery programmes in Zimbabwe. It is a modification of the CF planting basin approach that includes the precision application of small doses of nitrogen fertiliser (Twomlow et al 2008b: 3), 'irrespective of the quantity of surface residues retained as mulch' (Twomlow et al 2008a: 41). As mulch is not required, it is not always considered CA.

The Sahelian *Zaï* **pit system**, described as an indigenous strategy for soil rehabilitation, originating from Burkina Faso (Roose et al 1999), combines water harvesting and targeted application of organic amendments by the use of shallow pits (diameter 20–30 cm, 10–15 cm deep) dug into the hardened soil (Fatondji et al 2001; Mando et al 2006). As no mulch is used, it is generally not considered CA.

Planting basins, as promoted as part of CF and PCA in Zimbabwe, are smaller than *Zaï* pits. Recommended dimensions are 15 × 15 × 15 cm, spaced at either 75 × 60 cm for Natural Region II and either 75 × 75 or 90 × 60 cm for Natural Regions III, IV and V (Twomlow et al 2008a, 2008b; ZCATF 2009: 37). In Zambia, farmers adapted Oldreive's planting basins by making them wider (30–40 cm) and deeper, breaking plough or hoe pans that may form at a depth of 15–20 cm. As planting basins involves a degree of soil inversion, some do not consider it proper CA.

FIGURE 2.2 Foundations for Farming (formerly Farming God's Way) demonstration plot in Harare, 2010 (photo: J.A. Andersson).

Combining the promotion of the gospel and CF (Oldreive 2009), Oldreive's Foundations for Farming (formerly Farming God's Way) organisation became a hub in a regional network of faith-based NGOs extending CF to smallholder farmers.[8] The inclusion of an adapted version of his CA approach in donor-funded relief and recovery programmes in Zimbabwe in 2004 (Twomlow et al 2008b) provided further legitimisation, as it resulted in close collaboration with donors, NGOs and international research institutes. Participation in this emergent epistemic community arguably contributed to the profile and success of Oldreive's organisations.

From adaptive research to faith in blanket recommendations

The apparent epistemological contradiction between scientific experimentation and Oldreive's faith-based approach to CA can only be understood through an appreciation of Zimbabwe's political and economic crisis and the politics of humanitarian relief and development aid. While Zimbabwe's government had isolated itself internationally through a violent land redistribution programme and the controversial 2002 presidential elections, the pace of the country's economic decline increased rapidly. In response to this and drought conditions in 2001/02 and 2002/03 (Andersson 2007), donors used NGOs to distribute food aid and seed for planting (Rohrbach et al 2004b). These initial responses lacked coordination, but staff from the donors, NGOs, government and international agricultural research institutes soon began to work together through an Agriculture Coordinating Committee. Coordination of short-term relief programmes was vested in the FAO emergency office. Donors such as the EU and USAID were only willing to fund short-term relief programmes that assisted people in re-establishing their livelihoods; they would not provide development assistance or collaborate actively with the government. Other donors, such as the UK's DFID, were more concerned with the longer-term impacts of relief programmes (Rohrbach et al 2004a: 3, 35). In 2003 they began to add technical advice to fertiliser support aimed at poor and vulnerable farmers, including testing of ICRISAT's micro-dose fertiliser technology (Twomlow et al 2010). Subsequently, relief programmes became more encompassing and of longer duration, and the distinction between short-term relief and development became blurred, as reflected in the DFID-initiated Protracted Relief Programme of 2004 (PRP 2010). This programme, which channelled donor funding to crisis-ridden Zimbabwe while minimising direct collaboration with the country's government, evolved into a col-laborative multi-donor and NGO initiative. Its main aim is to 'reduce extreme poverty in Zimbabwe'.[9] In this way, new agricultural interventions were added to the relief agenda, including improving seed markets, the introduction of new open-pollinated varieties, improving extension advice, and enhancing farming and land-use systems through CA. The FAO had become more involved in CA promotion a few years before, co-organizing the first world congress on CA in Spain in 2001 (Vaneph and Benites 2001).

Meanwhile, ICRISAT's monitoring of the seed relief programmes revealed that yields improved where fertiliser and technical support were provided alongside the seed. It was also found that access to draught power, rather than the availability of seed, determined the area that poorer households could cultivate (Rohrbach et al 2004b). Such findings resonated well with ICRISAT's interest in the fertiliser micro-dose technology and planting basins (with or without mulching) for water harvesting in semi-arid areas (Mazvimavi et al 2008). The basin technology was attractive because it appeared to enable farmers without draught power to plant early.

Within DFID and the FAO, both key organisations within the concerted relief effort for Zimbabwe, there was excitement about work being done on CA in Zambia.[10] Inspired by Oldreive's planting basins in Zimbabwe, the Zambia National Farmers Union had formed a Conservation Farming Unit (CFU) in 1995 'to adapt the hand hoe basin system to Zambian conditions and to actively promote it among smallholders' (Haggblade and Tembo 2007: 14–15). DFID and FAO initiated the Zimbabwe Conservation Agriculture Taskforce (ZCATF), a broad-based partnership in which the FAO, CGIAR institutes such as CIMMYT and ICRISAT, and Oldreive's River of Life Church play prominent roles (Twomlow et al 2008a, 2008b). Members of these different policy, scientific and religious institutions may thus be seen as institutionalising an epistemic community on CA. Funded by the EU and DFID, the ZCATF monitors and disseminates information on CA to NGOs and government agencies, advocates for and coordinates research and training in CA, and has developed standardised CA packages for extension to smallholder farmers (Twomlow et al 2008b; ZCATF 2008). The River of Life Church, through its subsidiary Foundations for Farming, became an important training centre for NGO extension staff implementing the combined relief and CA efforts. Wide-scale CA promotion was further supported by demonstration plots, monitoring and evaluation, and research undertaken by CGIAR institutes.

The specific CA package that was developed and promoted by this epistemic community – Conservation Farming (CF) – targeted vulnerable households with limited access to draught power. It encompassed four major principles: (1) a high management standard (for instance, frequent weeding and timely operations); (2) minimum-tillage planting basins dug with a hand hoe to concentrate limited water and nutrient resources; (3) fertiliser micro-dosing to achieve higher nutrient efficiency (especially in areas where ICRISAT operated); and (4) improved seed for higher productivity (Twomlow et al 2008b). Notably, mulching (God's blanket), a major element in Oldreive's original CF work is not stressed in ZCATF or ICRISAT publications, but is often actively promoted in the field by NGO staff trained by the River of Life Church. Labour-saving technologies such as herbicides and farm implements are not included in these combined food security/CA extension programmes, while input support is often conditional on the use of planting basins (Figure 2.3). In local vernacular, CF is sometimes referred to as '*hondavation* agriculture' (*kuhonda* means 'to slim') or *diga-ufe* (dig-and-die) (Andersson et al 2011).

Understanding policy success: CA as the only way to go

The previous sections have described the institutional development of a distinct epistemic community around CA and the emergence of a particular CA policy package based on basins and mulching. While evidence-based policy is nowadays the watchword in development policy discourse, this standardised package (promoted by all but a few organisations) was a result of negotiations between research, faith-based and policy organisations. The basin/mulch package thus represents a disconnect with earlier science-based experimentation with minimum tillage, which had revealed

FIGURE 2.3 'Have you come to bring me fertiliser?' asked this farmer on arrival of visitors. Fertiliser support is often conditional on farmers' digging of planting basins. Murehwa district, Zimbabwe, November 2010 (photo: Jens A. Andersson).

problems with mulching and the need for a diversified, farmer-oriented approach. This section focuses on the successful diffusion of the CF policy model in southern Africa, acknowledging that this success may not be driven by empirical evidence of CF 'working in practice' (Latour 1987) – for example, that CA works in smallholder farming systems. As Rap (2006: 1304) has argued, policies and their success 'are subject to a continuing process of production and promotion aiming to mobilise and maintain political consent among the epistemic community to which they are directed and which they shape' (see also Haas 1992). In addition, there is a material component, as the production of policy success requires the mobilisation of substantial financial resources.

The concurrence of both processes – the promotion of policy and resource mobilisation – is central for our understanding of the policy success of CA in southern Africa. Powerful international donors and agencies, including DFID and FAO, were critical in the formation of this epistemic community. First, they provided the resources that allowed its institutionalisation in the ZCATF. Second, their strategic position in the coordination of humanitarian relief enabled them to link CA promotion to the humanitarian relief effort. Third, in the process they extended and reformulated the aims of these humanitarian programmes, which in turn increased the resource base for CA promotion through them. Fourth, the engagement of international research organisations in the formulation, implementation and evaluation of combined input support and CA programmes had a significant, if unintended, legitimising effect. While building on scientific work by international agricultural research institutes, the large-scale promotion of CF provided scientific legitimation for Oldreive's faith-based approach.

At the level of policy implementation, monitoring and evaluation, the CF model has proven equally powerful. First, the input-supported extension practices have affected CF adoption rates among resource-poor farmers, and confounded the effects of fertiliser application and CF (Mazvimavi and Nyamangara 2010). Claims of rapid yield increases thus feature prominently in the promotion of CA in southern Africa, while in capital-intensive systems elsewhere in the world (where fertiliser rates used are often higher), the benefits of CA mostly revolve around cost reductions and the possibility of an additional crop in the season. Second, the fact that CA is promoted as a package obscures the effects of individual practices and technologies. It also allows disappointing results to be explained away because of 'not implementing all components'. Third, and closely related to the latter point, is the inclusive nature of the CA policy discourse. While CA involves only three main principles, other agronomic practices and technologies are often claimed as CA practices. Examples are the FAO's and Oldreive's emphasis on a high level of agronomic management (Figure 2.2; ZCATF 2009), and the adding-on of technologies such as micro-dosing ('precision CA', Twomlow et al 2008a), agroforestry and biofuel crops, as in the Zambian Conservation Farming Unit's definition of CA.[11] Thus many different interventions can be sold to donors as CA. Fourth, to understand the policy success of CA for African smallholders requires an appreciation of the ways in which this epistemic community creates consensus. Festinger et al's seminal work on cognitive dissonance – an uncomfortable feeling caused by holding conflicting ideas simultaneously – provides useful insights. In *When Prophecy Fails*, Festinger et al (1956) analysed the responses of a cult group to the failure of their prediction that the world would end on a certain date. Instead of disintegrating, the group expanded as members started to share their beliefs with others. Thus they gained wider acceptance and, in doing so, reduced their own dissonance. Observations made by the first author during one of the meetings of Zimbabwe's CA Taskforce suggest that a similar mechanism may be at work.

Some weeks after the first rains of the 2010/11 season the ZCATF met in Harare. Among those gathering was Brian Oldreive as well as representatives of the FAO, CIMMYT, ICRISAT, USAID and Agritex (the national research and extension service). The meeting commenced with an update on the CA strategy document as formulated by the taskforce. It was reported that it was with the Ministry of Agriculture, and that a CA strategy was expected to be officially launched in 2011.

Then, an ICRISAT scientist presented results of an ongoing panel study of Conservation Farming uptake in Zimbabwe. Started in 2004/05, this study of over 200 vulnerable households covered 15 districts across Natural Regions II to V (Mazvimavi and Dimes 2009; Mazvimavi and Twomlow 2009). The presentation focused on the uptake of eight CA components during the 2005/06 to 2009/10 seasons: more than 20 per cent of households in the study had quit CF altogether, and with the exception of crop rotation, the uptake of seven other practices associated with CF showed a strong downward trend. Since 2005/06, the sharpest declines had been for winter weeding (from 87 to 46 per cent); mulch application (from 75 to 30 per cent); timely weeding (from 98 to 54 per cent); application of basal fertiliser (from 75 to 42 per cent); and application of top dressing fertiliser (from 92 to 60 per cent). The percentage of households digging planting basins reduced only marginally, from 99 per cent in 2005/06 to 86 per cent in 2009/10. A university professor at the meeting suggested that this was because farmers may get, or hope for, input support on the basis of having prepared basins. The meeting agreed with this interpretation.

In the ensuing discussion, a representative of the River of Life Church wondered whether the study was not misleading. He suggested that it dilutes uptake 'if you keep the same denominator when the numbers are decreasing'. Another taskforce member wanted to know how uptake is measured, for instance in relation to mulching. Is it yes/no adoption, or on a scale? An FAO representative suggested that since the relief efforts started, there had been a shift in the category of farmers targeted. By stressing that the emphasis of the CA extension effort is no longer on the poorest of the poor, he seemed to suggest that this panel study was not (or was no longer) representative for CA adoption in the country. '*These people are not even farmers!*' he exclaimed, and the meeting agreed. Another member seemed more concerned with moving forward: 'Let's accept that mulch is a problem, but let's look at ways to create mulch.' Concern was also raised about the distribution of the presentation. It was felt that the data may be misinterpreted as outsiders would 'not have the background info you give us here'.

Then the meeting left the discomforting findings of the panel study and continued with the next agenda items: the institutionalisation of CA in a governmental CA unit instead of the ZCATF; a new publication for a CA training module in agricultural colleges (Nyamangara and Matizha, 2010); and an update on imported CA equipment that was to be tested during the 2010/11 season.

Obviously, these observations are not representative for the whole epistemic community on CA, however defined. Yet the dynamic that emerges from them illustrates how people with shared vested interests may respond to incongruent information and gravitate towards a (new) public consensus. Confronted with evidence of farmers abandoning CA, the group did not question the value of particular technologies, but rather the commitment or 'mindset' of smallholder farmers.

Stewardship and changing mindsets: the legitimisation of CA by higher powers

Although the use of chemical inputs such as fertilisers and herbicides has been central to the success of CA in large-scale agriculture, the positive ring of 'conservation' is a strong mobilising force within both environmental and development circles. Soil conservation and better husbandry also resonate with the concept of sustainability. Further, the idea of conservation speaks to the religious psyche as stewardship is a central tenet in the Judeo-Christian tradition: people are the custodians of God's Earth and should not despoil it (Passmore, 1974).

Several evangelical churches promote CA with what can only be described as missionary zeal, referring to the misguided ways of non-believers. Arguably, the convergence of religious discourse, environmentalism and development is most visible in the widespread call to change farmers' 'mindsets' (FAO 2008a, 2008b), as if those promoting and practising CA are the chosen ones, the pioneers who are breaking from the mould into new territory. Thus the less innocent aspects of the CA epistemic community come to the fore as the (scientific) professionals who legitimise CA policy portray 'non-believers' as unqualified, ignorant and intransigent, stuck in the 'mindset of the plough' and in need of 'conversion'. Such evangelical language is common in the literature promoting CA. The ACT Network website reports 'Currently more than 100,000 small-scale farmers in Zambia have *converted* to conservation agriculture' (emphasis added).[12]

Contesting the suitability of CA in African smallholder farming systems

So why should CA not work in Africa? The simple answer is that it does, as evidenced by the uptake of CA on large-scale commercial farms in southern Africa during the 1990s (Giller et al 2009). The arguments concerning the potential benefits of CA for smallholder farmers have been rehearsed by Giller et al (2009), and in a subsequent electronic debate.[13] Here we address the question: Is CA suited to the circumstances of smallholder farmers in Africa? However, we are acutely aware that, in addressing this question in general terms, we run the risk of being trapped by our own arguments. Africa has a huge diversity of smallholder farms and farming systems (Giller et al 2011), in terms of soils, climate, crops, livestock and grazing areas, which makes any generalisations dangerous and potentially misleading. But having acknowledged this, poor productivity and a dominance of cereal crops, notably maize, typify smallholder farming systems where CA is being promoted actively. The discussion that follows therefore focuses on these.

God's blanket is rather thin ... the problems of mulching

In CA, successful erosion control requires the soil to be covered with a mulch of organic matter. Mulching has a number of advantages: the erosive energy of rainfall is reduced as it is intercepted by the mulch; the mulch protects soil particles from being dislodged; and soil porosity tends to increase due to old root channels and the activity of earthworms and termites, so runoff is reduced as most rainfall infiltrates directly into the soil. A thick layer of mulch can also help to suppress weeds. The retention of crop residues leads to increased soil organic matter that, in turn, enhances soil structure, infiltration and the supply of nitrogen for crop growth through mineralisation.

In mechanised CA where fertiliser is used, it is largely crop residue that provides the mulch, although sometimes green manure crops are grown specifically to provide soil cover. But in African smallholder farming, this is not so straightforward. The poor productivity of many smallholder farming systems means that the amount of crop residue produced is limited. Cereals such as maize often yield only 0.5–2 t ha^{-1} of grain and 1.5–3 t ha^{-1} of stover. A rule of thumb often used with CA is that 30 per cent of the soil should be covered at the beginning of the cropping season (FAO 2008a), which requires roughly 2–3 t ha^{-1} of plant material (Giller et al 2009). Thus, to ensure adequate soil cover, all available crop residues would need to be returned to the soil, but in many situations this is impossible because of competing uses, most notably as livestock feed. For instance, farmers with cattle remove crop residue from the field at harvest and store it at their homesteads for use as feed.

Given the long dry season in southern Africa, any crop residue left in the field disappears between crop harvest and the start of the next season due to the action of termites (Baudron et al 2012). Termites can have positive benefits – in West Africa it was found that particular soil-dwelling termites (*Odontotermes* and *Macrotermes*) improve nutrient release and crop performance on crusted soils (Mando 1998). These species are responsible for the formation of macropores in *Zaï* pits (Mando et al 2006: 393), which improves infiltration and capture of rainfall into the soil. However, farmers in Zimbabwe complain that leaving maize residue as mulch attracts termites that, especially in drier areas or during dry spells, feed on the next crop causing lodging and yield loss.

The practice and benefits of reduced tillage and mulching are interdependent. Tillage helps to control weeds. In the absence of mulch, runoff and erosion can be exacerbated by not tilling the soil. Tillage increases surface roughness and infiltration, particularly if soils are poor in organic matter. Tillage also has other benefits: the soil disturbance stimulates a flush of mineralisation, releasing nitrogen from the soil organic matter, which is then available for crop growth (Chikowo et al 2004). Thus not tilling can translate into yield penalties on poor soils (Guto et al 2012). Without a thick mulch cover, not tilling also leads to increased weed pressure.

Weeds – the Achilles' heel of CA

Smallholder farming is labour-constrained due to seasonal peaks in labour demand. Inversion tillage with a mould-board plough is effective in burying and controlling weeds. Although reduced tillage may alleviate the peak labour demand for land preparation and planting, if herbicides are not available, it increases the peak in labour demand at weeding. Especially on more fertile soils in hot areas, weed pressure can lead farmers to abandon up to a third of the area planted (Baudron et al 2012). Where weeding is done primarily by women, their labour burden may increase with reduced tillage (Giller et al 2009). Thus the benefits of CA for smallholders are restricted by the expense and availability of herbicides and knapsack sprayers. Even in high-input, large-scale agriculture, weed control in CA is not without problems. In Australia, over-dependence on the herbicide glyphosate has led to build-up of herbicide-resistant weeds, so that occasional cultivation is recognised as a better management option than no cultivation at all (Kirkegaard 1995).

CA-rbon sequestrated or overrated?

It is claimed that CA leads to increased soil carbon, but the scientific evidence is ambiguous. Two detailed meta-analyses failed to find consistent increases in soil organic carbon (SOC) with reduced or zero-tillage (Govaerts et al 2009; Luo et al 2010). It is well known that increasing the amount of organic residue returned to the soil increases SOC. This is why crop fertilisation that results in greater residue production can increase SOC (Vanlauwe and Giller 2006). The effect of tillage on soil C is less clear, however. Although soil disturbance causes a flush of microbial activity and mineralisation of C and N, this effect is short-lived and the rate of decomposition falls back to that of undisturbed soil within a matter of days. This means that the stimulation of decomposition rates has a relatively small effect on SOC. As physical protection of soil organic matter depends on binding to clay particles or entrapment in aggregates, the effect of tillage on SOC is greater in clay soils, but there is little effect on the sandy soils that predominate in Zimbabwe (Chivenge et al 2007).

So why is it so commonly claimed that CA increases soil organic matter? On the face of it, simply measuring the effect of CA on soil C stocks appears to be a trivial problem: take before-and-after soil samples and measure SOC. In many cases, observers say they can see the difference – the top layer of soil is darker. But, unfortunately, the situation is more complex than this. The lack of tillage leads to increased soil C in the surface horizons, whereas ploughing mixes organic matter into the surface 15–25 cm of soil. Thus the concentration of SOC is diluted. Further, untilled soil tends to become compacted and the bulk density increases. This means that sampling to the same depth in tilled and untilled soils may actually sample a different mass of soil, leading to the artefact that there is more SOC with CA. Thus sampling on a soil-mass basis appears to be the only way of ensuring valid comparisons of soil C stocks under different tillage treatments (Ellert and Bettany 1995).

There also seems to be a sweeping assumption with regard to soil organic matter that 'the more the better'. But increasing the amount of organic matter inputs, particularly via legume green manures, can lead to crop loss due to infestation with cutworms (Chikowo et al 2004). These white insect grubs thrive when large inputs of readily decomposable material – either as mulch or incorporated – are added to soil. As the name suggests, they cut the roots and can wipe out the following crop completely.

Crop rotations: an old problem resurfaces

A clear example of the mismatch between CA and smallholder agriculture relates to the third principle of CA – crop rotation, preferably with legumes. The technical benefits of growing legumes in rotation with cereals or root crops to break a monoculture are well known (Giller 2001). As early as the late 1920s, the colonial Department of Agriculture promoted crop rotation in Zimbabwe's African farming areas (Kramer 1997), but uptake has proved problematic ever since (Baudron et al 2012). A standard recommendation is for one season of a grain legume to be followed by two seasons of cereals, which would require a third of the land area to be cropped to legumes. Yet the labour requirement for the cultivation of common legumes such as groundnuts and Bambara nuts (*Vigna subterranea*) is higher than for cereals, and farming households need only a small area of grain legumes to meet their food needs. Unless there is a market for the extra produce, there is little incentive to grow more legume grain than the household will consume.

CAWT by one's own petard

Recently, the World Agroforestry Centre (ICRAF) has joined the push for what it is calling 'CAWT – Conservation Agriculture with Trees', or 'Evergreen Agriculture' (Garrity et al 2010). It proposes various approaches for integration of mainly nitrogen-fixing trees into CA. Some approaches, notably in parklands, where trees such as *Faidherbia albida* are maintained within cropped fields and managed for firewood and fodder, are common in West Africa and a few parts of East and southern Africa. Learning from the Conservation Farming Unit in Zambia, ICRAF now proposes to extend CA under *F. albida*, and is providing tree seedlings to NGOs. Little regard seems to be paid to the ecology of *F. albida* – its reverse phenology means that crops under it are not shaded, but the tree has a full canopy during the long dry season when growth depends on its roots being able to reach a permanent water table. It is therefore unlikely that it will grow well in many of the areas where it is being promoted, where shallow soils predominate.

Conclusion

One of the most prolific authors on reduced tillage agriculture in Africa, Rattan Lal, once bemoaned the lack of organic residues and manure available in smallholder systems. In an editorial, he concluded:

> Under these conditions, loosening of soil by any tillage (manual by a hoe, animal drawn traditional and/or tractor driven mouldboard plow or sub-soiler)

improves porosity and structural characteristics of a compacted soil, albeit temporarily. In addition, plowing also enhances mineralisation of whatever little soil organic matter still remains in the soil. The enhanced mineralisation releases essential nutrients (N, P, K), which also improves plant growth especially in traditional agriculture where chemical fertilizers are rarely or minimally used. … *resource-poor farmers will have to continue practicing plow tillage while fully realizing that it is not a sustainable practice.*

(Lal 2007; emphasis added)

Other authors have also highlighted how little consideration is given to what Sumberg (2005) calls 'adoption constraints that are endogenous to the fit between the innovation and the target group', or whether CA 'actually fulfils a concrete need from the point of view of targeted smallholders' (Bolliger 2007). Yet others continue to propose the best approaches to promote and extend CA (e.g. Kassam et al 2009) without questioning *if* (where and for whom) modified tillage systems and the CA 'package' are indeed appropriate.

The aim of this chapter is neither to add to nor resolve contestation around the agronomic basis of CA. Rather, the focus is on the ways in which science, development policy and religion have become intertwined. One result is that questions about the workings and appropriateness of CA have been labelled 'irrelevant', and farmers' tillage practices labelled as 'ignorance'. This chapter illustrates the silencing effects of a powerful epistemic community as it pursues a specific policy enterprise. This represents a rupture in the trend towards more farmer-oriented, participatory approaches to technology development.

Although CA promotion in southern Africa may be regarded as an extreme case, the analysis demonstrates that agronomic knowledge is produced within a particular political arena. Agronomy and agronomic research are not apolitical. This case of CA promotion in southern Africa demonstrates the power of an epistemic community when it becomes institutionalised. With its policy enterprise financed by development-oriented donors and policy organisations, and producing knowledge that is sanctioned by higher powers (God), such an epistemic community may operate largely independently of state institutions, yet may strongly influence national policy. The widespread endorsement of CA by governments in southern Africa evidences this dynamic (FAO 2009).

While CA increasingly dominates debates about agricultural development in Africa, we wonder whether international organisations should be so active and univocal in their promotion of CA. Although supported by committed and sincere scientists and development practitioners, only time will tell whether the missionary zeal of the 'blanket salesmen' warrants the disregarding of farmers' practices.

Acknowledgment

The authors gratefully acknowledge the very useful comments and suggestions made by Steve Twomlow and Jankees van Donge on an earlier draft of this chapter.

Notes

1 This is the most widely accepted definition, although there is considerable confusion, and many different approaches and practices are referred to as CA (Giller et al 2009).
2 For instance, in Zimbabwe alone the FAO channelled some $US20 million to smallholder CA projects during the period 2008–12 (FAO 2010: 49–50). This figure is an underestimate as it excludes natural resource management and food security projects that also promote CA.
3 See http://kenya.careofcreation.net, www.farming-gods-way.org, www.foundations forfarming.org. The notion of *Man's Responsibility for Nature* (Passmore 1974), or environmental stewardship, is a particular interpretation of the statement in *Genesis* (1: 26) that God gives man dominion over all creatures. Proponents of this view, including faith-based organisations promoting CA, differ from 'deep ecologists' (Naess, 1973), who reject the inherent anthropocentrism of this perspective.
4 Although their academic and professional backgrounds may vary, members of an epistemic community have shared sets of normative, principled and causal beliefs, shared notions of validity, and a common policy enterprise (Haas 1992: 3). Members of an epistemic community may thus be regarded as sharing a particular mindset.
5 As the opening quote suggests, Friedrich and Kassam (2011) appear to define as sustainable those situations in which natural soil formation rates are equal to or higher than soil erosion rates.
6 'The plough is an enemy of sustainability … [To] suggest its adoption as a possibility seems to be based on the fact that ploughs gain adoption easily. So does Fast Food, but it's not necessarily a good thing.' (Robert M. Boddey, Embrapa Agrobiologia, Brazil, email, 23/09/08)
7 Unlike ploughing, ripping does not involve soil inversion, merely the opening of the soil. Mulch ripping involves ripping mulch-covered soil. The no-till tied ridging technology makes use of ridges that are cross-tied at regular intervals with small dams. The basins formed between the ties and ridges prevent water from flowing off the field. Once the ridges are established, the land is not ploughed for a number of years.
8 See http://kenya.careofcreation.net and www.farming-gods-way.org, which incorporates activities of the South African Bountiful Grains Trust. Other examples include the 'Growing Nations' organisation in Lesotho (www.new-ag.info/en/focus/focusItem.php?a=485).
9 www.prpzim.info
10 Steve Twomlow, former ICRISAT scientist, email, 06/03/11.
11 www.conservationagriculture.org/CFU
12 www.act-africa.org
13 http://conservationag.wordpress.com/2009/12/01/ken-gillers-paper-on-conservation-agriculture

References

Andersson, J.A. (2007) 'How much did property rights matter? Understanding food insecurity in Zimbabwe: a critique of Richardson', *African Affairs*, 106(425): 681–90.
Andersson, J.A., Giller, K., Mafongoya, P. and Mapfumo, P. (2011) Diga-Udye *or* Diga-Ufe? *(Dig-and-Eat or Dig-and-Die): Is Conservation Agriculture Contributing to Agricultural Involution in Zimbabwe?*, Regional Conservation Agriculture Symposium for Southern Africa, 8–10 February 2011, Johannesburg, South Africa. http://fao-reosa.org/index.php?option= com_phocadownload&view=category&download=39:03-ca-posters-consolidated-theme-2-part-2&id=18:downloads&Itemid=137
Baudron, F., Andersson, J.A., Corbeels, M. and Giller, K.E. (2012) 'Failing to yield? Ploughs, conservation agriculture and the problem of agricultural intensification: an example from the Zambezi Valley, Zimbabwe', *Journal of Development Studies* (in press).
Beinart, W. (1984) 'Soil erosion, conservationism and ideas about development: a southern African exploration, 1900–1960', *Journal of Southern African Studies*, 11(1): 52–83.
Benites, J. and Steiner, K.G. (1998) *Conservation Tillage for Sustainable Agriculture: International Workshop*, Harare, Zimbabwe, 22–27 June 1998. Proceedings, Deutsche Gesellschaft für Technische Zusammenarbeit.

Bolding, A. (2004) 'In hot water: a study on sociotechnical intervention models and practices of water use in smallholder agriculture, Nyanyadzi catchment, Zimbabwe', PhD thesis, Wageningen University.

Bolliger, A. (2007) 'Is zero-till an appropriate agricultural alternative for disadvantaged smallholders of South Africa? A study of surrogate systems and strategies, smallholder sensitivities and soil glycoproteins', PhD thesis, University of Copenhagen.

Bolliger, A., Magid, J., Amado, T.J.C., Skorá Neto, F., Ribeiro, M.F.S., Calegari, A., Ralisch, R. and Neergard, A. (2006) 'Taking stock of the Brazilian "zero-till revolution": a review of landmark research and farmer's practice', *Advances in Agronomy*, 91: 49–110.

Chikowo, R. (2011) *Climatic Risk Analysis in Conservation Agriculture in Varied Biophysical and Socio-economic Settings of Southern Africa*. Johannesburg: FAO, 1–48.

Chikowo, R., Mapfumo, P., Nyamugafata, P. and Giller, K.E. (2004) 'Mineral N dynamics, leaching and nitrous oxide losses under maize following two-year improved fallows on a sandy loam soil in Zimbabwe', *Plant and Soil*, 259: 315–30.

Chivenge, P.P., Murwira, H.K., Giller, K.E., Mapfumo, P. and Six, J. (2007) 'Long-term impact of reduced tillage and residue management on soil carbon stabilization: implications for conservation agriculture on contrasting soils', *Soil & Tillage Research*, 94: 328–37.

Chuma, E. and Hagmann, J. (1995) 'Summary of results and experiments from on-station and on-farm testing and development of conservation tillage systems in semi-arid Masvingo', in Twomlow, S., Ellis-Jones, J., Hagmann, J. and Loos, H. (eds) *Soil and Water Conservation for Smallholder Farmers in Semi-arid Zimbabwe: Transfers between Research and Extension*, Proceedings of a technical workshop, April 1995. Harare: Integrated Rural Development Programme (IRDEP), 61–69.

Ellert, B.H. and Bettany, J.R. (1995) 'Calculation of organic matter and nutrients stored in soils under contrasting management regimes', *Canadian Journal of Soil Science*, 75: 529–38.

Elwell, H.A. (1980) *Design of Safe Rotational Systems*. Harare: Agritex.

Elwell, H.A. and Norton, A.J. (1988) *No-till Tied Ridging: A Recommended Sustainable Crop Production System*. Harare: Institute of Agricultural Engineering.

FAO (2008a) 'Conservation Agriculture', www.fao.org/ag/ca/1a.html

——(2008b) *Investing in Sustainable Agricultural Intensification. The Role of Conservation Agriculture. A Framework for Action*. Rome: Food and Agriculture Organization.

——(2009) 'Governments in Southern Africa endorse Conservation Agriculture as a pathway to food security', Food and Agricultural Organization, http://appablog.wordpress.com/2009/04/11/governments-in-southern-africa-endorse-conservation-agriculture-as-a-pathway-to-food-security

——(2010) 'Field Programme Management Information System', https://extranet.fao.org/fpmis/index.jsp

Fatondji, D., Martius, C. and Vlek, P. (2001) '*Zaï*: A traditional technique for land rehabilitation in Niger', *ZEF News* 8: 1–2.

Festinger, L., Riecken, H. and Schachter, S. (1956) *When Prophecy Fails: A Social and Psychological Study of A Modern Group that Predicted the Destruction of the World*. Minneapolis, MN: University of Minnesota Press.

Friedrich, T. and Kassam, A. (2011) 'Conservation Agriculture: global perspectives and developments', presentation at the Regional Conservation Agriculture Symposium, Johannesburg, South Africa, 8–10 February. Rome: FAO. See under 'Events' on http://www.fao.org/ag/ca/

Garrity, D.P., Akinnifesi, F., Ajayi, O., Weldesemayat, S., Mowo, J., Kalinganire, A., Larwanou, M. and Bayala, J. (2010) 'Evergreen Agriculture: a robust approach to sustainable food security in Africa', *Food Security*, 2: 197–214.

Giller, K.E. (2001) *Nitrogen Fixation in Tropical Cropping Systems*. Wallingford: CAB International.

Giller, K.E., Witter, E., Corbeels, M. and Tittonell, P. (2009) 'Conservation agriculture and smallholder farming in Africa: The heretics' view', *Field Crops Research*, 114: 23–34.

Giller, K. E., Tittonell, P., Rufino, M. C., van Wijk, M. T., Zingore, S., Mapfumo, P., Adjei-Nsiah, S., Herrero, M., Chikowo, R., Corbeels, M., Rowe, E. C., Baijukya, F., Mwijage, A., Smith, J., Yeboah, E., van der Burg, W. J., Sanogo, O. M., Misiko, M., de

Ridder, N., Karanja, S., Kaizzi, C., K'ungu, J., Mwale, M., Nwaga, D., Pacini, C. and Vanlauwe, B. (2011) 'Communicating complexity: integrated assessment of trade-offs concerning soil fertility management within African farming systems to support innovation and development', *Agricultural Systems*, 104: 191–203.

Govaerts, B., Verhulst, N., Castellanos-Navarrete, A., Sayre, K.D., Dixon, J. and Dendooven, L. (2009) 'Conservation agriculture and soil carbon sequestration: between myth and farmer reality', *Critical Reviews in Plant Sciences*, 28: 97–122.

Grant, P.M. (1995) 'Soil fertility and organic matter management', in Twomlow, S., Ellis-Jones, J., Hagmann, J. and Loos, H. (eds) *Soil and Water Conservation for Smallholder Farmers in Semi-arid Zimbabwe: Transfers between Research and Extension*, Proceedings of a technical workshop, April 1995. Harare: Integrated Rural Development Programme (IRDEP), 164–71.

Guto, S.N., Pypers, P., Vanlauwe, B., de Ridder, N. and Giller, K.E. (2012) 'Socio-ecological niches for minimum tillage and crop-residue retention in continuous maize cropping systems in smallholder farms of Central Kenya', *Agronomy Journal*, 103: 1–11.

Haas, P.M. (1992) 'Epistemic communities and international policy coordination', *International Organization*, 46(1): 1–35.

Haggblade, S. and Tembo, G. (2007) *Conservation Farming in Zambia*. Washington, DC: International Food Policy Research Institute.

Hagmann, J. (1993) *Farmer Participatory Research in Conservation Tillage and Approach, Methods and Experiences from an Adaptive On-farm Trial Programme in Zimbabwe*, Project Research Report No. 8. Agritex/GTZ.

Hagmann, J., Chuma, E., Murwira, K. and Moyo, E. (1995) 'Transformation of agricultural extension and research towards farmer participatory approach and experiences in Masvingo Province, Zimbabwe', in Twomlow, S., Ellis-Jones, J., Hagmann, J. and Loos, H. (eds) *Soil and Water Conservation for Smallholder Farmers in Semi-arid Zimbabwe: Transfers between Research and Extension*, Proceedings of a technical workshop, April 1995. Harare: Integrated Rural Development Programme (IRDEP).

IIRR/ACT (2005) *Conservation Agriculture: A Manual for Farmers and Extension Workers in Africa*. Boulder, CO: Westview Press and International Institute of Rural Reconstruction/African Conservation Tillage Network.

Kassam, A., Friedrich, T., Shaxson, F. and Pretty, J. (2009) 'The spread of Conservation Agriculture: justification, sustainability and uptake', *International Journal of Agricultural Sustainability*, 7: 292–320.

Kirkegaard, J. (1995) 'A review of trends in wheat yield responses to conservation cropping in Australia', *Australian Journal of Experimental Agriculture*, 35: 835–48.

Kramer, E. (1997) 'The early years: extension services in peasant agriculture in colonial Zimbabwe, 1925–29', *Zambezia* 24(2): 159–79.

Lal, R. (2007) 'Constraints to adopting no-till farming in developing countries', *Soil & Tillage Research*, 94: 1–3.

Latour, B. (1987) *Science in Action: How to Follow Scientists and Engineers through Society*. Cambridge, MA: Harvard University Press.

Luo, Z., Wang, E. and Sun, O.J. (2010) 'Can no-tillage stimulate carbon sequestration in agricultural soils? A meta-analysis of paired experiments', *Agriculture, Ecosystems and Environment*, 139: 224–31.

Mando, A. (1998) 'Soil-dwelling termites and mulches improve nutrient release and crop performance on Sahelian crusted soil', *Arid Land Research and Management*, 12: 153–63.

Mando, A., Fatondji, D., Zougmoré, R., Brussaard, L., Bielders, C.L. and Martius, C., (2006) 'Restoring soil fertility in semi-arid West Africa', in Uphoff, N., Ball, A.S., Fernandez, E., Herren, H., Husson, O., Laing, M., Palm, C., Sanchez, P., Sanginga, N. and Thies, J. (eds) *Biological Approaches to Sustainable Soil Systems*. Boca Raton, FL: CRC Press.

Marongwe, L. S., Kwazira, K., Jenrich, M., Thierfelder, C., Kassam, A. and Friedrich, T. (2011) 'An African success: the case of conservation agriculture in Zimbabwe', *International Journal of Agricultural Sustainability*, 9: 153–61.

Mazvimavi, K. and Dimes, J. (2009) 'Trends in Conservation Farming adoption and impacts', presentation to the CA Task Force meeting, 10 July 2009. Bulawayo: ICRISAT.

Mazvimavi, K. and Nyamangara, J. (2010) 'Dynamics in Conservation Farming Adoption Intensity, 2007–10', Presentation to the CA Task Force meeting, Institute of Agricultural Engineering, Harare, 7 December 2010. ICRISAT, Bulawayo.

Mazvimavi, K. and Twomlow, S. (2009) 'Socioeconomic and institutional factors influencing adoption of conservation farming by vulnerable households in Zimbabwe', *Agricultural Systems*, 101: 20–29.

Mazvimavi, K., Twomlow, S., Murendo, C. and Musitini, T. (2008) *Science in Agricultural Relief and Development Programs: The Case of Conservation Farming in Zimbabwe*, African Association of Agricultural Economists' Second International Conference, 20–22 August 2007, Accra. Nairobi: AAAE, pp. 321–25. http://ideas.repec.org/p/ags/aaae07/52129.html

McClymont, D. and Winkfield, R. (eds) (1989) *Conservation Tillage*, Commercial Grain Producers Association Handbook. Harare: Cannon Press.

Munyati, M. (1997) 'Conservation tillage for sustainable crop production: results from on-station and on-farm research in Natural Region II, 1988–96', *Zimbabwe Science News*, 31(2): 27–33.

Mupangwa, W., Love, D. and Twomlow, S. (2006) 'Soil-water conservation and rainwater harvesting strategies in the semi-arid Mzingwane Catchment, Limpopo Basin, Zimbabwe', *Physics and Chemistry of the Earth*, 31: 893–900.

Naess, A. (1973) 'The shallow and the deep, long-range ecology movement: a summary', *Inquiry* 16(1): 95–100.

Nehanda, G. (1999) 'Soil and water conservation, soil moisture management and conservation tillage in Zimbabwe', in Nabhan, H., Mashali, A.M. and Mermut, A.R. (eds) *Integrated Soil Management for Sustainable Agriculture and Food Security in Southern and East Africa, Proceedings of the Expert Consultation*, Harare, 8–12 December 1997: 153–67.

Norton, A.J. (1987) 'Improvement in tillage practices', paper for FAO/SIDA sponsored seminar on *Increased Food Production through Low-cost Food Crops Technology*, Harare, Zimbabwe, 2–17 March 1987, in Holmes, J.C. (ed.) *Improving Food Crop Production on Small Farms in Africa*. Rome: FAO: 314–23.

Norton, A. (1988) 'A systematic method of selecting and recommending tillage systems in Natural Regions III, IV and V', in *Cropping in the Semiarid Areas of Zimbabwe*, Proceedings of a workshop held in Harare, 24–28 August 1987. Agritex/DR&ss/gtz: 495–530.

Nyagumbo, I. (1999) 'Conservation tillage for sustainable crop production systems: experiences from on-station and on-farm research in Zimbabwe, 1988–97', in Kaumbutho, P.G and Simalenga, T.E. (eds) *Conservation Tillage with Animal Traction*. Harare: Animal Traction Network for Eastern and Southern Africa: 108–15.

Nyamangara, M.E. and Matizha, W. (2010) *Principles of Conservation Agriculture: Module for Diploma in Agriculture*. Harare: Ministry of Agriculture, Mechanization and Irrigation Development.

Nyamapfene, K. (1991) *The Soils of Zimbabwe*. Harare: Nehanda Publishers.

Nyamudeza, P. and Nyakatawa, E.Z. (1995) 'The effect of sowing crops in furrow of tied ridges on soil water and crop yields in NRV of Zimbabwe', in Twomlow, S., Ellis-Jones, J., Hagmann, J. and Loos, H. (eds) *Soil and Water Conservation for Smallholder Farmers in Semi-arid Zimbabwe: Transfers between Research and Extension*, Proceedings of a technical workshop, April 1995. Harare: Integrated Rural Development Programme (IRDEP), 32–40.

Okali, C., Sumberg, J. and Farrington, J. (1994) *Farmer Participatory Research: Rhetoric and Reality*. London: Intermediate Technology Publications.

Oldreive, B. (1993) *Conservation Farming for Communal, Small-Scale, Resettlement and Co-operative Farmers of Zimbabwe, A Farm Management Handbook*. Zimbabwe: Mazongororo Paper Converters (Pvt) Ltd.

——(2009) *Trainer's Manual, Beginner's Course*. Harare: Foundations for Farming, 7–9.

Passmore, J. (1974) *Man's Responsibility for Nature: Ecological Problems and Western Traditions*. London: Duckworth.

Prestt, A.J. (1986) 'Basin tillage – a review', *Zimbabwe Agricultural Journal*, 83(1): 11–17.

PRP (2010) 'Livelihoods, Food Security & Nutrition Programme', www.prpzim.info/default/default.cfm?linkid=28

Rap, E. (2006) 'The success of a policy model: irrigation management transfer in Mexico,' *Journal of Development Studies*, 42(8): 1301–24.

Rohrbach, D., Charters, R. and Nyagweta, J. (2004a) *Guidelines for Emergency Relief Projects in Zimbabwe: Seed and Fertilizer Relief*. Bulawayo: ICRISAT/Rome: FAO.

Rohrbach, D., Mashingaidze, A.B. and Mudhara, M. (2004b) *The Distribution of Relief Seed and Fertilizer in Zimbabwe: Lessons Derived from the 2003/04 Season, Bulawayo, Zimbabwe*. Bulawayo: ICRISAT.

Roose, E., Kabore, V. and Guenat, C. (1999) 'Zaï practice: A West African traditional rehabilitation system for semiarid degraded lands, a case study in Burkina Faso', *Arid Land Research and Management*, 13(4): 343–55.

Shumba, E.M., Waddington, S.R. and Rukuni, M. (1992) 'Use of tine-tillage, with atrazine weed control, to permit earlier planting of maize by smallholder farmers in Zimbabwe', *Experimental Agriculture*, 28: 443–52

Smith, R.D. (1988) *Tillage Trials in Zimbabwe 1957 to 1988*. Harare: Institute of Agricultural Engineering, Department of Agricultural Technical and Extension Services, Ministry of Land, Agriculture, and Rural Resettlement.

Sumberg, J. (2005) 'Constraints to the adoption of agricultural innovations – is it time for a re-think?', *Outlook on Agriculture*, 34: 7–10.

Taonezvi, P.H. (1994) 'Agricultural research policy', in Rukuni, M. and Eicher, C.K. (eds) *Zimbabwe's Agricultural Revolution*. Harare: University of Zimbabwe Publications, 92–103.

Thierfelder, C. and Wall, P.C. (undated) *The Problem of Soil and Land Degradation*. Harare: CIMMYT.

Twomlow, S.J., Steyn, T. and du Preez, C.C. (2006) 'Dryland farming in Southern Africa', in Peterson, G.A., Unger, P.W. and Payne, W.A. (eds) *Dryland Agriculture*, Agronomy Monograph No. 23 (2nd edn). Madison, WI: American Society of Agronomy, Crop Science Society of America, Soil Science Society of America, 769–836.

Twomlow, S., Hove, L., Mupangwa, W., Masikati, P. and Mashingaidze, N. (2008a) 'Precision conservation agriculture for vulnerable farmers in low potential zones', in *Proceedings of the Workshop on Increasing the Productivity and Sustainability of Rainfed Cropping Systems of Poor, Smallholder Farmers*, Tamale, Ghana, 22–25 September 2008. Bulawayo: ICRISAT.

Twomlow, S., Urolov, J.C., Jenrich, M. and Oldrieve, B. (2008b) 'Lessons from the field: Zimbabwe's Conservation Agriculture Task Force', *Journal of SAT Agricultural Research*, 6: 1–11.

Twomlow, S., Rohrbach, D., Dimes, J., Rusike, J., Mupangwa, W., Ncube, B., Hove, L., Moyo, M., Mashingaidze, N. and Mahposa, P. (2010) 'Micro-dosing as a pathway to Africa's Green Revolution: evidence from broad-scale on-farm trials', *Nutrient Cycling in Agroecosystems*, 88: 3–15.

Vaneph, S. and Benites, J. (2001) *First World Congress on Conservation Agriculture: A World-wide Challenge*, Madrid, 1–5 October, pp. 1–21.

Vanlauwe, B. and Giller, K.E. (2006) 'Popular myths around soil fertility management in sub-Saharan Africa', *Agriculture, Ecosystems and Environment*, 116: 34–46.

Vincent, V. and Thomas, R.G. (1961) *An Agricultural Survey of Southern Rhodesia: Part I Agro-ecological Survey*. Harare: Government Printer.

Vogel, H. (1994) 'Weeds in single-crop conservation farming in Zimbabwe', *Soil and Tillage Research*, 31(2–3): 169–85.

Winkfield, R. (1993) 'Foreword', in Oldrieve, B., *Conservation Farming for Communal, Small-Scale, Resettlement and Co-operative Farmers of Zimbabwe, A Farm Management Handbook*. Zimbabwe: Mazongororo Paper Converters (Pvt) Ltd.

ZCATF (2008) *Conservation Agriculture Toolbox for Zimbabwe* (version 2). Harare: Zimbabwe Conservation Agriculture Task Force.

——(2009) *Farming for the Future; A Guide to Conservation Agriculture in Zimbabwe*. Harare: Zimbabwe Conservation Agriculture Task Force.

3

CONSERVATION AGRICULTURE-BASED TECHNOLOGIES AND THE POLITICAL ECONOMY

Lessons from South Asia

Olaf Erenstein

Introduction

There has been an increasing global interest in Conservation Agriculture (CA) to rebuild soil health and make agricultural systems in the developing world more sustainable (FAO 2007; Hobbs et al 2008; Giller et al 2009). But the suitability of CA and reported impacts have been contested by research and development (R&D) stakeholders.

The contested agronomy argument (see Chapter 1 in this volume) posits that neoliberalism, participation and the environmental agenda have radically changed the context of agronomic research in the developing world since the mid-1970s. In the case of South Asia, liberalisation drastically reconfigured economies and accelerated growth – but perhaps had less far-reaching effects on agronomic research *per se*. There has been increasing private-sector investment in agro-dealer networks (e.g. Bell et al 2007), but private-sector investment in agronomic R&D remains limited – particularly when contrasted with the increasing investments in breeding proprietary crops such as hybrid maize. In part, this also reflects the inconsistent way in which liberalisation was implemented. In India, for example, strategic commodities such as wheat and rice continued to receive particular protection and emphasis by the public sector. This helped create the intensive rice–wheat systems, but also thwarted private-sector investment in related R&D. In the late 1990s, Monsanto did support no-till research at public universities in India and Pakistan, but subsequently discontinued this as the potential market for its herbicide glyphosate was considered too limited.

Participatory approaches in South Asia have become mainstream in the NGO/ development community but have had less transforming effects on the agricultural research establishment. Indeed, the latter still adheres to plot- and animal-level research and would benefit from a shift towards 'more people-centered, participatory and holistic methods and to interdisciplinary and multi-institutional approaches which link people, innovations and policy' (Erenstein and Thorpe 2011). Liberalisation and the associated retrenchment of the public sector also set the stage for new partnerships between major private and public stakeholders, but so far progress has been limited, not least because of persistent mutual distrust.

The developing world's changing context is expected to have changed agronomic research practice and opened new spaces for contestation, with subsequent impacts on rural development policy and practice and livelihoods and the environment (see Chapter 1). This chapter contributes to the debate by focusing on the contestation and impact part of the contested agronomy argument using the case of CA-based technologies in South Asia's Indo-Gangetic Plains (IGP). There are three intertwined levels of contestation in this case study: farm, science, and politics. At the farm level, debates revolve mainly around the operationalisation of CA – the numerous technical challenges of applying it within the prevailing rice–wheat systems. At the scientific level, the debate is about the evidence in support of CA. At the policy level, debate revolves around the prospects and contribution of CA *vis-à-vis* the political economy, some promoting it as a technological fix whereby more painful political adjustments can be avoided, whereas others perceive it as an insignificant drop in the ocean.

Innovation is not a neutral process. Past, current and future stakeholders at the various levels have diverging interests in how a specific system has evolved and will – or will not – evolve in the future. The introduction of CA practices into South Asia's IGP is no exception. A political economy perspective can thereby help to understand and disentangle some of the associated blockages and implications for agricultural R&D. This chapter does not seek to delve into the vast political economy literature. Instead, we use the term here to refer to interdisciplinary study of the dynamics between politics, institutions and CA, and particularly how the former has shaped and influenced CA development and uptake.

The chapter reviews the development and promotion of CA-based practices in South Asia's IGP and how these have fed into the multi-tiered contestation of suitability and impact. It first sets the scene by introducing the case of CA in the study area. It subsequently reviews the agronomic challenges, including nomenclature and the issues associated with each of the CA principles. This is followed by a review of the impact challenges in terms of measurement, profitability, equity and environment. The argument is that both the complexity of the innovation and the political economy go a long way in terms of explaining the associated contestation. The chapter ends with a discussion of lessons and implications.

The case study: CA-based technologies in the Indo-Gangetic Plains

The Green Revolution transformed the IGP – spreading from Pakistan through northern India and the Nepal Terai region to Bangladesh – into South Asia's granary. The combination of improved seed, chemical fertiliser and irrigation with a supportive environment for agricultural transformation led to rapid productivity growth, and resulted in rice–wheat systems covering an estimated 14 million ha in the region, with the bulk (10 million ha) in India (Timsina and Connor 2001). Productivity growth in these intensive systems started to stagnate towards the end of the twentieth century, thereby re-igniting concerns over national food security. This stagnation is widely attributed to soil and water degradation induced by the prevailing crop management practices, and this narrative has contributed to strong advocacy for CA-based technologies to rebuild soil health and enhance sustainability and profitability (Hobbs et al 2003; Abrol et al 2005; Gupta and Sayre 2007; Hobbs et al 2008; PACA 2008; WCCA 2009).

The Rice–Wheat Consortium (RWC) of the IGP has been one of the more vocal and influential advocates of CA. It was established in 1994 as an eco-regional program of the Consultative Group for International Agricultural Research (CGIAR). This consortium is a research network of national and international agricultural researchers that seeks to enhance agricultural productivity and environmental sustainability. The RWC was commended in its latest external review as a successful institutional innovation (Seth et al 2003). It is credited as being nationally led and facilitating agronomic research through new partnerships, new resources and new interests at the time the Indian economy started liberalising. The consortium was thereby able to bypass some initial institutional resistance to CA and collaborate with farmers and the private sector (particularly agricultural machinery manufacturers) to create interest and momentum.

The RWC was instrumental in the adaptation, promotion and diffusion of zero-tillage (ZT) wheat in South Asia, the most successful CA-based component technology in the IGP to date (Gupta and Sayre 2007; Erenstein and Laxmi 2008; Hobbs et al 2008). The RWC is thus widely perceived as a success story (Ekboir 2002; Seth et al 2003; Erenstein and Laxmi 2008; Harrington and Hobbs 2009; Erenstein 2010d).

Progress has, however, not been uniform. Conservation Agriculture has been taken up most markedly in India, and within India in the north-west IGP. This differential pattern of adoption can be explained by the presence of the RWC, but also by divergent political and economic factors (e.g. Erenstein 2010a; Erenstein and Thorpe 2011). There are also critical differences between the two crops. Advances with CA have largely been limited to wheat, with the adaptation to rice still problematic. From a CA perspective, a number of potential benefits are thwarted as tillage is reduced only for wheat – with subsequent intensive (wet) tillage for rice – and crop residues may not be retained as mulch. What is more, progress has been limited where it is most needed, as from a sustainability perspective it is primarily the environmental footprint of rice – in terms of soil and water management – that most threatens the sustainability of South Asia's cereal basket.

In the aftermath of the Green Revolution, there was a paradigm shift from commodity-centric towards more multidisciplinary and systems agricultural research. The initial interest in ZT wheat thereby originated from diagnostic studies that highlighted time conflicts between rice harvesting and wheat planting (Byerlee et al 1984; Fujisaka et al 1994). As ZT R&D progressed, the agenda also evolved to include resource-conserving technologies and eventually CA. The evolution reflected an increased emphasis on soil health and broader concerns over agriculture's environmental impacts. The research agenda was further broadened by increasing calls for more holistic and poverty-focused agricultural R&D (e.g. Seth et al 2003). The technological entry point of ZT evolved – 'conservation agriculture is probably one of the best ways to increase production, increase food security, improve farmer livelihoods and create environmental benefits while undertaking efficient natural resource use' (Hobbs et al 2003). The changing scope, in turn, broadened the array of stakeholders, from the agronomists and engineers working on ZT wheat to an array of scientists and development agents concerned with rice, other crops, crop breeding, livestock and social science.

Champions play a critical role in the successful deployment of innovations. Yet RWC's interest in and advocacy of CA was also influenced by its evolving institutional set up. The RWC was initially convened by ICRISAT but, because of the nature and extent of ICRISAT's mandate, it was never likely to give priority to supporting irrigated rice–wheat systems (Harrington and Hobbs 2009). CIMMYT convened RWC from 1999 to 2007, after which IRRI stepped in. CIMMYT had long been interested in and an advocate of ZT/CA, and its staff have contributed to its development. Although no longer the convening centre, CIMMYT continues to promote CA in the IGP and beyond (Lumpkin and Sayre 2009). IRRI has been a somewhat less enthusiastic CA advocate.

As with all disciplines, agronomists are, to a large extent, shaped by their professional training. There is strong continuity in approaches to both research and practice. Paradigm shifts require conclusive evidence against the zero hypothesis that current practice is best. CA challenges the agronomic establishment (for example, 'the mindset of the plough') and needs to be substantially superior to existing practices to win over sceptics. The problem with CA is that providing such conclusive evidence can be challenging due to a number of potentially confounding factors. Costly, long-term trials are needed, and are instrumental in documenting degradation processes and of the rebuilding of soil health. Until recently, a challenge to CA in South Asia was the absence of such long-term trials (CSISA 2009). A particular problem for CA is that its benefits become visible and substantial only after a number of years, especially in irrigated systems. Thus, because of the lack of conclusive evidence, opinion remains divided.

This chapter does not aim to settle the scientific disputes around CA or to take sides in those debates. Instead, given the strong CA advocacy in South Asia's IGP, the chapter highlights some of the blockages or constraints that advocates would need to address if their calls for widespread CA use are to be heeded. The subsequent sections review the agronomic challenges of CA in rice–wheat systems, and then move on to the impact challenges.

Agronomic challenges of CA-based technologies

Nomenclature

The technical principles of CA – minimal soil disturbance; retention of crop residue as mulch; and the use of crop rotations – are increasingly recognised as essential for sustainable agriculture (FAO 2007; Hobbs et al 2008). However, the operationalisation of CA has proven problematic.

A major problem is nomenclature: when we use the term CA, what are we talking about? CA means different things to different people and thereby provides a fertile ground for misunderstanding and contestation. In fact, CA is best conceived of as a basket of cultural practices around a common concept.

Nomenclature issues are exacerbated by the coexistence of various definitions that have evolved over time, leading to disputes as to whether reported results can actually be attributable to CA. This, in turn, leads to evolving nomenclature as terms are discredited and discarded. Nomenclature has been a challenge for some time, with CA emerging as the preferred label [for example, over 'conservation tillage' (Erenstein 2002), or the RWC's recent evolution from 'resource-conserving technologies' to 'CA-based technologies' (Gupta and Sayre 2007)].

The nomenclatural issue is particularly problematic for CA because it has three principles that typically translate into different and variously named technological components. This makes CA complex and calls for adaptive R&D, but also makes it highly site-specific as potential trade/pay-offs are dependent on specific biophysical and socio-economic conditions (Erenstein 2002). The several required changes in farmers' cultural practices also make it knowledge-intensive (Erenstein 2002; Wall 2007).

This inherent complexity is a major handicap. A simple innovation is easier to convey and explain to stakeholders, including farmers, R&D practitioners, policy-makers and the media, particularly where there are language barriers, limited human capital and other resource constraints (Erenstein 2002). An additional problem is over-simplification: in a quest to keep it simple, the complexity and nuances of the technology can be lost.

Reduced tillage

Minimal soil disturbance is a central CA tenet and typically implies the need to reduce physical tillage. Pioneering calls to this effect were made by Faulkner (1943) and have led to over half a century of R&D. Uptake of reduced tillage systems in the USA was enabled by the development of both herbicides and suitable planting equipment, and driven by favourable market developments (Erenstein 2002). The interest in reduced tillage is reflected in the portfolio of tillage-associated names – including conservation tillage, no-till(age), minimum till(age) and direct sowing.

In South Asia, ZT has been on the research agenda for over three decades. In wheat–rice systems, ZT wheat has a number of advantages: it permits earlier wheat planting, helps control obnoxious weeds such as *Phalaris minor*, reduces costs and saves water (Erenstein and Laxmi 2008). Pivotal to the success of ZT in the IGP was the development of delivery pathways for ZT seed drills, including the creation of a local manufacturing capacity. Concerted efforts by an array of public- and private-sector stakeholders were championed by key individuals (Erenstein 2010d).

The initial ZT R&D efforts were met with disdain at all levels, from farmers to policy-makers. This reaction was associated with a long-standing tradition of intensive tillage. Pioneering farmers faced numerous challenges and social pressures (Malik et al

2005). Agricultural R&D in the region remains largely funded through public resources, and some research institutions and university departments maintain a strong emphasis on station research and an inherent scepticism of innovation. Despite the research establishment not being very supportive, there were some initial champions who persevered with RWC support. Indeed, the reliance on local champions and the different levels of resistance they met helps explain the substantial differences in diffusion within and between countries (Erenstein 2010b). For instance, in India, the renowned Punjab Agricultural University was never very supportive of ZT, which contrasts with active promotion by the Haryana Agricultural University (the latter also being a member of the Professional Alliance for Conservation Agriculture; PACA 2008). In the case of the Pakistan Punjab, there were two government departments with one advocating and the other opposing ZT (Iqbal et al 2002). This had unfortunate consequences for farmers and the technology alike.

Despite increasing evidence of the potential of ZT wheat, the perceived need to till still persists among many farmers and extension agents, who believe there is a positive association between tillage intensity and yield. Indeed, even in north-west India, extension agents often still recommend reversion to tillage after some years of ZT wheat.

A further confounding factor is the development and promotion of rotavator tillage (Erenstein 2010c). Perhaps somewhat unexpectedly, ZT has opened up prospects for this single-pass technology, but the associated soil pulverisation goes against CA principles. Paradoxically, the Indian Government provides an investment subsidy for both ZT drills and rotavators – that is, for implements that respectively reduce and increase tillage intensity. In part, this reflects the confusion associated with the complexity and nomenclature highlighted above. It also reflects a subsidy syndrome that has thwarted innovation as farmers wait and see if a subsidy materialises.

From a CA perspective, tillage reduction in the IGP has only been partially successful, as ZT is typically only applied to wheat, whereas for the subsequent rice, intensive wet-land preparation followed by transplantation still prevails. Reducing rice tillage intensity presents major challenges, particularly in terms of water, weed management and available germplasm. Ongoing research is addressing these challenges to viable 'double no-till' rice–wheat systems (Ladha et al 2009).

Crop residue management

The maintenance of soil cover is another CA principle, and relies primarily on the retention of crop residue as mulch. However, in the mechanised production systems of the USA, where much of the pioneering R&D was undertaken, reduced tillage typically meant that substantial quantities of residues remained as mulch. In situations where crop residues have alternative uses, such as in much of the developing world, crop residue management is less straightforward and implies additional trade-offs (Erenstein 2002, 2003).

Zero-tillage wheat in the IGP does not necessarily retain crop residues as mulch. In fact, the prevailing ZT seed drills do not work well in the presence of mulch, but for better or worse, this has not been a major issue in view of the limited biomass remaining after rice (Erenstein and Laxmi 2008). Leaving more crop residue as mulch would require adaptation of ZT drills. Ongoing R&D has already generated some second-generation drills that are able to handle significant residues, but their cost is still relatively high.

Moving rice–wheat systems towards CA will require new approaches to crop residue management so as to ensure adequate soil cover and address potential trade-offs with alternative residue uses. The *ex-situ* use of crop residues as livestock feed is near universal (Erenstein and Thorpe 2010): wheat is the traditional food crop in the north-west IGP, and wheat residues are the basal feed for ruminant livestock. Proceeding to the eastern plains, rice becomes the staple food and rice straw the preferred feed for ruminant livestock. In the north west, this implies significant imbalances in terms of seasonal residue extraction, with surplus rice straw being burned *in situ* (Erenstein 2011). The widespread use of crop residues as feed shows they have significant value, and markets and institutional arrangements have developed accordingly (Erenstein and Thorpe 2010). There are also important regional variations in non-feed residue uses (e.g. as fuel and construction material). The increasing mechanisation of cereal harvesting creates new trade-offs in terms of residue use and management, and has led to the development and rapid uptake of a tractor-pulled straw reaper that chops the loose wheat straw and standing stubble into the preferred length for feeding (*bhusa*) and collects this in an enclosed trailer (Erenstein 2011).

In theory, the retention of crop residue as soil cover is imperative in continuous ZT systems (Erenstein 2003; Govaerts et al 2005). However, to date cultivation of ZT wheat in the IGP in the absence of some soil cover has resulted in limited perceivable negative consequences (Erenstein and Laxmi 2008). This is probably a consequence of the seasonal nature of ZT use, with plots still being seasonally tilled for the subsequent rice. However, with year-round or double no-till, residue retention will probably become critical.

Any recommendation to retain crop residue as mulch also confronts the 'clean-fields' mindset that still persists in the IGP farming community. The long-standing tradition of intensive tillage is associated with a preference not only for pulverised soils, but also for homogeneous, residue-free fields. Standing rice stubble that remains visible in the emerging wheat field is considered an eyesore, and early ZT adopters were labelled as lazy and faced social pressure (e.g. Malik et al 2005). Crop residue retention is also an important part of the ZT controversy in Pakistan Punjab. Basmati rice is a major export crop there, and the extension service fears that without ploughing, ZT wheat may encourage overwintering of stem borers in the rice stubble, undermining productivity and competitiveness. However, there is no scientific evidence of such risk (Erenstein and Laxmi 2008).

Another major issue affecting crop residue retention is that there are no immediate pay-offs in rice–wheat systems. Positive short-term yield effects associated with mulch often reflect improved water-holding capacity and reduced drought stress (Erenstein 2002). This is of particular interest in less intensive and rainfed systems, and could induce more stable and higher yields (Erenstein 2003; Govaerts et al 2005). But rice–wheat systems are typically irrigated, and drought stress is correspondingly limited.

Failing a short-term water-conservation pay-off, a longer term is typically needed for mulching to translate into soil improvements and tangible medium- to long-term yield effects.

Crop rotation

Diversified crop rotation, particularly the inclusion of legumes, is widely acknowledged as a central tenet of good agronomy. However, in developing countries, crop rotation can be more challenging, particularly if production is to a large extent for home consumption or undeveloped agricultural markets. Diversified crop rotation is not widely practised in the IGP's rice–wheat systems. Granted, the system itself is already a seasonal rotation of two crops, but both are cereal grains and are continuously cultivated on the same plot. These systems reflect a public incentive structure geared towards these two staple grains, including widespread public intervention with assured produce prices and state-controlled marketing channels. This is so particularly in India (Erenstein 2010a). The combination of secure produce markets and irrigation makes rice and wheat production a low-risk venture that has proven difficult to displace. Underlying the political economy of rice and wheat is the long-standing concern over food security in the sub-region and the reluctance to return to dependence on cereal imports. These concerns helped spark the Green Revolution, but were raised again during the recent world food price crisis. There have been some R&D initiatives to diversify rice–wheat systems but, in face of the prevailing political economy, these provide prime examples of the limitations of technological solutions without an enabling environment. Still, there is an increasing scope for diversifying rice–wheat systems, particularly in the north-west IGP, whether in response to technological developments (Jat et al 2006), rapidly evolving domestic markets (due to economic growth, urbanisation and emerging marketing chains), or increasing water scarcity (Erenstein 2009a).

Impact challenges of CA-based technologies

The above-mentioned agronomic challenges to CA-based technologies in the IGP suggest that there is no substantial area under year-round CA. Instead, the CA-based technologies have made partial inroads in the rice–wheat system: ZT wheat is the most highly developed and its impacts are most widely documented.

Profitability

A review of the impacts of ZT wheat in India's rice–wheat systems has shown that it generates substantial benefits at the farm level by enhancing income from wheat cultivation (US$97 ha^{-1}) through the combined result of a yield effect and a cost-saving effect (Erenstein and Laxmi 2008). The cost saving is robust and largely undisputed, with numerous studies reporting substantial fuel and time savings for land preparation and seeding (see Erenstein and Laxmi 2008). An average saving of

US$52 ha^{-1} primarily reflects the drastic reduction in tractor time as the number of passes over the land is reduced from eight to one. This implies a significant, immediate and recurring cost saving, corresponding to a 15–16 per cent saving on operational costs (Erenstein et al 2008).

The potential yield enhancement is more ambiguous. A review of ZT in India found an average yield effect of only 5–7 per cent for wheat across on-station trials, on-farm trials and surveys (Erenstein and Laxmi 2008). A short-term yield effect, if any, is closely associated with enhanced timeliness of wheat establishment. Heat stress at the end of the wheat season can mean that the potential wheat yield is reduced by 1–1.5 per cent per day if planting occurs after mid-November. Hence a positive yield effect of ZT hinges on the ability to translate the time savings at land preparation into an earlier seeding. Failing that, the potential yield enhancement is largely forfeited. In some early agronomic trials, planting dates of conventional and ZT were purposively aligned, thereby undermining ZT's relative performance. Some surveys also found that farmers sometimes failed to turn the time saving into earlier wheat establishment (Erenstein et al 2008). A better understanding of why farmers do not capitalise on ZT's potential to sow wheat earlier merits follow-up research.

The cost-saving effect alone makes ZT profitable, but profitability is greatly enhanced by a positive yield effect, which markedly reduces adoption risk (Erenstein and Laxmi 2008). The lack of a positive yield response was a major contributor to the slower adoption in Pakistan Punjab, and also merits follow-up research. A further confounding factor and inherent challenge is the 'yield paradigm' that still pervades in the agricultural R&D establishment and the farming community. Producing the same with less can still be a very attractive proposition for enhancing farmers' bottom line (although it may not alleviate concerns about food security), but it implies a shift in the mindset that has traditionally focused on producing more per unit of area. So far, the economic incentives for a shift to dry direct rice seeding have been relatively weak, but the recent oscillations in international prices of oil, fertiliser, rice and wheat have only increased the relevance of resource-conserving technologies such as ZT. The ability to minimise tilling and fuel use has been attractive for wheat: increasing rural wage rates and increasing regional water scarcity may make dry direct seeding of rice more attractive.

If CA is to spread, new germplasm will be required. Most crop-breeding efforts have selected germplasm under intensive tillage conditions. As a result, the wheat and rice varieties currently available are not particularly well suited to ZT conditions. Varieties specifically selected under and for CA conditions – including direct seeding and aerobic conditions for rice – are likely to boost both productivity and profitability (Joshi et al 2007; Rajaram et al 2007).

Survey results show that ZT wheat had limited spillover effects on the productivity and management of the subsequent rice crop (Erenstein et al 2008). However, from a CA perspective, this partial adoption means that the system benefits are largely for-feited. At the same time, shifting rice towards CA is likely to result in significant positive spillovers for wheat productivity and profitability, in terms particularly of improved soil structure, but also of enhanced timeliness. Double no-till would also increase returns to investment in ZT drills. Indeed, currently some farmers refrain from investing in a ZT drill as it can only be used in the winter season.

Measuring adoption

The importance of reliable indicators of agricultural technology uptake is generally acknowledged, yet there is a relative lack of adoption studies, in part reflecting the level of resources they require. Without evidence-based adoption estimates, there is a tendency for initial technology promoters to put out their own estimates. Overly positive assessments of the extent of adoption can backfire by undermining the credibility of actual achievements. It has been argued that the research funding cycle contributes to this dynamic (Orr et al 2008).

Measuring adoption has long been a particular challenge for agronomic practices, particularly where these practices vary across farmers' fields. This complexity adds to the difficulty of measurement and interpretation, further compounded by the spatial and dynamic dimensions of technology use (Erenstein 2010b). The objective assessment of the adoption of agronomic packages such as CA is exacerbated when the package and/or its component technologies can be variously used, measured and interpreted (Erenstein 2010b).

The ZT case adequately illustrates some of the problems of reliably estimating, let alone measuring, adoption. It is a cultural practice that is sparsely reported in agricultural statistics and studies. It is also ambiguously interpreted, with the term often used interchangeably for the cultural practice and the seeding implement. Yet, whereas most ZT depends on the use of a ZT seed drill, the practice is not simply embodied in this machinery, as the drills are also used on fields that have had reduced or intensive tilling. Furthermore, ZT is also variously used, including over seasons and within farms, with some farmers using it for one part of their farm while adhering to more intensive tillage elsewhere (Erenstein 2010d).

Adoption of ZT wheat in South Asia started in the second half of the 1990s and accelerated in the early years of the twenty-first century. Experts estimated that the combined zero/reduced tillage wheat area in the IGP amounted to some 2 million ha in 2004/05. But the actual extent of ZT diffusion is not known precisely, and the initial estimates were based in part on the sales of ZT drills. Research studies on ZT, and the associated data collection and reporting, have both increased and improved in the past several years. However, most studies report primarily on the technical aspects of ZT at the plot level, and often are based on trial data (Erenstein and Laxmi 2008). Many farm surveys are not based on a robust sampling frame that would allow for unbiased diffusion estimates; instead, most farm surveys contrast a sample of ZT adopters with non-adopters (e.g. Singh 2008). Reliable and empirically based ZT diffusion indicators are scarce and problematic. Lacking other estimates, the expert estimates of ZT adoption are often repeated and cited. However, in the process, two important underlying qualifications are often omitted – they are estimates and not empirically grounded; and they reflect estimated ZT drill use irrespective of tillage intensity.

A first systematic attempt to estimate ZT diffusion through a random village sample across the north-west IGP confirmed earlier reports of significant ZT diffusion. It found the combined zero/reduced tillage wheat amounted to 22 per cent of the wheat area in the communities surveyed in 2007/08, which, extrapolated to Indian Punjab and Haryana, would imply 1.26 million ha (Erenstein 2010c).

Farm surveys have also revealed some ZT dis-adoption (Erenstein 2010b), apparently due to a combination of factors including technology performance, technology access and seasonal constraints. Claims of (dis-)adoption need to be evaluated systematically: a case in point is ZT wheat in Pakistan, where original claims of adoption were based on extrapolation and were not necessarily in line with empirically based diffusion indicators, which showed slower diffusion and higher dis-adoption (Erenstein 2010b).

Measuring impact

Erenstein and Laxmi (2008) provide a comprehensive review of the impacts of ZT wheat in India's rice–wheat systems, including effects on land preparation and crop establishment, water use, soils and biotic stresses, yields, and cost savings and profitability. The most commonly reported performance indicators include yield and production costs, which were already reviewed.

Ceteris paribus, there is a decreasing ability to control for noise as one proceeds from on-station trials, to on-farm trials, to farmer use. We would thus expect a decreasing likelihood of finding significant differences in terms of performance indicators. Yet the review found a more consistent ZT yield gain in on-farm trials compared with on-station work, which was hypothesised to be associated with the fact that these trials did not benefit from subsequent enhancements in ZT drills, knowledge and skills. An additional factor may have been that the on-station trials maintained the same sowing date for tillage treatments, thereby eliminating a major source of ZT yield gain (Erenstein and Laxmi 2008). A confounding factor was the site-specificity of the ZT yield gains: both on-station and on-farm trials showed a marked ZT yield effect that increased from the Indian Punjab in the north west towards the middle Gangetic plains, reflecting the increasing importance of timeliness (Erenstein and Laxmi 2008).

An additional complication is that some of the ZT-induced changes in performance are easily dwarfed by the inability to control other sources of variation in field surveys. Hence surveys typically confirm the cost savings associated with ZT, but are less apt to confirm water savings. The amount of background variation is aggravated further by the fact that partial adoption is widespread, be it of technology components or in terms of area, whereby farmers use ZT on only a part of their farm. A major challenge in measuring the impact of any technological package is the fact that farmers unpack them and use only those components that are attractive. In the end, the prime driver for adoption of ZT is monetary gain, not water savings or soil health (Erenstein et al 2008). The complexity of ZT also makes it knowledge-intensive, to the extent that its success may depend more on the 'how' of management rather than the level of inputs applied (Wall 2007). Structural differences between adoption categories are also important (Erenstein and Farooq 2009a, 2009b); as are specification effects in terms of how tillage options are contrasted (Erenstein 2009b).

Equity

Zero-tillage wheat has been adopted primarily in the north-west IGP (Erenstein and Laxmi 2008), an area that typically has more intensive and productive rice–wheat systems, more favourable institutional support, and markedly less poverty than the densely populated eastern plains (Erenstein et al 2010; Erenstein and Thorpe 2011). Nevertheless, the potential yield gains and cost savings associated with ZT should be greater in areas with less intensive agriculture such as the eastern plains (Erenstein and Laxmi 2008). The initial R&D results in the eastern plains are encouraging but not well documented or widely published. Most references to ZT and the rice–wheat systems in the IGP are still based on or extrapolated from the experience in the north west, tending to ignore significant biophysical and socio-economic gradients (Erenstein and Thorpe 2011).

Benefits of ZT have been reported to be scale-neutral, with both larger-scale farms and smallholders adopting (Erenstein and Laxmi 2008). This is facilitated by the ability of smallholders to contract ZT drill services, just as they do for their tillage services in general, which makes the tractor-based machinery divisible. Adoption surveys have revealed that 60–74 per cent of ZT adopters did not own a ZT drill (Erenstein and Farooq 2009a). Drill providers have the added advantage of having hands-on experience and self-interest in promoting the technology. Still, ZT tends to be adopted first by the better endowed farmers (Erenstein and Farooq 2009a, 2009b). The differential ZT adoption calls for a closer consideration of equity implications in future R&D, with particular attention to smallholders' access to ZT knowledge and drills. Timely access to a ZT drill is the key to ensuring timely wheat establishment and consequent yield gains. Differential access to ZT implements and knowledge may therefore have contributed to the differential yield performance of ZT wheat in Pakistan Punjab, where ZT resulted in lower yields only on smallholder farms (Erenstein 2009b).

Despite increasing talk of participation, a technocentric approach to R&D still prevails, and as a result the implications of technical change for disadvantaged segments of society are often ignored. Labour-saving technologies inherently shift income from labourers to producers. The IGP's mainly mechanised land preparation, however, implies that the labour savings associated with ZT wheat are limited, but could be substantial if direct seeding of rice were to substitute for transplanting. The class and gender segmentation in the labour market would impose social costs. There would also be a regional equity dimension, as the intensive north-west systems still rely on migrant labour from the eastern plains.

Technology developed for the capital-abundant north-west IGP is not necessarily appropriate for the eastern plains, where capital is more limited. The popularity of two-wheel tractors in Bangladesh and Nepal is a case in point, these being less capital-intensive than four-wheel tractors and more appropriate for the small farms and plots.

There is thus a need for local adaptation of ZT, and initial results along these lines are encouraging (e.g. Hossain et al 2006).

Environmental aspects

From a CA perspective, ZT wheat represents partial adoption and thus implies relatively limited environmental gains. Most of the environmental gains associated with CA are forgone because reduction in tillage, retention of mulch, and crop rotation are only partial. Nevertheless, ZT still implies some positive effects, including lower fossil fuel and water use, and reduced greenhouse gas emissions. The fuel savings produce relatively undisputed gains in terms of carbon emissions, but the effects on soil organic C are less clear cut (Govaerts et al 2009). Further research is needed to substantiate and value these environmental impacts (Erenstein and Laxmi 2008).

CA helps regulate the soil ecology (Erenstein 2002; 2003), which is relevant as an adaptation strategy to climate change. Climate change is expected to exacerbate the heat stress at the end of the wheat season, enhancing the potential payoff to ZT wheat if seeding is timely. However, climate change also raises serious questions about the future of rice–wheat systems and agriculture in the IGP more generally.

Zero-tillage wheat after rice does not necessarily entail an increased reliance on herbicides because rice fields are relatively weed-free at harvest time (Erenstein and Laxmi 2008). In fact, by reducing soil movement, ZT serves as an effective control measure for *Phalaris minor*, an important weed that has reduced wheat yields, and that in the mid-1990s showed emerging resistance to the herbicide isoproturon. The ability to control herbicide-resistant *Phalaris* thereby became one of the drivers for ZT adoption in north-west India; ZT combined with new herbicides eventually proved effective in controlling *Phalaris* (Erenstein 2010d). However, an increased use of dry rice seeding is likely to increase reliance on herbicide.

The unfolding water crisis in the north-west IGP (e.g. Briscoe and Malik 2006) has led to concern about agricultural water productivity and calls for water-saving technologies. Water savings in farmers' fields with ZT wheat are relatively small, and less than initially expected (Erenstein and Laxmi 2008). Yet, from a system perspective, any savings from wheat are dwarfed by the potential water savings associated with a shift to direct seeding of rice in dry soil (Erenstein 2009a). Water shortage may eventually drive the change toward direct rice-seeding methods. In the eastern plains, irrigation infrastructure is less well developed and rice is often rainfed or only partially irrigated. Here, too, direct-seeded rice may be an increasingly attractive alternative to transplanting, particularly in view of the erratic onset of the monsoon and frequent incidence of drought.

Discussion

The adoption of ZT wheat in the IGP can be explained because it is financially attractive and was promoted through a process that combined elements of persistence, flexibility, inclusiveness and facilitation (Erenstein 2010d). To enhance its potential contribution to soil health and system sustainability, there is a need to use ZT wheat as a stepping stone to CA by addressing several outstanding challenges. These include the existing knowledge gaps regarding socio-economic and environmental impacts that would enhance the ability to out- and up-scale in a cost-effective, equitable and sustainable manner (Erenstein 2010d). To succeed, the R&D establishment needs to acknowledge more emphatically that the political economy typically ensures the playing field is not level for agronomic innovations such as CA.

The adoption dynamics of CA in the IGP are governed by two key factors: the complexity of the technological package, and the political economy. The former opens up the interpretation of results and impacts to contestation, producing different and contending 'facts' and knowledges. The latter creates vested economic and political interests that some stakeholders seek to safeguard and some innovations may erode.

The IGP's political economy is a major impediment to change. Policies that favoured the creation and intensification of the rice–wheat system during the Green Revolution shifted the political economy in such a way that the system has become a victim of its own success. Indeed, the prevailing policy environment has been a major contributor to making the rice–wheat system unsustainable (Erenstein and Thorpe 2011): it undervalues ecosystem services and has introduced numerous market distortions, including assured staple commodity markets and prices, and substantial subsidies for fertiliser and irrigation. The extent of these distortions varies both between countries (Erenstein 2010a) and within countries – for example, relatively rich north-west India still receives the lion's share of policy support and subsidies (World Bank 2005; Jha et al 2007). Vested interests are now such that policy change implies political suicide: to date, no elected government has dared to push through the much-needed reforms. Ironically, the prevailing political economy has dug itself into an ever deeper hole by producing a highly stable *status quo* despite the natural resource base being stretched to the limit (Erenstein and Thorpe 2011). With the vested interests – including farmers, R&D or policy-makers – having limited incentive for change, what options are there to break the log-jam other than a full-blown agro-ecological crisis?

Innovations that create enough interest and momentum among selected stakeholders to become self-sustaining appear the most promising option – thereby potentially surmounting any unfavourable political economy environment. A major obstacle, though, is that any such innovation still needs to be introduced somehow, whereas the agricultural R&D establishment already tends to be part and parcel of the political economy. The RWC played an important facilitating role in the introduction of ZT by dovetailing into local research institutions without being similarly bound by the domestic political economy.

From a CA perspective, the introduction of ZT wheat is a piecemeal innovation approach. The development and promotion of ZT wheat instead of outright CA allowed for some initial progress, but the overarching question remains whether this will suffice in the face of the magnitude of change required. Such a technocentric entry point could be complemented by a regulatory approach, but the relative reluctance of the political establishment to bite the bullet so far is a bad omen. Also, enforcement of mandatory agronomic practices is particularly problematic – although the use of social group control has been more successful. The quest therefore remains for technological options that are attractive from both private and social perspectives. Such options need to be worth their while for farmers – that is, to have substantial short-term benefits and relatively limited up-front costs.

Conservation Agriculture remains a problematic sell, particularly in irrigated systems such as the IGP, where it typically needs a multi-year time frame to build up soil health and concomitant productivity increases. Still, there is a need to establish and demonstrate unambiguously the pay-off to CA over the long term through well-designed long-term trials. The long-term CA trials in Mexico are a case in point, and provide a continuing stream of scientific and hands-on visual evidence of CA's potential. The integrated nature of CA is also problematic. First, this makes the adaptation and adoption of CA-based practices complex and knowledge-intensive, with important roles for agricultural extension, farmer education and training; yet there has been a general breakdown of publicly funded providers of such services. Second, farmers have an outstanding ability to unpack technological packages and adopt only those components that best fit their needs and interests. In this regard, CA as a package has not been successful, as only individual component technologies have been adopted. This reiterates the need for substantial synergies between components and/or the need for institutional innovations that ensure components remain coupled.

In the end, agronomists in the IGP and elsewhere need to provide options that create enough interest and deliver sufficient benefits to create a self-sustaining dynamic of technical change. The case of CA in the IGP illustrates the numerous challenges that agricultural innovations must surmount.

Acknowledgement

This chapter draws from and builds on earlier work (particularly Erenstein 2010d) and subsequent papers cited above, derived from when the author was based in South Asia for CIMMYT. The chapter benefited from comments by Philip Woodhouse and Ian Scoones. The views expressed in this chapter are the author's and do not necessarily reflect the views of the author's institution.

References

Abrol, I.P., Gupta, R.K. and Malik, R.K. (2005) *Conservation Agriculture – Status and Prospects.* New Delhi: Centre for Advancement of Sustainable Agriculture.

Bell, D.E., Sanghavi, N., Fuller, V. and Shelman, M. (2007) *Hariyali Kisaan Bazaar: A Rural Business Initiative.* Cambridge, MA: Harvard Business School.

Briscoe, J. and Malik, R.P.S. (2006) *India's Water Economy: Bracing for a Turbulent Future.* New Delhi: Oxford University Press.

Byerlee, D., Sheikh, A.D., Aslam, M. and Hobbs, P.R. (1984) *Wheat in the Rice-Based Farming System of the Punjab: Implications for Research and Extension*, NARC/CIMMYT Reports Series No. 4. Islamabad: NARC/CIMMYT.

CSISA (2009) *Cereal Systems Initiative for South Asia.* http://sites.google.com/site/csisaportal.

Ekboir, J. (2002) 'Developing no-till packages for small-scale farmers', in Ekboir, J. (ed.) *CIMMYT 2000–2001 World Wheat Overview and Outlook*. Mexico, DF: CIMMYT, 1–38.

Erenstein, O. (2002) 'Crop residue mulching in tropical and semi-tropical countries: an evaluation of residue availability and other technological implications', *Soil & Tillage Research*, 67(2): 115–33.

——(2003) 'Smallholder conservation farming in the tropics and sub-tropics: a guide to the development and dissemination of mulching with crop residues and cover crops', *Agriculture, Ecosystems & Environment*, 100(1): 17–37.

——(2009a) 'Comparing water management in rice–wheat production systems in Haryana, India and Punjab, Pakistan', *Agricultural Water Management*, 96(12): 1799–1806.

——(2009b) 'Specification effects in zero tillage survey data in South Asia's rice–wheat systems', *Field Crops Research*, 111(1–2): 166–72.

——(2010a) 'A comparative analysis of rice–wheat systems in Indian Haryana and Pakistan Punjab', *Land Use Policy*, 27(3): 869–79.

——(2010b) 'Triangulating technology diffusion indicators: case of zero tillage wheat in South Asia's irrigated plains', *Experimental Agriculture*, 46(3): 293–308.

——(2010c) 'Village surveys for technology uptake monitoring: case of tillage dynamics in the Trans-Gangetic Plains', *Experimental Agriculture*, 46(3): 277–92.

——(2010d) 'Zero tillage in the rice–wheat systems of the Indo-Gangetic Plains: a review of impacts and sustainability implications', in Spielman, D.J. and Pandya-Lorch, R. (eds) *Proven Successes in Agricultural Development: A Technical Compendium to Millions Fed*. Washington, DC: IFPRI.

——(2011) 'Cropping systems and crop residue management in the Trans-Gangetic Plains: issues and challenges for conservation agriculture from village surveys', *Agricultural Systems*, 104(1): 54–62.

Erenstein, O. and Farooq, U. (2009a) 'A survey of factors associated with the adoption of zero tillage wheat in the irrigated plains of South Asia', *Experimental Agriculture*, 45(2): 133–47.

——(2009b) 'Factors affecting the adoption of zero tillage wheat in the rice–wheat systems of India and Pakistan', *Outlook on Agriculture*, 38(4): 367–73.

Erenstein, O. and Laxmi, V. (2008) 'Zero tillage impacts in India's rice–wheat systems: a review', *Soil & Tillage Research*, 100(1–2): 1–14.

Erenstein, O. and Thorpe, W. (2010) 'Crop–livestock interactions along agro-ecological gradients: a meso-level analysis in the Indo-Gangetic Plains, India', *Environment, Development and Sustainability*, 12(5): 669–89.

——(2011) 'Livelihoods and agro-ecological gradients: a meso-level analysis in the Indo-Gangetic Plains, India', *Agricultural Systems*, 104(1): 42–53.

Erenstein, O., Farooq, U., Malik, R.K. and Sharif, M. (2008) 'On-farm impacts of zero tillage wheat in South Asia's rice–wheat systems', *Field Crops Research*, 105(3): 240–52.

Erenstein, O., Hellin, J. and Chandna, P. (2010) 'Poverty mapping based on livelihood assets: a meso-level application in the Indo-Gangetic Plains, India', *Applied Geography*, 30(1): 112–25.

FAO (2007) 'Conservation Agriculture', www.fao.org/ag/ca

Faulkner, E.F. (1943) *Plowman's Folly*. Stillwater, OK: University of Oklahoma Press.

Fujisaka, S., Harrington, L. and Hobbs, P.R. (1994) 'Rice–wheat in South Asia: systems and long-term priorities established through diagnostic research', *Agricultural Systems*, 46: 169–87.

Giller, K.E., Witter, E., Corbeels, M. and Tittonell, P. (2009) 'Conservation agriculture and smallholder farming in Africa: the heretics' view', *Field Crops Research*, 114(1): 23–34.

Govaerts, B., Sayre, K.D. and Deckers, J. (2005) 'Stable high yields with zero tillage and permanent bed planting?', *Field Crops Research*, 94(1): 33–42.

Govaerts, B., Verhulst, N., Castellanos-Navarrete, A., Sayre, K.D., Dixon, J. and Dendooven, L. (2009) 'Conservation agriculture and soil carbon sequestration: between myth and farmer reality', *Critical Reviews in Plant Science*, 28: 97–122.

Gupta, R. and Sayre, K. (2007) 'Conservation agriculture in South Asia', *Journal of Agricultural Science*, 145(3): 207–14.

Harrington, L.W. and Hobbs, P.H. (2009), 'The Rice–Wheat Consortium and the Asian Development Bank: a history', in Ladha, J.K., Yadvinder-Singh, O., Erenstein, B. and Hardy, B. (eds) *Integrated Crop and Resource Management in the Rice–Wheat System of South Asia*. Los Baños, the Philippines: IRRI, 3–67.

Hobbs, P.R., Gupta, R., Malik, R.K. and Dhillon, S.S. (2003), 'Conservation agriculture for the rice–wheat systems of the Indo-Gangetic Plains of South Asia: a case study from India', in Garcia-Torres, L., Benites, J., Martinez-Vilela, A. and Holgado-Cabrera, A. (eds) *Conservation Agriculture: Environment, Farmers' Experiences, Innovations, Socio-Economy, Policy*. Dordrecht, the Netherlands: Kluwer Academic.

Hobbs, P.R., Sayre, K. and Gupta, R. (2008) 'The role of conservation agriculture in sustainable agriculture', *Philosophical Transactions of the Royal Society B: Biological Sciences*, 363(1491): 543–55.

Hossain, Md. I., Sufian, M.A., Haque, M.E., Justice, S. and Badruzzaman, M. (2006) 'Development of power tiller operated zero tillage planter for small land holders', *Bangladesh Journal of Agricultural Research*, 31(3): 471–84.

Iqbal, M., Khan, M.A. and Anwar, M.Z. (2002) 'Zero-tillage technology and farm profits: a case study of wheat growers in the rice zone of Punjab', *Pakistan Development Review*, 41(4): 665–82.

Jat, M.L., Gupta, R.K., Erenstein, O. and Ortiz, R. (2006) 'Diversifying the intensive cereal cropping systems of the Indo-Ganges through horticulture', *Chronica Horticulturae*, 46(3): 27–31.

Jha, S., Srinivasan, P.V. and Landes, M. (2007) *Indian Wheat and Rice Sector Policies and the Implications of Reform*, Economic Research Report 41. Washington, DC: USDA, iv.

Joshi, A., Chand, R., Arun, B., Singh, R. and Ortiz, R. (2007) 'Breeding crops for reduced-tillage management in the intensive, rice–wheat systems of South Asia', *Euphytica*, 153(1): 135–51.

Ladha, J. K., Yadvinder-Singh, O., Erenstein, B. and Hardy, B. (2009) *Integrated Crop and Resource Management in the Rice–Wheat System of South Asia*. Los Baños, the Philippines: IRRI.

Lumpkin, T.A. and Sayre, K. (2009), 'Enhancing resource productivity and efficiency through Conservation Agriculture', in WCCA (ed.) *Proceedings 4th World Congress on Conservation Agriculture*, 4–7 February 2009, New Delhi, India. New Delhi: WCCA, 3–9.

Malik, R.K., Gupta, R.K., Yadav, A., Sardana, P.K. and Singh, C.M. (2005) *Zero Tillage – The Voice of Farmers*, Technical Bulletin No. 9. Hisar, India: CCS Haryana Agricultural University, Directorate of Extension Education.

Orr, S., Sumberg, J., Erenstein, O. and Oswald, A. (2008) 'Funding international agricultural research and the need to be noticed: a case study of NERICA rice', *Outlook on Agriculture*, 37(3): 159–68.

PACA (2008) 'Professional Alliance for Conservation Agriculture', www.conserveagri.org

Rajaram, S., Sayre, K.D., Diekmann, J., Gupta, R. and Erskine, W. (2007) 'Sustainability considerations in wheat improvement and production', *Journal of Crop Improvement*, 19(1/2): 105–23.

Seth, A., Fischer, K., Anderson, J. and Jha, D. (2003) *The Rice–Wheat Consortium: An Institutional Innovation in International Agricultural Research on the Rice–Wheat Cropping Systems of the Indo-Gangetic Plains (IGP)*, Review Panel Report. New Delhi: RWC.

Singh, N.P. (2008) *Adoption and Impact of Resource Conserving Technologies on Farm Economy in Indo-Gangetic Plains*, India. New Delhi: IARI.

Timsina, J. and Connor, D.J. (2001) 'Productivity and management of rice–wheat cropping systems: issues and challenges', *Field Crops Research*, 69(2): 93–132.

Wall, P.C. (2007) 'Tailoring conservation agriculture to the needs of small farmers in developing countries: an analysis of issues', *Journal of Crop Improvement*, 19(1/2): 137–55.

WCCA (2009) *Proceedings 4th World Congress on Conservation Agriculture*, 4–7 February 2009, New Delhi, India. New Delhi: WCCA.

World Bank (2005) *India – Re-energizing the Agricultural Sector to Sustain Growth and Reduce Poverty*. New Delhi: Oxford University Press.

4

ANTHROPOGENIC DARK EARTHS AND AFRICA

A political agronomy of research disjunctures

James Fairhead, Melissa Leach and Kojo Amanor

Introduction

Anthropogenic dark earths (ADE) and biochar are current foci of extraordinary levels of technological optimism, agricultural research and political debate. ADE comprise both black soils associated with long enduring settlement sites and their depositions, and slightly lighter coloured soils that have also been rendered more enduringly fertile than the soils on which they are formed through deposition and cultivation practices. These anthropogenically enriched soils can sustain permanent farming; their fertility is thought to be due in part to their high biochar content. Biochar refers to the carbon-rich products that result when biomass is burned under oxygen-deprived conditions and then buried in the ground (Lehmann and Joseph 2009).

Interest in ADE and biochar is linked to a double promise held by the purposeful creation of ADE through applying biochar: enduringly improving the productivity of highly weathered tropical (and other) soils, while at the same time capturing atmospheric carbon dioxide and locking it up in the soil. This potential 'win–win' is now generating intense research interest, and private-sector and NGO investments. At the same time, the agronomy of ADE and biochar has become the focus of critique and of counter-politics in a sometimes heated and polarised debate.

This chapter examines how research into ADE and biochar in the tropics has developed. We take a political agronomy lens to analyse how our particular objects of study – ADE and biochar – have emerged and become politicised within a wider history of agronomy, whose broader trends we can only sketch. Political agronomy, we note, is closely related to the vibrant research field of 'political ecology', and can be enriched with two insights from it. First, while political ecologists examine how ecological processes are shaped by political and economic forces, some also attend to how ecology leaves its mark on politics. Second, political ecologists reveal not only how political and economic forces shape the conduct of science, but also how ecology is understood – the politics of ecological knowledge (Forsyth 2003). There is no question that research into ADE has developed from observations of soils in Amazonia (there termed Terra preta and Terra mulata) originating in pre-Colombian settlement and farming practices, and few would contest that it was originally Terra preta research that animated wider research into biochar as a soil conditioner. Yet beyond this consensus, we want to consider how ADE and biochar research has responded to, and been reframed by, changing political and economic contexts – now shaped strongly by climate change debates and the new political economy of carbon. We also argue that the history of ADE and biochar is a story about disjunctures drawn between Amazonia and Africa in academic and policy communities. These disjunctures have been written into the way African soils are understood and researched, are shaping how the significance of ADE and biochar for Africa is being portrayed, and opening the field of ADE and biochar to new, and sometimes highly polarised, contestations.

The story we tell unfolds over four episodes. First, following a brief introduction to ADE and its significance, we consider how and why ADE was for so long ignored and occluded in agronomic research. Second, we explore the emergence of ADE and Terra preta research in Amazonia from the 1980s. Third, we examine why this interest was not paralleled in Africa during this period, and reasons for the continued profound silence about African ADE until around 2005. Finally, we explore the implications of the sudden interest in ADE in Africa from this time, now reframed as 'biochar', a technology to be transferred into African settings.

Our political agronomy analysis of each of these episodes is 'political' in relation to three theories of power. First, we attend to the politics of knowledge, using a broadly Foucauldian optic to consider the structuring of inquiry within and between academic disciplines and how this shapes the discourses put into play – and what they include and occlude. Just as there are disjunctures between the disciplines of soil and agronomic sciences, and of archaeology, history and the social sciences, in their methods, reasoning and communities, so there are particular conjunctures between them in their reliance upon each other's findings. We examine how ADE and biochar research has been structured by these disciplinary configurations, but also how individual researchers have been able to subvert them.

Second, we explore the changing political–economic context in which new ideas and disciplinary combinations become appealing and fundable. Over the past century, different agricultural, food and environmental issues have attracted policy attention and research funding. The relative prominence of colonial and global players, and of state, non-governmental and business actors, have all been enwrapped with shifting economic and political interests. These shape the ways in which ADE and biochar have been framed and reframed at different stages.

Third, our political agronomy approach recalls a more subtle form of power – residing not just in knowledge and political economy, but in the practices they put into play. Ideas about soils do not exist just in journals and research, but become vested in (encoded in) landscape features (such as 'watershed protection reserves', 'fire curtain reserves' or 'permanent sample plots'); in the laws, institutions and cartography that govern their use; in the tools and chemicals used to manipulate them; and in networks and communities of collaboration (such as those now linking biochar researchers). Ideas that are put into practice in this way acquire a quality very different from those that are not. Scientists may have disproved the idea that the Sahara is advancing because of anthropogenic influence, but the idea that it does so lives on in the international desertification convention and the myriad of programmes extolling inhabitants to change their ways. If the idea of human-induced desertification had never been institutionalised, its refutation would be much less challenging. Particular ideas about soils have become embedded in, and reproduced through, everyday practices of science and intervention, and in the very soil and landscape features and processes produced through these (Fairhead and Leach 2003).

At the same time, we are interested in how ecologies and soils, however framed, make their presence felt. What comes to be known (and what remains unknown) is thus conditioned not only by the politics of knowledge, political economy and practice, but by these in a dialectical relation with ecological forces.

The chapter thus argues that the paradigms and practices through which ADE and biochar have become objects of study can be traced to broader political economic orders. Our own arrival at the door of ADE and biochar is a case in point. As social science researchers with interdisciplinary backgrounds and interests in agriculture and ecology, we have long-standing concerns with African landscapes, farmers' knowledge and investments in productivity in certain sites, but – in keeping with dominant priorities and practices in the 1990s – had focused on their anthropogenic vegetation (Amanor 1994; Fairhead and Leach 1996, 1998). After exposure to the Terra preta and biochar literature, we realised that these sites could be investigated as much for their anthropogenic soils as for their enriched forests and fallows. Given that ADE research was being framed as a phenomenon only of Amazonia, we reconfigured our own research interests to look at ADE in Africa (Fairhead and Leach 2009), aiming to initiate a conversation between ADE research communities in Amazonia and researchers in Africa. Yet in entering this debate we encountered three concerns. First, those researching ADE in Amazonia had established ADE as exclusive to Amazonia or the neo-tropics. Second, ADE and biochar research had acquired a dominating global carbon focus. Third, we realised how quickly and how far agronomic research around biochar was itself becoming politicised and commoditised. We found ourselves contributing to a field that was being criticised for its distributional implications; as playing into industrial solutions to climate change and 'land grabs' associated with it. In none of these domains, however, were the interests and perspectives of the African farmers we knew being addressed. Our overriding concern driving this analysis of the political agronomy of ADE and biochar research is to divest it of these shackles.

ADE (Terra preta) and biochar

The existence of extensive areas of ADE in the Amazon was first documented in the 1870s, and until the early 1900s it was uncontroversial to understand these as associated with depopulated Amerindian settlements and as anthropogenic (Woods and Denevan

2009). Yet for most of the twentieth century, these soils attracted little attention and most observers understood them as natural.

Recent research on the Amazon basin, however, has led to a fundamental reappraisal of its social and natural history. Earlier arguments that the region's poor soils had restricted pre-Hispanic social formations to small, semi-permanent settlements (Meggers 1971) have been undermined by archaeological evidence of large sedentary settlements throughout the Amazon basin (Heckenberger et al 2008; Mann 2008; Schaan et al 2008). Areas of dark, highly fertile soils able to support intensive farming have been found to cover 1.2–1.8 million ha of forested lowland Amazonia, undermining earlier interpretations that its infertile soils could not support large settled populations (e.g. contributions to Woods et al 2009). These soils are anthropogenic; the darkest (Terra preta) are usually the middens of pre-Hispanic settlements, while others (Terra mulata) are probably the outcome of pre-Hispanic agricultural practices (Lehmann et al 2003a; Glaser et al 2004a,b; Woods et al 2009). Pre-Hispanic populations are now known to have been far greater than earlier thought, their decline far more precipitous, and their impact on modern Amazonian forests far more significant (Clement 1999; Lehmann et al 2003a; Balée and Erikson 2006; Woods et al 2009).

The significance of these soils extends beyond a reappraisal of history. First, modern farmers value them, and many have developed distinct agricultural practices on them that contribute to more sustainable livelihoods (German 2003; Fraser 2009). Second, soil scientists are excited by their complex soil biology and its implications for soil fertility and agriculture (e.g. Uphoff et al 2006). Amazonian ADE contrast strongly with the soils in which they develop. They generally have about three times the soil organic matter (SOM) and, more importantly, the component of SOM consisting of charred residues from incomplete combustion (carbons and charcoal) can be up to 70 times greater than that of background soils (Glaser et al 2004a,b; Liang et al 2006). This is chemically stable and resistant to microbial degradation, so remains in the soil for centuries. This biochar improves soil structure and aggregation, water infiltration and retention, and nutrient storage capacity (Lehmann et al 2003b). Third, because the secret to these soils lies partially in their high proportion of biochar, farming technologies that seek to create ADE could sequester enormous quantities of carbon.

The existence of ADE in Africa has been less apparent in the agronomic literature. The most obvious example lies in the exploitation of the middens of the cities of Pharaonic Egypt as a source of fertiliser during the early nineteenth century. The remains of mud-brick structures (bricks themselves being made of nutrient-laden Nile silt), which form the ancient mounds of Egyptian cities and villages, are referred to as *sebakh* and are sought out by farmers. Nitrogen-rich material in courtyard work areas, rubbish dumps and unpaved streets also contributes to *sebakh* formation. In larger cities, household rubbish and animal excreta were dumped over hundreds (and thousands) of years, causing the streets to rise ever higher so that the ground floors of houses gradually became basements (Bailey 1999). The importance of these middens as a fertiliser was recognised in the early nineteenth century, when the soil was transported and sold throughout the Nile Valley, and large companies mined them on an industrial scale. Fields throughout Egypt are nowadays 'archaeologically polluted' as they are full of ceramic shards removed from mounds. In the 1930s, *sebakh* digging was officially banned, although its removal in small and substantial quantities still occurs to the present.

Farming practices that generate biochar through the slow burning of vegetation under anaerobic conditions were also observed in Africa from the mid-nineteenth century. In many locations, colonial observers noted how grass or bush vegetation was cut, dried, covered with soil and burnt. Farmers would craft the conditions such that the vegetation burned very slowly and 'without a flame', often for a week or two. Afterwards, the soil, char and ash mix could be farmed *in situ*, or distributed more widely over the field. This practice acquired assorted names in European languages, including 'burn-beating', 'denshering', 'soil burning', 'sod burning' and, in French, '*ecobuage*'. This technique was described in the Fouta Djallon (Guinea), in Chad and Cameroon, Ghana, Ethiopia, Congo, the Democratic Republic of Congo, and Malawi. But while these practices produce biochar, contemporary observers understood their logic to lie in other benefits: the nutrients released in the ash; the reduced soil acidity; the improved soil texture; and the destruction of weed seed banks and insect pests. None saw any significance in the accumulation of biochar (Livingstone 1875; Portères 1972; Mesfin 1981, 1982; Roorda 1984; Pulschen and Koch 1990; Mboukou-Kimbatsa 1997; Mpangui 1997; Sohi and Yeboah 2009).

Histories of occlusion

Why was the significance of ADE and biochar largely ignored – at least until the 1980s? Focusing first on the politics of knowledge, the significance of ADE was downplayed by the structuring of scientific disciplines. In both Amazonian and African settings, soil scientists, historians, archaeologists, foresters and social anthropologists generally conducted research separately, yet drew on each other's assumptions.

Foresters examining the Amazonian forest considered it 'pristine' and a climatic climax. Soil scientists found the region's soils to be highly weathered and unable to sustain intensive agriculture. Anthropologists cast its people's longer-term history in evolutionary rather than social and political terms. And archaeologists accepted the agronomists' conclusions that Amazonian soils were inevitably too poor to have supported dense, settled populations; accepted from foresters that if the forest had a history, it was a natural history; and accepted from anthropologists more timeless interpretations of social form. In short, the disjuncture between forestry, soil science, anthropology and archaeology structured the ways in which the Amazon was interpreted, and the conjuncture (mutual reliance on each other's analysis) stabilised a reading of the Amazon that occluded its human history. These patterns were not totalising, but critique when it happened was ignored. For instance, Sombroek made arguments in the 1960s about Amazonian ADE and their capacity to support large populations, but these fell on deaf ears in both archaeological and agronomic circles. Where ADE were observed, they were generally interpreted as 'natural'; where they were associated with artefacts, it was assumed that they had attracted settlements.

Such 'naturalisation' of ADE was also important in African settings, but linked to a slightly different analysis stabilised in the configuration of these disciplines. Here, patches of 'dark earths' are associated with woody vegetation. Foresters understood these as 'more natural', less degraded landscape features, in line with 'climatic climax' assumptions that 'natural' African vegetation was more forested. Soil scientists accepted this, considering the richer soils under 'forest patches' either to be naturally different, or to be the more original soils of landscapes otherwise degraded by people. So, far from seeing ADE as improved relative to surrounding 'unimproved' soils, these patches of good soil came to be considered as the natural soils, and a baseline against which surrounding soil degradation could be assessed. For example, when Ramsay and Innes (1963) searched for 'original' vegetation during research on controlled burning in African savannas, they drew a blank but, finding sacred groves with dense closed woodland on old settlement sites, took this as evidence of the possibility of establishing undisturbed woodlands in the savanna zone. Crucially, however, they considered that 'the vigour of the trees in these groves may be ascribed in the first instance to higher soil fertility levels of old village sites than on impoverished eroded soils of surrounding farms' (p. 50) – thus downplaying any effects of positive investment in settlement soils in relation to 'natural' background soils, by considering the latter as degraded. Examples of such misrecognition of upgraded soils occurred throughout West Africa (see Fairhead and Leach 1996, 1998).

Within the prevailing politics of knowledge during this period, there was little attention to farmers' indigenous knowledge and practices, and their possible significance in upgrading soils. In Amazonia, this is because indigenous settled farming populations are rare now, and were assumed not to have existed. In African settings, farmers evidently did exist – but pejorative and sometimes racist colonial assumptions about the backwardness of their techniques and practices deterred interest in indigenous knowledge.

Second, these histories of occlusion reflected particular political-economic and policy contexts that shaped the prisms, and funding, of agronomic research. In Amazonia, settlement and clearance for agriculture – and associated agronomic interest – dates only from the 1960s, and was driven by concerns with large-scale mechanisation and modernisation. In Africa, the political economy of agronomic research has a deeper history, with several discernible phases. Until the great depression in the 1930s, the principal colonial interest in African agriculture focused on the expansion of export crops such as rubber, cotton, groundnut, coffee, cocoa and palm oil. The possible importance of ADE to the production of these crops went unnoticed.

From the 1930s, colonial researchers began to conduct research on food crops in the context of famines and food shortages linked to the expansion of export crops, and (in southern and eastern Africa) of white settlement (Faulkner and Mackie 1933; Cooper and Packard 1997; Hodge 2007). Colonial researchers' attention came to be dominated by soil erosion and by a set of crisis narratives constructed around deforestation, desertification and overpopulation. Soil conservation emerged as central to colonial agricultural policy, through the promotion of soil terracing and mixed farming to replace shifting cultivation, control of bush burning, and the introduction of local land-planning systems. Studies began to be conducted on the relationship between shifting cultivation and the soil, and the relationship between soil organic matter, vegetation and agricultural practice came to be of agronomic interest, taken up at the Third Inter-African Soils Conference at Dalaba in Guinea in 1959, for example. Studies and debates compared the relative merits of attempts to improve soil humus through green manures, cover crops, bush fallowing and other African farming methods (e.g. Vine 1953), culminating in Nye and Greenland's (1960) *The Soil Under Shifting Cultivation* and Ahn's (1970) *West African Soils*. In these approaches it was surmised that fallowing led to a growth in the 'nutrient capital' of the soil, which declined during cultivation. Two possible methods of dealing with decline in nutrient levels were investigated: use of fertilisers, and use of leguminous trees and cover crops, both of which attracted debate and scepticism (Ahn 1970: 245).

After the Second World War, research refocused in support of agricultural modernisation and mechanisation, with the emphasis on inorganic fertiliser and improved seeds (Hodge 2007) – a focus that continued after independence. Narratives of a looming population explosion justified increasing marginalisation of research on farmers' soil management techniques. Research on soil fertility became concerned largely with the optimal application of inorganic fertilisers to different soil types and farming regimes involving mechanised land clearance and line planting. During the 1970s, the main focus in agricultural policies was on extending Green Revolution technologies to smallholder farmers, including packages of seeds and fertilisers. A second branch of research in international agricultural institutions experimented with insights into fast regenerating fallow species and agroforestry. This, however, resulted in the commodification of farm–fallow interactions and farmers' management practices, which were appropriated and redesigned on experimental sites as packages – such as alley-cropping – to be disseminated to farmers to 'solve' the problem of shifting cultivation. This sat uneasily with existing labour constraints and gender relations, and with the diversity of farming systems. Thus insights gained from research into the soil under shifting agriculture from an earlier era were marginalised within policy, which sought to replace farmers' knowledge and practice with new technologies created on experimental stations.

With the economic crises and Sahelian droughts of the late 1970s and early 1980s, many international and church-based NGOs moved into agricultural development with a focus on the environment, tree planting and agroforestry. In addition to disseminating Green Revolution technologies, such agencies supported technologies that were a throwback to the 'conservation'-focused land planning of the 1930s, including composting, soil bunding, terracing and tree planting.

The dominant policies within agricultural research during the 1980s did not encourage attention to indigenous soil fertility management. However, new paradigms also emerged, based on participatory approaches and indigenous knowledge (Chambers 1983; Richards 1985). These responded to critiques of both state planning in agriculture (Lipton 1977; Bates 1981) and the development of neoliberal anti-statist policies. They questioned the top-down nature of agricultural policies, and their failure to tailor recommendations to the conditions and needs of farmers or to build research on farmers' existing practices, strategies and knowledge. The advances made by soil science in the 1950s and 1960s in understanding the rationale of fallow cultivation were important in the emergence of participatory frameworks and validation of farmers' knowledge. However, approaches were also influenced by the environmental concerns of the late 1980s with deforestation and biodiversity, and used the insights from earlier soil research to address these concerns. As a consequence, knowledge of soils continued to be structured by processes related to nitrogen, phosphorous, potassium and pH, and the significance of soil carbon and old settlement sites did not feature. Even 'ethnopedology' – which gained ground in this period in detailing indigenous soil classifications and understandings of soil processes (Barrera-Bassols and Zinck 2000, 2003) – remained entirely silent on both the soils of old settlement sites and processes involving soil carbon.

Throughout these shifting political-economic contexts, it is notable that those shifts in policy concern that might have been attentive to ADE were not (e.g. the early periods of interest in tree crops, which often focused on peri-village ADE, and the period of participation and attention to indigenous knowledge). This did not simply reflect the hazards of discovery. After all, ADE had been observed in the 1870s in Amazonia, and biochar-liberating agricultural techniques had been observed in Africa. Instead, it indicates why it is important to consider the different dimensions to ways in which power operates – including Foucauldian perspectives already discussed, and the embedding of power/knowledge in practice.

In this third dimension to our political agronomy framework, the occlusion of ADE reflected embedded practices in research and intervention: ideas of soils being natural unless degraded were not only reproduced in theories of soil genesis based on background geology, climate and 'catena', but also were incorporated into regional soil mapping and land classification, and the regional agricultural planning and even legislation based on it.

We can see that the 'agency' of ADE and biochar itself was either misrecognised as a feature of natural soil (if soils were dark, they were dark for all the reasons except the addition of pyrolised materials, which could hardly be 'natural'). Or, in the case of biochar, its effects were masked by all the other transformations that pyrolising vegetation under the soil might effect. That ADE made itself known to Amazonian farmers, and that African farmers considered it as banal and an inevitable corollary of settlement, was rarely, if ever, observed.

The new significance of Terra preta in Amazonia

In Amazonia, appreciation of ADE among agronomists began to change from the late 1970s. These soils came again to be understood as anthropogenic, and a new and vibrant era of research and interest in Terra preta and Terra mulata was born.

The political-economic context was crucial to this new appreciation as it coincided with the increased settlement and use of Amazonia. As roads were built, Amazonian forests were cleared and small-scale farmers moved into them in a complex relationship with loggers and ranchers, so they found and used ADE. As colonisation proceeded apace, so its environmental and social effects began to show, and this threw up a critical counter-current to the rapid clearance and unsustainable use of Amazonian soils. As they endeavoured to develop permanent agricultural systems, several researchers began to see a potential model in Terra preta. This critique developed in the context of indigenous people's movements, and more global appreciation of indigenous knowledge and agro-ecological paradigms for small farm development. ADE research thus became configured within, and framed as, an alternative to massive, and destructive, forest clearances.

This 'struggle' was also associated with new disciplinary configurations in the production of knowledge. Anthropologists, agronomists and archaeologists were by now starting to work together more closely. Rather rapidly, a new and mutually appreciative community of discovery developed around Terra preta. This linked Amazonia-based researchers with others in universities and research institutes in the Latin American region and the USA, extending to Europe. They organised into networks and funded programmes, and found common purpose in reasoning that came to be labelled as historical ecology, political ecology and agro-ecology.

This emerging research located Terra preta in the context of indigenous practices, and in the knowledge of the small-scale farmers who appreciated these soils (although not indigenous knowledge *per se*, as the processes leading to Terra preta formation appeared to have been 'lost' with the region's European conquest). Nevertheless, some researchers (e.g. Hecht 2003; Steiner et al 2009) were interested in indigenous knowledge and agro-ecology, and researched exemplars of ADE creation by contemporary farmers. One line of research and debate asked whether ADE were produced intentionally as part of livelihood strategies, or were accidental legacies of past peoples. Another set aside the question of origins to focus on how today's farmers value and use Terra preta (Fraser 2009, 2010).

When Sombroek articulated the vision of mimicking the creation of ADE in 'terra preta nova' (Sombroek et al 2003), it was largely in the context of searching for alternatives to shifting cultivation. Yet, as research revealed that the secret of these soils lay in part in their biochar content, it became clear that, in mimicking ADE, one would sequester atmospheric carbon. It was at this point, and in the context of new concerns with climate change and carbon sequestration, that attention shifted from ADE to biochar.

Several soil scientists who were already prominent in Terra preta research picked up on and led work on biochar, suggesting a high-potential 'win–win' for climate change mitigation as well as soil conditioning (Sombroek et al 2003; Lehmann 2007; Gaunt and Lehmann 2008; Lenton and Vaughan 2009). This, in turn, gave a boost to Amazonian Terra preta research. Finding that pyrolised organic material has a much greater average stability than uncharred organic matter, researchers argued that burying biochar creates a long-term carbon sink that can last from hundreds to thousands of years (Cheng et al 2008; Lehmann et al 2009), with evidence of Terra preta soils that have retained their carbon since pre-Hispanic times adduced to support these claims (e.g. Lehmann et al 2009: 184). It was argued that most soils already contain char generated through vegetation fires and settlement practices during the past few thousand years, and that these – ADE and ADE-like soils – make up several per cent of total soil organic carbon worldwide (e.g. Gonzalez-Perez et al 2004). Biochar soil management offered the potential to add significantly to these pre-existing chars, with some proponents quoting a potential global carbon sink of 5.5–9.5 Gt C year^{-1} by 2100, larger than the annual quantity of carbon currently produced by the burning of fossil fuels (Lehmann et al 2006).

The argument that biochar buried in soil offers large potential for sequestering carbon rapidly linked Amazonian soil scientists and agronomists with an expanding global network of researchers and political advocates. This included prominent individuals such as James Hansen, head of the NASA Goddard Institute for Space Studies, and James Lovelock, originator of the Gaia theory, who claimed that 'There is one way we could save ourselves and that is through the massive burial of charcoal. […] Then you can start shifting really hefty quantities of carbon out of the system and pull the CO_2 down quite fast.' Johannes Lehmann of Cornell University, a long-standing researcher in the Amazonian ADE field, was in this context named by social enterprise Re:char as the 'biochar hero'.[1] An expanding epistemic community that had built around Terra preta now refocused around biochar, and was formalised in organisations and networks such as the International Biochar Initiative and a growing suite of biochar-focused panels at soil science conferences in the Latin American region and beyond. Thus ADE – which initially had attracted interest as a conservation-inspired alternative to Amazonian destruction, emerging as a reaction to experiences of state-led agricultural modernisation – was now reframed as a solution to a global climate problem.

Continued silence about ADE in Africa

New interest in Terra preta and biochar among agronomists and others working on Amazonia during the 1980s and 1990s, and even into the early 2000s, was not paralleled in Africa. Africanist researchers did not pick up on the Terra preta/biochar debate during this period, and in some quarters these lines of agronomic research were actively constructed as being irrelevant to Africa. Again, the reasons for this relate to the politics of knowledge, to prevailing political-economic contexts, and to communities of practice.

Partly at stake was a strong regionalism in the practices of research communities and partnerships, in which crossover between those concerned with the Amazon – mainly from Latin American and US institutions – and those concerned with Africa was relatively infrequent. Moreover, some Amazonianists and Africanists alike discouraged such interaction, contributing to discursive disjunctures through claims about the 'exceptionalism' of their regions' agro-ecology and history. Thus Amazonianists argued that because pre-Hispanic Amazonian farmers had only stone axes, they could not practise shifting cultivation – as African farmers, who had iron technologies, were able to – and so were forced into the kind of intensive practices that build Terra preta (Denevan 1992, 2006). It was also argued that, as Amazonia (unlike Africa) did not have domestic animals, aquatic environments were more important, and that the qualities of Terra preta may be linked to fish diets and their calcium additions to soils (Neves et al

2003). For some Africanists, importing an 'Amazonian model' into Africa was an analytical sin; indeed, Nyerges and Green (2000) made this critique of Fairhead and Leach's research that revealed the significance of old settlement sites to farming practices in the West African forest zone in the early 1990s (Fairhead and Leach 1996). These arguments asserting the uniqueness of Amazonian and African agro-ecological history are wholly overstated. Although Africa had a much earlier iron age, many African agro-ecological systems (or parts of them) have long involved intensive forms of cultivation not reliant on the efficiencies of iron technology – while fish, freshly caught or dried – have long been central to livelihoods and diets in many parts of the continent. It has also become evident that basic ecological and soil distinctions cannot provide a basis for Amazonian exceptionalism. ADE are found over a wide range of ecological conditions in Amazonia, many of which are common to the lowland humid tropics of Central and West Africa, including the highly weathered and leached soils (Oxisols and Ultisols). Amazonian ADE are now understood to comprise a family of carbon-enriched soil types, which is not a singular basis for comparison (Hecht 2003, 2009; Schmidt and Heckenberger 2009). Nevertheless, throughout the 1980s and 1990s, exceptionalist arguments prevailed and helped to construct Terra preta and biochar research as irrelevant in African settings.

Disciplinary divides also contributed to the continuing silence about ADE in African settings. There were certainly many interdisciplinary engagements and partnerships between agronomists and social scientists in this era. Indeed, this combination was actively promoted by many Africa-based centres within the CGIAR system, for instance. Yet archaeologists – whose contributions had been so important to the Terra preta debate in Amazonia – largely worked apart. Thus, while Africanist archaeologists frequently encountered dark earths on the settlement sites they investigated, and observed farmers using them, their focus was on the sites and their artefacts – not on the soils, their qualities and agro-ecological significance.

Contradictory tendencies emerged within soil science, in which an increasingly influential 'nutrient balance' model dating back to the 1960s was in tension with a broader agro-ecological model critical of it, yet neither has been attentive to anthropogenic soil transformation. At its most extreme, the former is highly reductionist, imagining African 'soil fertility' as if the soil was simply a bank account, with the fertility status being understood as the balance between the nutrients added (through fallows, manuring or fertiliser) or removed through cropping. Economic metaphors infuse this powerful strand of soil science work on nutrient balances, their measurement and modelling (Fairhead and Scoones 2005).

Those pioneering agro-ecological approaches to farming in Africa at this time, and urging appreciation of indigenous knowledge and practices, also overlooked enduring anthropogenic soil transformations. The 'soil under shifting cultivation' paradigm framed social science inquiries into farmers' own knowledge and logics – in attuning crops to particular site, soil nutrient and fallow conditions, and enriching and managing fallows (e.g. Richards 1985; Amanor 1994). Their focus expands far beyond soil nutrients, reflecting on soil structure, weed competition and pests and diseases, and wider ecological and social factors shaping their management. Yet with the major focus on the maintenance of soil fertility through fallows, and through the management and recycling of vegetation into crop production, greater attention has been paid to the more temporary factors impacting on crop fertility, rather than on the more permanent soil transformations associated with ADE. We are not arguing that a focus on ADE should question the pertinence of these approaches. Indeed, farmers' management of trees in short land-rotation systems, and their selection of trees in fallows and root-mat management through pollarding and rapid coppice regrowth, may be more significant for soil processes over much larger areas than ADE formation. ADE is just one of many relationships between people and the environment. All we are arguing is that these agro-ecological approaches have also overlooked the soil transformations associated with ADE.

Such discursive constructions of African soil fertility also fitted the prevailing political-economic context of the 1980s and 1990s, with the embedding of neoliberal policies and market arrangements. This was an era in which metaphors of soils as nutrient banks, and of nutrients themselves as 'natural capital', made sense; framings that also facilitated the assimilation of chemical fertilisers, provided through emerging market and public–private arrangements, into farming as additions to the nutrient balance. This was also an era of growing environmental concern, shaping political-economic and funding contexts for agronomic and agro-ecological research. Yet at this time, leading up to and just after the 1992 Earth Summit conference in Rio de Janeiro, preoccupying concerns were with desertification, biodiversity loss, deforestation and land degradation. Dominant policy and donor narratives, and many projects, highlighted crises of land and soil degradation linked to loss of vegetation cover – and much research was framed in response or resistance to such views (Leach and Mearns 1996). This was not a context that encouraged a research focus on long-term anthropogenic soil transformations. Indeed, when Fairhead and Leach explored farmers' long-term creation of village 'forest islands' in Guinea in the early 1990s (Fairhead and Leach 1996), they did examine soil effects, but relatively cursorily; they framed their research as primarily significant to understanding vegetation and forest cover change (not soil), in keeping with the key environmental debates of the time.

The early 2000s have seen a renewed interest in agricultural intensification, refashioned in the context of promoting private input dealers and the expansion and concentration of capital in agribusiness and supermarket chains. The state's role is increasingly limited to developing enabling conditions for private investment in agriculture. At the same time, large philanthro-capitalist initiatives and public–private partnerships seek to roll out and scale up the use of improved seeds and inorganic fertilisers in order to stimulate Africa's own Green Revolution. These tendencies have resulted in a decline of funding for more ecologically focused and participatory research in agriculture. It is likely that indigenous African agro-ecologies, such as ADE and the wider cropping practices and vegetation suites associated with them, are simply not on the radar of a policy world where fertiliser and GM crops are increasingly seen as the solution to farming problems. Robert Paarlberg's (2009) *Starved for Science: How Biotechnology is Being Kept Out of Africa* exemplifies this framing. Paarlberg is dismissive of indigenous agro-ecology as being not only unworthy of scientific study, but also responsible for soil degradation and poor crop yields. Such discourses help to shape the interests of agricultural science in Africa, and explain in part why many institutions, researchers and policy-makers overlook the existence and significance of indigenous agronomic practices around ADE.

Transferring biochar to Africa

Nevertheless, and even in this apparently unwelcome agricultural political-economic and policy context, from around 2005 Africa saw an expansion of biochar research and development. Arguments began to be made that the Amazonian research on Terra preta was relevant to Africa (Sillitoe 2006). A number of prominent soil scientists and agronomists in the Amazonian biochar field expanded their attention to more global, including African, settings (Lehmann and Joseph 2009). There, they began to work with partners in African soil science institutions (e.g. Sohi and Yeboah 2009), joined by new generations of international biochar researchers who are focusing their work on Africa.

In accounting for this sudden interest in biochar in Africa, its timing and the particular form it has taken, again an analysis must link political economy with political ecologies of practice, and with the politics of knowledge. The political economy of environment and climate change as it has emerged in the 2000s is undoubtedly central. This has created new political and policy imperatives to mitigate climate change, and new carbon markets and opportunities linked to them. In this context, a host of new companies, NGOs, partnerships and business initiatives have emerged, seeking to promote biochar as a 'win–win' that will simultaneously address African climate and farming challenges – and benefit from what Spash has called the 'brave new world' of carbon funding (Spash 2009).

Biochar is thus seen as a way to tap into carbon markets, offering high market potential 'as a long-term and readily measurable sequestration product, [that] will provide additional revenue in any market or jurisdiction where C is traded or C sequestration outcomes are valued' (Glover 2009: 378). Funding from carbon trading is argued to be essential to finance the research and development necessary to discover and exploit the full potential of biochar to contribute to climate change mitigation, and to enable scale-up to sequester carbon at globally significant levels. Others argue that, if farmers receive payments for sequestered carbon, this can provide an income stream and justify the financial and time investments necessary to adopt biochar systems (Palmer 2009) – a model tested by the Biochar Fund in Central Africa. Pro-biochar advocates have been at pains to bring biochar into the UN Framework Convention on Climate Change process, and to argue the case for biochar to be included as an offset mechanism in formal carbon trading schemes under the Kyoto Protocol and in its Clean Development Mechanism. Meanwhile, biochar is included in various voluntary carbon markets – or at least the promise of these, in an unfolding and uncertain market scene. Through 'farming carbon' – sequestering carbon in soils, including those that are desertified or degraded – and selling carbon credits just like any other farm-produced commodity, it is argued, carbon trading could generate significant profits, whether for businesses, farmers or both (Lal 2010).

The potential of generating profits through carbon trading has enticed many small companies and commercial initiatives onto the biochar scene, where they form a subset of the dizzying array of commercial ventures forming around the new carbon economy in general. Commercial ventures specialising in or including biochar are many and varied. Examples include BioChar Products, 'a start up company dedicated to the demonstrating and testing of the fast pyrolysis concept for use in small communities near forested landscapes'[2;] and Carbon Gold, a UK-based company that manufactures biochar-based products for gardening and has a portfolio of projects in developing countries including Ghana[3]. These examples are only a small handful among the many business initiatives seeking to profit from biochar technologies and offering advice about them amidst the political economy of carbon. In this context, even publicly funded research such as our own is easily reframed in terms of its 'impact' in contributing to carbon agendas, and the business relationships linked to these (Leach et al 2010).

In this political-economic context, emerging NGO–business partnerships are implementing a rapidly expanding number of practical biochar projects. African Biodiversity Network, Biofuelwatch and Gaia Foundation (2009) list 19 such projects, and the list is growing fast. These have all started since 2005 and most describe themselves as 'trials', illustrating both the novelty of biochar applications and the status of many as simultaneous research sites for the development of biochar science. They include a project by the French Centre for Rural Innovations (in Côte d'Ivoire and Burkina Faso), involving biofuel and biochar trials on 2500 hectares, and field trials in Cameroon and DR Congo run by the Biochar Fund (Belgium); research projects/ trials in western Kenya linked to Cornell University, targeting 20 households with cookstoves and carrying out biomass assessments on 50 households; small pilot pyrolysis plants and biochar trials in Mali, Niger and Senegal supported by the NGO Pro-Natura; a study in west-central Ghana aiming to develop 'biochar-based soil management strategies for smallholder agriculture' run by Rothamsted Research (UK) and the Soil Research Institute in Kumasi; and an EU-funded project linking Italian researchers with institutions in Sierra Leone and Togo to produce biochar in cookstoves, and its effects on soils both in field stations and on farmers' fields. Emerging networks, websites and databases, such as those managed by the International Biochar Initiative, connect these and other projects, contributing to a growing community of experimental practice around biochar in Africa and beyond.

As in these examples, most contemporary African biochar projects focus on the transfer of biochar technology, and on the rapid production of biochar for application to soils through the use of 'improved' (often imported) stoves and kilns. However, in the context of such projects, there is a nascent interest in African Terra preta: in the carbon-enriched soils of old settlement sites which are valued and used across the continent, the history of their production, and the significance of farmers' knowledge and practices in using and possibly mimicking them today. Our own research has helped to stimulate this interest among biochar researchers working in Ghana and Sierra Leone, for example, leading to new PhD and master's student projects.

As the justifications for these projects emphasise, biochar offers prospects of contributing to small farmers' priorities and agendas without upsetting the prevailing political economy of food and agriculture. This has been key to its promotion in African settings. Supporting small farmers and contributing to livelihoods and poverty reduction is a central motivation for the interest in biochar among many researchers – ourselves included – and hitching to carbon agendas and funding can be seen as strategically valuable in achieving these aims. For example, the Biochar Fund describes its mission as 'fighting hunger, energy poverty, deforestation and climate change – *simultaneously*', and its impact – through projects such as those in Cameroon and DR Congo – as creating 'a synergy that radically changes the livelihoods of some of the world's poorest communities in multiple ways'.[4]

The NGO Pro-Natura, whose central concern is 'fighting rural poverty', describes how it took the decision 'to encourage the use of its green charcoal as a biochar and has launched pilot projects on its intervention sites. […] It is thus possible to render the carbon footprint globally negative (by taking more carbon from the atmosphere than is emitted), while fighting effectively against poverty and hunger'.[5] This framing of biochar as contributing simultaneously to soil enhancement, poverty reduction, wellbeing and livelihoods along with climate change has been key to the growing research and development interest in it in African settings – among businesses, NGOs and universities alike.

Nevertheless, there are tensions in this biochar debate, which is unfolding and being shaped by a high-stakes political economy chasing new carbon money. One set of tensions is around the politics of scale. While those promoting small farmer agendas generally favour small-scale schemes that recycle agricultural wastes (Lehmann and Joseph 2009; Pratt and Moran 2010), those seeking to sequester sufficient carbon to make a difference to climate change mitigation (and engender sufficient carbon-trading profits) emphasise large-scale schemes involving plantations of biochar feedstocks (Read 2009). Yet this spectre of large-scale biochar development is being roundly questioned by NGOs and researchers as unsustainable and liable to lead to poverty and deprivation – in an era shaped by concerns with 'land grabs' in Africa and by recent debates over 'biofuels versus food' as competing uses of rural lands (African Biodiversity Network et al 2009; Paul et al 2009). There is, as yet, no evidence of large-scale, commercial biochar developments in Africa, yet critics suggest that all biochar projects are currently small-scale simply because there has been no opportunity to scale them up. In this way, and as happened with biofuels, it is argued, small-scale participatory schemes are both a smokescreen for, and an opening to pave the way for, large-scale biochar monocultures that will displace farmers from their land (TNI 2009).

Another set of tensions concerns the most appropriate strategies for addressing Africa's supposed soil productivity crisis. Here, amidst a complex and again highly politicised debate, as we have seen, many of those arguing for a new Green Revolution for Africa (AGRA 2009) emphasise the importance of packages including chemical fertilisers, to be delivered at scale – including through new business–state partnerships and philanthropic funding. In contrast, others emphasise approaches that are claimed to be more attuned to small farmers' diverse livelihood and agro-ecological contexts. While such debates about African agricultural futures are heated and often polarised, biochar notably offers opportunities to both 'sides'. Thus organisations favouring an increased role for small farmer agendas and organic, biomass-based pathways see biochar strategies as offering one route of this kind (e.g. Woodfine 2009). Yet, because additions of biochar may help soil to retain nutrients and fertilisers (Hansen et al 2008; Lehmann and Joseph 2009), biochar can be framed as not an alternative to inorganic fertilisers, but a complement – enhancing fertiliser efficiency. This is potentially an attractive scenario for companies and organisations that profit from fertiliser production and distribution, which can expect greater demand for fertilisers from farmers who see their application resulting in larger crop productivity gains. Of course, not all advocates of a fertiliser-led revolution are interested in biochar. Yet the potential for biochar to be mobilised across diverse parts of the contemporary soil politics spectrum has certainly contributed to interest in it, and to difficulties in rejecting its potential out of hand. However, it is also the case that biochar promoted in this way might come to be seen by farmers as another commodity fertiliser, and perhaps rejected in favour of other soil fertility management practices. There is even a danger that an alliance of ADE and biochar with carbon sequestering and climate change agendas may lead to a marginalisation of other aspects of farmers' management of soil fertility and fallows.

This contemporary political-economic context has interlocked with a politics of knowledge in shaping interest in biochar in Africa. The promise of carbon sequestration and the transfer of biochar technology seems to be breaking down the regional exclusivity that dominated during earlier decades. Thus soil scientists with a background in Amazonian research are increasingly becoming involved in African research and partnerships. In some instances, they are working with social scientists – such as ourselves – who once framed their interests in African environments in terms of their vegetation, but, inspired by social and ecological research on Amazonian Terra preta, are now asking similar questions about African soils. In parallel, and significantly, global climate change concerns are inspiring Africanist archaeologists to turn their attention more closely to environmental questions, so that in some places at least, archaeology on the continent is becoming environmental archaeology. This is creating new potential for the kinds of interdisciplinary engagement between archaeologists, agronomists, ecologists and social scientists which were so significant to Terra preta research in the Amazon. In a few instances, such interdisciplinary alliances are now being mobilised to explore ADE in Africa.

The place of indigenous knowledge in contemporary biochar debates in Africa is ambiguous, but may be shifting. Amidst the interest in African biochar from around 2005, little attention has been paid to indigenous knowledge. Despite general arguments about participation, there is very little attention to the potential for working with, and seeking to build on, farmers' existing ADE knowledge and practices. The dominant modus operandi is of transferring in biochar technologies and strategies from outside. This presumed gap between farmers' existing practices and biochar strategies seems, at first sight, to jar with the origins of biochar interest in work on Amazonian Terra preta. Yet there is a presumed disjuncture between Terra preta creation – part of a pre-Hispanic past – and today's farming. This narrative of disjuncture deters interest in the implications of today's farming systems for the implantation of biochar practices. More significantly, it also deters interest in the possibility that today's farmers might themselves be creating ADE; that recent, extant indigenous knowledge might include acknowledgement, value and use of – or even practices to create – char-enriched soils. Research led by social scientists in Africa is now exploring just this possibility (Fairhead and Leach 2009; Fairhead et al 2009), seeking to investigate more widely and systematically practices that have so far been reported only as isolated cases and anecdotes (e.g. Zech and Haumaier 1990; Leach and Fairhead 1995; Sohi and Yeboah 2009). If evidence builds, it may lend support to those arguing for small-scale, locally appropriate approaches to biochar strategies for soil enhancement. It may be open to mobilisation by public and private organisations seeking to profit from the new political economy of carbon, which will be able to add to the sustainability credentials of their initiatives a romantic appeal to indigenous, African authenticity – as some already do with respect to Amazonian Terra preta. It is likely also that new lines of agronomic and ecological research will open up, as well as new dialogues across disciplines and regions, and with Amazonian Terra preta research communities.

Conclusions

This chapter has tracked the rise of ADE and biochar research in both Amazonia and Africa against the background of historical occlusion. In Amazonia, interest in ADE offered a conservationist counter to destructive agricultural expansion. By the time the debate was picked up in African settings, more than twenty years later, environmental preoccupations had shifted to global climate change and ADE was reframed as biochar, a win–win that could link soil enhancement with climate change mitigation in a profitable new carbon economy. Political agronomy has thus produced and re-produced its objects in a range of contrasting and contested ways.

In explaining these shifting foci, framings and timings, we have required a political agronomy analysis attentive both to changing politics of knowledge and to shifting political-economic contexts. As we have shown, most recently, agronomic research is being shaped to some degree by the new business opportunities associated with carbon pricing and potential profits. We have shown the importance of political-economic drivers of research, and the inverse: the ways in which research findings support lobbying within and for market opportunities. The financing of research is predicated on driving that economy forward – now so visible in the way researchers obtain funding by emphasising climate mitigation impacts. Many scientists have been sceptical of ADE, and especially of biochar, as a soil conditioner. Yet precisely because biochar research is enwrapped in political economic forces, such critique is now inevitably politicised.

Thus, today, alongside positive narratives about the potential of biochar, an array of alternative narratives can also be discerned. Critique is located in positions that see biochar research as locked into a research–business pathway that would support the establishment of biochar plantations that offer false promise to solve climate problems, and will have negative fall-out (e.g. land grabs). In a critical commentary in *The Guardian* newspaper in March 2009, the environmental journalist George Monbiot argued that 'the latest miracle mass fuel cure, biochar, does not stand up; yet many who should know better have been suckered into it' (Monbiot 2009a). At the very least, the so-called '"charleaders" need to cool their enthusiasm' (Monbiot 2009b). Biochar is thus becoming the focus of a – sometimes fraught and potentially high-stakes – political debate.

The importance of taking a political agronomy approach is thus in its ability to reveal the political economic forces shaping the encounter between scientists and the ecological world they probe, and to introduce reflexivity into the interpretation of their results. While this might be seen to be at the cost of debasing scientific results (shifting biochar research away from a simplistic 'realist' ontology), such reflexivity has the benefit of opening the research field to alternative pathways. The current political polarisation risks blocking alternative research. A political agronomy analysis, in helping to reveal reasons and contexts for such polarisation, also helps illuminate how it might be overcome. In particular, research need not be financed within the current win–win framing, but could look more empirically at soils and their use – not carbon-centric and linked to global agendas and a narrow view of soil ecology, but open to farmers' own knowledge and agendas. Such approaches might not meet the 'win–win' claims of proponents, but might still offer the prospects of benefits for farmers, livelihoods and landscapes as part of more diverse strategies to address soil fertility and environmental problems. In the long run, it may prove to be this kind of approach that delivers both agronomic and environmental wins, less as overt goals, but amidst multiple outcomes of processes attuned to livelihoods and landscapes – and thus likely to work in reality.

In many senses, current debates about biochar mirror earlier debates about soil and environment. Like the promotion of inorganic fertilisers during the Green Revolution era, and of agroforestry technologies during the environmental era, the current focus on carbon-fixing technologies during a climate-anxious era marginalises the complexity and diversity of agro-ecological and agronomic processes and interactions, and farmers' knowledge of these. Now that the silence about ADE in Africa has been broken, will the agenda be co-opted by big business and externally led 'solutions' to problems framed elsewhere? Or will ADE be properly acknowledged and researched as part of a rich, diverse repertoire of soil management processes and practices, with farmers' own perspectives and priorities centre stage?

Notes

1 'Biochar Hero, Johannes Lehmann, Testifies before 111th Congress', 9 July 2009, www.re-char.com/2009/07/09/biochar-hero-johannes-lehmann-testifies-before-the-111th-congress

2 www.biocharproducts.com
3 www.carbongold.com
4 www.biocharfund.org/index.php?option=com_content&task=view&id=14&Itemid=37
5 http://wordpress.pronatura.org/?page_id=31&lang=en

References

African Biodiversity Network, Biofuelwatch and Gaia Foundation (2009) 'Biochar land grabbing: the impacts on Africa', www.biofuelwatch.org.uk
AGRA (2009) Alliance for the Green Revolution in Africa, www.agra-alliance.org/section/work/soils
Ahn, P.M. (1970) *West African Soils*. London: Oxford University Press.
Amanor, K.S. (1994) *The New Frontier: Farmers' Responses to Land Degradation*. London: Zed Books.
Bailey, D.M. (1999) 'Sebakh, sherds and survey', *Journal of Egyptian Archaeology*, 85: 211–18.
Balée, W. and Erikson, C. (eds) (2006) *Time and Complexity in Historical Ecology: Studies in the Neotropical Lowlands*. New York: Columbia University Press.
Barrera-Bassols, N. and Zinck, J.A. (2000) *Ethnopedology in a Worldwide Perspective: An Annotated Bibliography*, Publication 77. Enschede, the Netherlands: ITC
——(2003) 'Ethnopedology: a worldwide view on the soil knowledge of local people', *Geoderma* 111(3/4): 171–95.
Bates, R.H. (1981) *Markets and States in Tropical Africa: The Political Basis of Agricultural Policies*. Berkeley, CA: University of California Press.
Chambers, R. (1983) *Rural Development: Putting the Last First*. London: Prentice Hall.
Cheng, C.-H., Lehmann, J. and Engelhard, M. (2008) 'Natural oxidation of black carbon in soils: changes in molecular form and surface charge along a climosequence', *Geochimica et Cosmochimica Acta*, 72: 1598–1610.
Clement, C.R. (1999) '1492 and the loss of Amazonian crop genetic resources, the relation between domestication and human population decline', *Economic Botany*, 53(2): 188–202.
Cooper, F. and Packard, R. (eds) (1997) *International Development and the Social Sciences: Essays on the History and Politics of Knowledge*. Berkeley, CA: University of California Press.
Denevan, W.M. (1992) 'The pristine myth: the landscape of the Americas in 1492', *Annals of the Association of American Geographers*, 82: 654–81.
——(2006) 'Pre-European forest cultivation in Amazonia', in Balée, W. and Erickson, C.L. (eds) *Time and Complexity in Historical Ecology: Studies in the Neotropical Lowlands*. New York: Columbia University Press, pp. 153–63.
Fairhead, J. and Leach, M. (1996) *Misreading the African Landscape: Society and Ecology in a Forest-Savanna Mosaic*. Cambridge: Cambridge University Press.
——(1998) *Reframing Deforestation: Global Analyses and Local Realities – Studies in West Africa*. London: Routledge.
——(2003) *Science, Society and Power: Environmental Knowledge and Policy in West Africa and the Caribbean*. Cambridge: Cambridge University Press.
——(2009) 'Amazonian Dark Earths in Africa', in Woods, W.I.T., Teixeira, W.G., Lehmann, J., Steiner, C., WinklerPrins, A.M.G.A. and Rebellato, L. (eds) *Terra Preta Nova: Wim Sombroek's Dream*. Dordrecht: Springer.
Fairhead, J. and Scoones, I. (2005) 'Local knowledge and the social shaping of soil investments: critical perspectives on the assessment of soil degradation in Africa', *Land Use Policy*, 22(1): 33–41.
Fairhead, J., Leach, M., Amanor, K.S. and Lehmann, J. (2009) Amazonian dark earths in Africa? Economic and Social Research Council Research Grant, Case for Support, www.steps-centre.org/ourresearch/biochar.html
Faulkner, O.T. and Mackie, J.R. (1933) *West African Agriculture*. Cambridge: Cambridge University Press.
Forsyth, T. (2003) *Critical Political Ecology*. London: Routledge.

Fraser, J. (2009) 'Agriculture and anthrosols in Central Amazonia', PhD thesis, University of Sussex.

Fraser, J.A. (2010) 'The diversity of bitter manioc (*Manihot esculenta* Crantz) cultivation in a whitewater Amazonian landscape', *Diversity* 2(4): 586–609.

Gaunt, J. and Lehmann, J. (2008) 'Energy balance and emissions associated with biochar sequestration and pyrolysis bioenergy production', *Environmental Science & Technology*, 42: 4152–58.

German, L. (2003) 'Historical contingencies in the coevolution of environment and livelihood: contributions to the debate on Amazonian Black Earth', *Geoderma*, 111: 307–31.

Glaser, B., Zech, G.W. and Woods, W.I. (2004a) 'History, current knowledge and future perspectives of geoecological research concerning the origin of Amazonian Anthropogenic Dark Earths (Terra Preta)', in Glaser B. and Woods, W.I. (eds) *Amazonian Dark Earths: Explorations in Space and Time.* Heidelberg: Springer.

Glaser, B., Guggenberger, G. and Zech, W. (2004b) 'Identifying the pre-Columbian anthropogenic input on present soil properties of Amazonian dark earths (*Terra preta*)', in Glaser B. and Woods, W.I. (eds) *Amazonian Dark Earths: Explorations in Space and Time.* Heidelberg: Springer.

Glover, M. (2009) 'Taking biochar to market: some essential concepts for commercial success', in Lehmann, J. and Joseph, S. (eds) *Biochar for Environmental Management: Science and Technology.* London: Earthscan.

González-Pérez, J.A., González-Vila, F.J., Gonzalo, A. and Knicker, H. (2004) 'The effect of fire on soil organic matter – a review', *Environment International*, 30(6): 855–70.

Hansen, J., Sato, M., Kharecha, P., Beerling, D., Berner, R., Masson-Delmotte, V., Pagani, M., Raymo, M., Royer, D. and Zachos, J. (2008) 'Target atmospheric CO_2: where should humanity aim?', *Open Atmospheric Science Journal*, 2: 217–31.

Hecht, S.B. (2009) 'Kayapo savanna management: fire, soils, and forest islands in a threatened biome', in Woods, W.I.T., Teixeira, W.G., Lehmann, J., Steiner, C., WinklerPrins, A.M.G.A. and Rebellato, L. (eds) *Terra Preta Nova: Wim Sombroek's Dream.* Dordrecht: Springer.

——(2003) 'Indigenous soil management and the creation of Amazonian Dark Earths: implications of Kayapó practices', in Lehmann, J., Kern, C., Glaser, B. and Woods, W. (eds) *Amazonian Dark Earths: Origin, Properties, Management.* Dordrecht: Kluwer.

Heckenberger, M.J., Russell, J.C., Fausto, C., Toney, J.R., Schmidt, M.J., Pereira, E., Franchetto, B. and Kuikuro, A. (2008) 'Pre-Columbian urbanism, anthropogenic landscapes, and the future of the Amazon', *Science*, 321(5893): 1214–17.

Hodge, J.M. (2007) *Triumph of the Expert: Agrarian Doctrines of Development and the Legacies of British Colonialism.* Athens, OH: Ohio University Press.

Lal, R. (2010) 'Beyond Copenhagen: mitigating climate change and achieving food security through soil carbon sequestration', *Food Security*, 2(2): 169–77.

Leach, M. and Fairhead, J. (1995) 'Ruined settlements and new gardens: gender and soil ripening among Kuranko farmers in the forest–savanna transition zone', *IDS Bulletin*, 26(1): 24–32.

Leach, M. and Mearns, R. (1996) *The Lie of the Land: Challenging Received Wisdom on the African Environment.* London: James Currey.

Leach, M., Fairhead, J., Fraser, J. and Lehner, E. (2010) *Biocharred Pathways to Sustainability? Triple Wins, Livelihoods and the Politics of Technological Promise*, STEPS Working Paper 41. Brighton: STEPS Centre.

Lehmann, J. (2007) 'Bio-energy in the black', *Frontiers in Ecology and the Environment*, 5: 381–87.

Lehmann, J. and Joseph, S. (eds) (2009) *Biochar for Environmental Management: Science and Technology.* London: Earthscan.

Lehmann, J., Kern, D.C., Glaser, B. and Woods, W.W. (eds) (2003a) *Amazonian Dark Earths: Origin, Properties, Management.* Dordrecht: Kluwer.

Lehmann, J., da Silva Jr, J.P., Steiner, C., Nehls, T., Zech, W. and Glaser, B. (2003b) 'Nutrient availability and leaching in an archaeological Anthrosol and a Ferralsol of the Central Amazon basin: fertilizer, manure and charcoal amendments', *Plant and Soil*, 249: 343–57.

Lehmann, J., Gaunt, J. and Rondon, M. (2006) 'Bio-char sequestration in terrestrial ecosystems – a review', *Mitigation and Adaptation Strategies for Global Change*, 11: 403–27.

Lehmann, J., Czimczik, C., Laird, D. and Sohi, S. (2009) 'Stability of biochar in soil', in Lehmann, J. and Joseph, S. (eds) *Biochar for Environmental Management: Science and Technology*. London: Earthscan, pp. 183–206.

Lenton, T. and Vaughan, N. (2009), 'The radiative forcing potential of different climate geoengineering options', *Atmospheric Chemistry and Physics Discussions*, 9: 2559–608.

Liang, B., Lehmann, J., Solomon, D., Kinyangi, J., Grossman, J., O'Neill, B., Skjemstand, J.O., Thies, J., Luizao, F.J., Petersen, J. and Neves, E.G. (2006) 'Black carbon increases cation exchange capacity in soils', *Soil Science Society of America Journal*, 70: 1719–30.

Lipton, M. (1977) *Why Poor People Stay Poor; Urban Bias in World Development*. Cambridge, MA: Harvard University Press.

Livingstone, D. (1875) *The Last Journals of David Livingstone in Central Africa*. Chicago, IL: James McClurg & Co.

Mann, C.C. (2008) 'Ancient earthmovers of the Amazon', *Science* 321(5893): 1148–52.

Mboukou-Kimbatsa, I.M.C. (1997) 'Les macroinvertebres du sols dans differents systèmes d'agriculture au Congo: cas particulier de deux systèmes traditionels (ecobuage et brulis) dans la vallée du Niari', These de Doctorat de l'Universite de Pierre et Marie Curie.

Meggers, B. J. (1971) *Amazonia: Man and Culture in a Counterfeit Paradise*. Washington, DC: Smithsonian Institution Press.

Mesfin, A. (1981) 'Soil burning in Ethiopia', *Ethiopian Journal of Agricultural Science (Addis Ababa)*, 3(1): 57–73.

——(1982) 'Uses of improved seed-bed and fertilizers as an alternative to soil burning or "guie"', *Ethiopian Journal of Agricultural Science (Addis Ababa)*, 4(1): 1–9.

Monbiot, G. (2009a) 'Woodchips with everything. It's the Atkins plan of the low-carbon world', www.guardian.co.uk/environment/2009/mar/24/george-monbiot-climate-change-biochar

——(2009b) 'Charleaders must cool enthusiasm for setting fire to the planet', www.guardian.co.uk/environment/georgemonbiot/2009/mar/27/biochar-monbiot-global-warming

Mpangui, A. (1997) 'Etude de l'Organisation et du comportement de sols Ferrallitiques agrileux de la Vallée du Niari (Congo)', Thèse de Doctorat de l'Université de P. et M. Curie.

Neves, E.G., Petersen, J.B., Bartone, R.N. and da Silva, C.A. (2003) 'Historical and socio-cultural origins of Amazonian Dark Earths', in Lehmann, J., Kern, D.C., Glaser, B. and Woods, W.I. (eds), *Amazonian Dark Earths: Origin, Properties, Management*. Dordrecht, the Netherlands: Kluwer.

Nye, P.H. and Greenland, D.J. (1960). *The Soil Under Shifting Cultivation*, Commonwealth Bureau of Soils Technical Communication 51. Farnham, UK: Commonwealth Agricultural Bureau.

Nyerges, A.E. and Green, G.M. (2000) 'The ethnography of landscape: GIS and remote sensing in the study of forest change in West African Guinea Savanna', *American Anthropologist*, 102(2): 271–89.

Paarlberg, R.L. (2009) *Starved for Science: How Biotechnology is Being Kept Out of Africa*. Cambridge, MA and London: Harvard University Press.

Palmer, A.S. (2009) '"Pay dirt" charcoal: financing local and global land conservation with carbon payments for biochar in agricultural soils', www.conservationcapitalintheamericas.org/students.html

Paul, H., Ernsting, A., Semino, S., Gura, S. and Lorch, A. (2009) 'Agriculture and climate change: real problems, false solutions', preliminary report by Econexus, Biofuelwatch, Grupo de Reflexion Rural and NOAH, Bangkok. www.econexus.info/sites/econexus/files/agriculture-climate-change-june-2009_summary.pdf

Portères, R. (1972) 'De l'écobuage comme un système mixte de culture et de production', *Journal d'Agriculture Tropicale et de Botanique Appliquée*, 19(6/7): 151–207.

Pratt, K. and Moran, D. (2010) 'Evaluating the cost-effectiveness of global biochar mitigation potential', *Biomass and Bioenergy*, 34: 1149–58.

Pulschen, L and Koch, W. (1990) 'The significance of soil burning "Guie" in Ethiopia with special reference to its effects on the Agrestal weed flora', *Journal of Agronomy and Crop Science*, 164: 254–61.

Ramsay, J.M. and Rose Innes, R. (1963) 'Some quantitative observations on the effects of fire on the Guinea Savannah vegetation of Northern Ghana over a period of eleven years', *African Soils*, 8: 41–85.

Read, P. (2009) 'Policy to address the threat of dangerous climate change: a leading role for biochar', in Lehmann, J. and Joseph, S. (eds) *Biochar for Environmental Management: Science and Technology*. London: Earthscan.

Richards, P. (1985) *Indigenous Agricultural Revolution: Ecology and food production in West Africa*. London: Hutchinson.

Roorda, T.M.M. (1984) *Effects of Soil Burning (Guie) on Physico-chemical Properties of Soils in the Sheno, Debre Berhan and Chacha Areas of Ethiopia*. Addis Ababa: International Livestock Centre for Africa.

Schaan, D., Alceu Ransi, A. and Pärssinen, M. (eds) (2008) *Aqueologia da Amazônia Ocidental: Os Geoglifos do Acre*. Belém: Editora Universitaria, UFPA.

Schmidt, M.J. and Heckenberger, M.J. (2009) 'Amerindian anthrosols: Amazonian dark earth formation in the Upper Xingu', in Woods, W.I.T., Teixeira, W.G., Lehmann, J., Steiner, C., WinklerPrins, A.M.G.A. and Rebellato, L. (eds) *Terra Preta Nova: Wim Sombroek's Dream*. Dordrecht: Springer.

Sillitoe, P. (2006) 'Ethnobiology and applied anthropology: rapprochement of the academic with the practical', *Journal of the Royal Anthropological Institute* (N.S.): S119–S142.

Sohi, S. and Yeboah, E. (2009) 'Traditional biochar-based management of tropical soil in subsistence agriculture', in Lehmann, J. and Joseph, S. (eds) *Biochar for Environmental Management: Science and Technology*. London: Earthscan.

Sombroek, W., Ruivo, M. d. L., Fearnside, P.M., Glaser, B. and Lehmann, J. (2003) 'Amazonian dark earths as carbon stores and sinks', in Lehmann, J., Kern, D.C., Glaser, B. and Woods, W.I. (eds) *Amazonian Dark Earths: Origin, Properties, Management*. Dordrecht: Kluwer.

Spash, C.L. (2009) *The Brave New World of Carbon Trading*, MPRA Paper No. 19114, http://ideas.repec.org/p/pra/mprapa/19114.html

Steiner, C., Teixeira, W.G., Woods, W.I. and Zech, W. (2009) 'Indigenous knowledge about Terra Preta formation', in Woods, W.I.T., Teixeira, W.G., Lehmann, J., Steiner, C., WinklerPrins, A.M.G.A. and Rebellato, L. (eds) *Terra Preta Nova: Wim Sombroek's Dream*. Dordrecht: Springer.

TNI (2009) 'Biochar, a big new threat to people, land and ecosystems', www.tni.org/article/biochar-big-new-threat-people-land-and-ecosystems

Uphoff, N., Ball, A.S., Fernandes, E., Herren, H., Husson, O., Laing, M., Palm, C., Pretty, J. and Sanchez, P. (2006) *Biological Approaches to Sustainable Soil Systems*. Boca Raton, FL: CRC Press.

Vine, H. (1953) 'Experiments and the maintenance of soils fertility at Ibadan, Nigeria, 1922–55', *Empire Journal of Experimental Agriculture*, 21(82): 65–85.

Woodfine, A. (2009) for TerrAfrica, *Using Sustainable Land Management Practices to Adapt to and Mitigate Climate Change in Sub-Saharan Africa*, Version 1.0.

Woods, W.I. and Denevan, W.M. (2009) 'Amazonian Dark Earths: the first century of reports', in Woods, W.I.T., Teixeira, W.G., Lehmann, J., Steiner, C., WinklerPrins, A.M.G.A. and Rebellato, L. (eds) *Terra Preta Nova: Wim Sombroek's Vision*. Dordrecht: Springer, pp. 1–14.

Woods, W.I.T., Teixeira, W.G., Lehmann, J., Steiner, C., WinklerPrins, A.M.G.A. and Rebellato, L. (eds) (2009) *Terra Preta Nova: Wim Sombroek's Vision*. Dordrecht: Springer.

Zech, W., Haumaier, L. and Hempfling, R. (1990) 'Ecological aspects of soil organic matter in tropical land use', in McCarthy, P., Clapp, C.E., Malcolm, R.L. and Bloom, P.R. (eds) *Humic Substances in Soil and Crop Sciences, Selected Readings*. Madison, WI: American Society of Agronomy and Soil Science Society of America.

5

CONTESTATION AS CONTINUITY?

Biofortification research and the CGIAR

Sally Brooks and Sarah E. Johnson-Beebout

Introduction

Biofortification, the development of nutrient-dense staple crops, has been promoted both as a solution to 'hidden hunger' among poor populations in the developing world (Nestel et al 2006) and as an exemplar of the kind of global public goods research for which the CGIAR system is renowned (Dalrymple 2008). As an interdisciplinary field of research and development linking crop science with human nutrition and public health (CIAT and IFPRI 2002), biofortification presents both challenges and opportunities for an international agricultural research system oriented towards genetics-led crop improvement (Anderson et al 1991). This chapter traces developments in biofortification research over a fifteen-year period during which it emerged from the margins of the CGIAR to become a priority for research investment (von Braun et al 2008).

Biofortification is a relatively new term which simultaneously refers to (i) a range of technologies designed to alter the grain nutrient levels in selected crop varieties; (ii) a development intervention combining goals of improved public health and poverty alleviation; and (iii) an idea linking agriculture, nutrition and health in new ways. It is a multi-dimensional 'project' contested on a number of levels, in terms of its technical feasibility and efficacy (in controlled conditions), effectiveness and impact (in the 'real world'), and appropriateness and desirability (in comparison with alternative solutions). This chapter analyses developments in biofortification research as an extended case study in contested agronomy[1], in which a body of knowledge about complex interactions between genotypes, soils, human bodies and populations has evolved over time, in ways that have both reflected and reinforced particular sets of interdisciplinary and inter-institutional relations. In the process, certain types of knowledge have presided over others, with the result that some dimensions of this complex, multi-dimensional project have been contested, while others have not.

This chapter traces successive stages of biofortification research within the CGIAR and among its partners, highlighting how these dimensions of potential contestation have played out at each stage, in ways that reflected the priorities of the time, location and particular characteristics of crops, nutrients and technologies. Despite these specificities, certain continuities can be identified. In particular, contestation has tended to focus on feasibility and efficacy questions that can be resolved within the confines of institutional science, at the expense of broader questions about effectiveness and appropriateness in the context of the needs, priorities and programmes of particular countries and populations. A notable exception is the contestation surrounding the controversial 'Golden Rice' project, which has been elevated to exemplary 'case study' status in the GM crop debate (Jasanoff 2005; Taverne 2007). In the process, a multiplicity of uncertainties about the less emotive, technical aspects of the project have been shielded from professional as well as public scrutiny (Brooks 2010).

One dimension that has gone remarkably uncontested, at least by the international nutrition community, is the question of the appropriateness of biofortification as a nutritional intervention (although there are notable exceptions; for example, see Johns and Sthapit 2004). This may be because biofortification does not, for this community, represent a fundamental change of paradigm. Since the mid-1990s, the field has been dominated by a 'goal-oriented nutrition' paradigm that is particularly amenable to scalable micronutrient delivery mechanisms such as industrial food fortification and pharmaceutical supplements (Gillespie et al 2004; Latham 2010). From this position, biofortification, despite its novelty, does not represent a significant point of departure. Instead, debates about impact are dominated by *ex ante* analyses extrapolating health and economic outcomes associated with a 'switch' from non-biofortified to biofortified varieties (Stein et al 2005). By and large, these analyses are based on frameworks from neoclassical economics, which do not take into account the diversity of ways in which rice is cultivated, processed and consumed within different cultural and agro-ecological contexts (Brooks 2010).

A glance back at the CGIAR's first biofortification project (long before the term appeared) suggests that this lack of debate about effectiveness and appropriateness, particularly with regard to addressing the nutritional needs of the poorest, was indeed problematic. Research began at the Mexico-based International Maize and Wheat Improvement Center (CIMMYT) on *opaque2* maize in the 1960s (Mertz et al 1964), providing the foundation for the Quality Protein Maize (QPM) programme that has continued from the 1970s to this day. Accounts of the trajectory of QPM research reveal repeated cycles of optimism inspired by each new 'breakthrough', only to be tempered by field results that were insufficiently conclusive to justify either full endorsement or closure (Mertz 1997; see also Prasanna et al 2001).[2] Today, QPM is grown extensively in East Africa, although the extent to which this is due to its nutritional qualities is uncertain (De Groote et al 2010). In India, the national maize breeding programme prioritizes QPM research (Prasanna et al 2001), although its work is increasingly oriented towards the livestock feed market rather than the nutritional deficiencies of the poor (Hellin and Erenstein 2009).

Will more recent biofortification initiatives, focused on the micronutrients iron, zinc and vitamin A, avoid these ambiguities and succeed in reaching the poorest? An example and oft-cited biofortification 'success story' has been the promotion of orange fleshed sweet potato (OFSP) in sub-Saharan Africa. Naturally high in beta-carotene (the precursor of vitamin A), its substitution for white-fleshed sweet potato has been a favoured food-based strategy of nutritionists for many years (Gichuki et al 1997; Hagenimama et al 2001; Low et al 2001, 2007). The untapped potential of OFSP to combat vitamin A deficiency led to the absorption of ongoing research activity into the HarvestPlus Biofortification Challenge Program as the basis for much of its early 'end-user' work.[3] In contrast to other crops targeted by the CGIAR for biofortification, the OFSP project utilises well developed products, the efficacy and desirability of which do not attract contestation. Nevertheless, questions remain about the effectiveness of a nutrition intervention, based on food items that still require intensive promotion, even after twenty years of research and development efforts.[4]

Perhaps because of the conspicuous yellow colour associated with the trait, research on biofortification of crops with beta-carotene has tended to have a higher profile than research focusing on other nutrients. Varieties enriched with beta-carotene exhibit a yellow-orange colour that makes it possible to segregate biofortified from non-biofortified products, while cultivars bred for increased iron or zinc density are visually indistinguishable from other varieties. This has implications for labelling and pricing, as well as the potential for targeting particular populations 'at risk' from malnutrition-related illness, raising a different set of challenges with regard to impact assessment. The focus of this chapter is on efforts, centred in the International Rice Research Institute (IRRI), to biofortify rice with the trace minerals iron and zinc. Contestation around this research has been relatively restrained, mainly because the research has relied largely (but not exclusively) on 'conventional' plant breeding rather than more controversial transgenic technologies. A key claim made for iron- and zinc-dense varieties is that they offer a 'win–win' solution combining nutritional benefits with improved agronomic performance (realising higher yields, particularly in nutrient-deficient soils; Bouis 1996), making this a particularly interesting case from a contested agronomy perspective.

This chapter traces the history of research aimed at producing iron- and zinc-dense rice varieties. It highlights, at each stage, which dimensions were contested and which were not, and how this contestation (or lack of it) was linked to particular config-urations of actors, disciplines and broader institutional factors. It explores how the problem to be addressed by the research was defined or 'framed' (Schön and Rein 1994) in ways that both reflected and reinforced particular sets of interdisciplinary relations. These dynamics are viewed through the lens of interdisciplinary relations and contests that emerged in each stage of the research. This analysis highlights how scale assumptions embedded in certain disciplines (or in particular approaches within disciplines) could be marshalled to tilt the interdisciplinary playing field, with impli-cations for research directions and science practice. Furthermore, these dynamics 'at the interface' (Long 2001) between epistemic traditions unfolded within a broader institutional context that was itself in a state of perpetual transformation. A key contribution of this chapter is that it offers a cross-scale analysis of contested agronomy linking the micropolitics of interdisciplinary 'boundary work' (Gieryn 1999) with the broader power-knowledge relations that characterize these increasingly globalised research networks.

The pre-breeding study – establishing feasibility (1994–99)

This section outlines the series of events through which plant breeding for micronutrient density found its way onto the CGIAR research agenda. This was due, in large part, to a small network of like-minded people who championed the approach at a time when it was perceived by many within the CGIAR as unrealistic and somewhat eccentric. It focuses on particular moments when the biofortification research agenda was subtly reframed to bring in different constituencies, particularly the CGIAR plant breeders on whom the approach (as conceived by its promoters) depended.

In 1993, the International Food Policy Research Institute (IFPRI) received funding from the USAID Office of Nutrition to identify ways in which CGIAR 'might undertake to join other international and national organisations in the fight against micronutrient malnutrition' (Bouis 1995a: 11). While this idea initially received a lukewarm response from CGIAR scientists (mindful of the early QPM experience), a breakthrough came with the discovery of a network of scientists advocating a 'food systems approach' to the problem of micronutrient malnutrition (Combs et al 1996). This was envisaged as a holistic and 'inherently interdisciplinary' approach in which plant breeding research was integrated with research into micronutrient bioavailability[5] and food technology. The institutional home of this approach was the Cornell-based Federal Plant, Soil and Nutrition Laboratory (PSNL), which 'had, since the 1930s, been investigating linkages between minerals in soils and the nutrition of plants, animals and humans in the United States' (Bouis 1995a: 12).

At this time, Ross Welch of the PSNL introduced Howarth Bouis, based at IFPRI and the CGIAR's main advocate of biofortification research, to Robin Graham of the Waite Agricultural Research Institute at the University of Adelaide.[6] Graham was conducting research on crops bred for more efficient uptake of trace minerals such as iron and zinc from deficient soils (Bouis 1995a: 12–13). Graham's aim was to use this trait to improve wheat yields in zinc-deficient soils in Australia. Meanwhile, a research programme was under way to adapt Australian zinc-efficient varieties for the zinc-deficient soils in Turkey, with the aim of improving plant and human nutrition simultaneously (Cakmak 1996). It was estimated that 'Turkish wheat farmers would save $100 million annually in reduced seeding rates alone' (Cakmak 1996: 13).[7] Graham, Welch and Bouis envisioned a 'win–win situation' (Graham and Welch 1996: 15–16) in which crop yields would be enhanced 'without additional farmer inputs' alongside improved nutritional quality (Welch and Graham 2004: 356), through a strategy of 'tailoring the plant to fit the soil'. However, the implied synergies between plant and human nutrition benefits were still unproven at this stage (Bouis 1995b: 18).

In 1994, IFPRI hosted a workshop entitled 'Agricultural Strategies for Micronutrients', which led to the establishment of the CGIAR micronutrients project (1994–99) (Bouis et al 1999). The merits of various breeding strategies were explored and mechanisms regulating plant and human nutrition were discussed. In the published output a strategic simplification was made, which proved critical in convincing CGIAR plant breeders to participate. It was articulated as follows: 'The genetics of these traits is generally simple, making the task for breeders comparatively easy ... the primary selection criterion is a simple and efficient one – the micronutrient content of the seed' (Graham and Welch 1996: 55). This problem redefinition spoke directly to the prevailing, genetics-led approach to crop research within the CGIAR by framing grain micronutrient content as an 'isolable problem' (Anderson et al 1991), which could be approached in the same way as other stress-tolerant traits. And so the 'food systems' framing was replaced by a familiar CGIAR narrative – the solution was 'in the seed' (Brooks 2010).

Meanwhile, a group of IRRI plant breeders led by Dharmawansa Senadhira were developing rice varieties for 'problem soils' characterised by salinity and mineral toxicity and deficiency. This group produced a cross called 'IR68144', an aromatic variety suited to 'cold elevated areas'. At this time, Senadhira became aware of the CGIAR micronutrients project, which prompted a shift to nutritional breeding objectives.[8] At the same time, the attention of his Filipino colleagues was drawn to a national campaign to combat iron-deficiency anaemia following the 'Ending Hidden Hunger' conference in Montreal in 1991 (Gregorio et al 2000: 382; see also Graham et al 1999). As a result, while IR68144 contained elevated levels of both iron and zinc, it was its identity as a high-iron cultivar that was emphasised. In 1999, an IRRI-convened conference, which brought together crop scientists and nutritionists to discuss strategies for 'improving human nutrition through agriculture', provided Sehandhira's team with an opportunity to showcase their recently discovered 'high-iron rice':

> A high-iron trait can be combined with high-yielding traits. This has already been demonstrated by the serendipitous discovery ... of an aromatic variety – a cross between a high yielding variety (IR72) and a tall, traditional variety (Zawa Bonday) from India – from which IRRI identified an improved line (IR68144–3B-2-2-3[9]) with a high concentration of grain iron (about 21ppm[10] in brown rice). ... yields are about 10% below those of IR72, but in partial compensation, maturity is earlier. This variety has good tolerance to soils deficient in minerals such as phosphorus, zinc and iron.
>
> *(Gregorio et al 2000: 383)*

While the 'serendipitous discovery' of IR68144 appeared to confirm the feasibility of rice biofortification, questions remained about its performance under different agro-ecological conditions. The question of genotype–environment interactions, however, would be dealt with through the usual process of varietal evaluation following multi-location trials, so these were put on hold. For the time being, the focus shifted to the nutrition parameters of bioavailability and bioefficacy (the extent to which adsorption of these nutrients effects a measurable change in human nutrition status) as representing 'the final unknown' (Brooks 2010). Bouis and Senadhira's team now looked to Angelita del Mundo, a nutritionist at the neighbouring Institute for Human Nutrition and Food at the University of Philippines, Los Baños, who had for many years advocated the incorporation of nutritional parameters into rice breeding programmes.[11] Del Mundo proposed a 'feeding trial' be conducted to test the bioefficacy of iron in IR68144; and proposed Catholic convents as an 'ideal' setting for such a study (Haas et al 2000: 442). Collaborators would include Jere Haas of the Division of Nutritional Sciences at Cornell and John Beard from the Department of Nutrition at Pennsylvania State University. Following this presentation, new funding was secured from the Asian Development Bank (ADB) for continued research on iron-biofortified rice – on the condition that the feeding trial formed an integral part of the programme.[12]

The feeding trial – focus on nutrition (2000–03)

This section focuses on the systematic nutrition study which, it was hoped, would convince the international nutrition and donor communities to support biofortification. The study that Del Mundo and her colleagues designed was an ambitious nine-month feeding trial which involved, as research subjects, more than 300 religious sisters in ten Catholic convents across Metro Manila. It was both a landmark study and a major logistical challenge which was extremely demanding of the small, close-knit inter-disciplinary team of nutritionists and plant breeders. This team, or 'research family' as they called themselves, displayed particular characteristics that shaped the study in ways that have tended to be overlooked during subsequent contestation.

With the prioritisation of the bioefficacy study, the emphasis of the project shifted to nutrition, using the 'high-iron rice' IR68144 as the material 'developed at the IRRI for experimental use' (Haas et al 2005: 2825). The feeding trial was a 'prospective, randomised, controlled, double blind, longitudinal (9 month) intervention trial involving 317 women. The study had two arms: low-iron rice and high-iron rice, which were the exclusive sources of rice consumed [by the research subjects] for nine months' (Haas et al 2005: 2824). In preparation for the feeding trial, crop scientists at IRRI conducted a series of experiments to measure the effects of production, milling and cooking of IR68144 in comparison with the proposed control. Thus far, the screening of varieties for iron content had been conducted on dehulled but unmilled 'brown' rice. However, in the Philippines (and elsewhere in the region) rice is usually consumed in its milled 'white' form. This was the first time that the research team had evaluated the effects of post-harvest processing (milling, rinsing, cooking) on grain iron content. They found that milling and rinsing had a far greater impact on the iron content of cooked white rice than previously assumed, to the extent that the differential between the 'high-iron' and 'low-iron' rice was reduced to a level that threatened the viability of the study:

> In effect, the differential between IR68144 and PSBRc28 [the original control] is largely based on milling and not genotype. ... The differential may be achieved

> if a commercially produced rice ... will be used opposite to IR68144 ...
> treatments such as milling of IR68144 and washing of rice prior to cooking
> should be taken into consideration to maximize the differential.
>
> *(Gregorio et al 2003: Conclusions and recommendations)*

Adjustments had to be made in order to engineer the iron differential required for the study to go ahead, including the selection of a new control and the development of a milling strategy that involved under-milling IR68144 and over-milling the control. Since under-milled rice does not store well, supplies of the 'high-iron' rice had to be delivered to the participating convents on a fortnightly basis. These adjustments placed demands on the researchers, which they absorbed willingly. The location of the research in Catholic convents held particular significance for the Filipino 'research family', who were all of the Catholic faith. Del Mundo, in particular, 'had always dreamed of working with religious sisters' in her research work (Del Mundo 2003: 82). This convergence of science and religion[13] was also reflected in the convent leaders' decision to accommodate the research, once convinced that participation constituted a form of 'humanitarian service'.[14]

Questions remained, however, about how the 'high-iron' status of IR68144 might be sustained beyond the carefully controlled feeding trial. The elaborate logistics required to maintain the identity of the 'high-iron' material was just a taste of the challenges to come in maintaining its integrity as a commercial variety with distinct (yet invisible) characteristics. Consideration of the implications for traceability, pricing and attributable nutritional impact in 'real-world' conditions was shelved. The seeds of future contestation were sown with the claim that such a partial and contingent success would represent 'proof of concept' (an ambiguous claim in itself); particularly since the IR68144 materials had, by then, been submitted for varietal testing, with the expectation that the conclusion of the feeding trial would coincide with the launch of the Philippines' first high-iron rice variety.

During routine varietal testing, the agronomic performance of IR68144 did not match expectations, so it was released with the more cautious certification of a 'special variety' and named MS13 (Padolina et al 2003: 11; Corpuz-Arocena et al 2004). Meanwhile, MS13 seeds were transferred to the Philippine Rice Research Institute (PhilRice) for seed multiplication and varietal promotion. It was at this point that agronomists began investigating the variability of the 'high-iron' character of MS13/ IR68144 more closely, discovering significant variation in grain iron content across contrasting agro-ecological conditions and between seasons.[15] It was in the context of these questions about the relative contribution of the genotype (G) and environmental (E) factors that some agronomists began to question the wisdom of privileging a genetic-led approach to biofortification. Surely these findings suggested that environmental testing might play a useful role in informing breeding strategies (cf. Simmonds 1991)? As one scientist explained: ' ... they identify genotypes first, without understanding the cultural practices that will optimise the expression of iron ... If they did an agronomic study first, then the true breeding parents would have been used'.[16]

Globalising biofortification: negotiating programme-wide breeding targets (2004–06)

In 2003, funding was secured for a joint proposal from CIAT and IFPRI for a biofortification 'Challenge Program' called HarvestPlus (CIAT and IFPRI 2002). This included funds from a new donor, the Bill & Melinda Gates Foundation (BMGF). This section charts the transformation of the ADB-funded regional rice biofortification initiative into the rice crop component of this new global programme. In the process, new actors congregated around a vision of a series of 'gold standard'[17] biofortified lines, developed according to a system-wide framework of breeding targets. Meanwhile, the outputs of earlier research – including the mixed performance of IR68144 – presented dilemmas for a new team of research managers poised to 'scale up' rice biofortification research.

The results of the feeding trial were published in 2005, with the conclusion that 'consumption of biofortified rice, without any other changes in diet, is efficacious in improving iron stores of women with iron-poor diets in the developing world' (Haas et al 2005: 2823). This was an important milestone, which coincided with a change in personnel involved in rice biofortification research at IRRI.[18] A 'research family' rooted in the Philippine context gave way to an internationally focused network of researchers now tasked with conducting iron-biofortified rice research under HarvestPlus.[19] Distancing themselves from IR68144/MS13, they asserted that, while as a variety it was far from 'gold standard', the feeding trial had provided the necessary 'proof of concept' to justify investment in further research.

But what had been proven? As discussed in the previous section, problems had emerged in the run-up to the feeding trial, and later in varietal testing, that cast doubts on the wisdom of a genetics-led approach to biofortification. While the former had highlighted the importance of post-harvest practices in determining grain iron content (Gregorio et al 2003), the latter suggested that environmental rather than genetic factors might be more significant. By this time, however, the HarvestPlus Program, which institutionalised a genetics-led strategy, had been endorsed by the newly established CGIAR Science Council. The Science Council was committed to a return to model of 'high-impact' public goods research (Science Council 2006), which within the CGIAR was equated with genetics-led research (Brooks 2011a). Furthermore, this equation linking 'impact at scale' with a genetics-led approach had been key to securing the support of the BMGF for biofortification at a time when the CGIAR's traditional donors were still cautious.[20] The next step would therefore be to resume the search for rice germplasm with higher grain iron content in accordance with centralised, programme-wide targets.[21] Having streamlined the problem definition thus, it was not long before IRRI scientists were debating whether transgenic methods might be a more efficient way to achieve these targets than conventional plant breeding.[22,23]

Those now tasked with steering rice biofortification research under HarvestPlus drew selectively from the previous research phase, claiming 'proof of concept' for the efficacy of iron-rice biofortification (as well as, even more questionably, a 'bioavailability number' for iron in rice-based diets[24]). At the same time, the question of technical feasibility with respect to biofortification through conventional plant breeding was being reopened – the key question now was whether HarvestPlus nutrient targets necessitated a transgenic approach. As a result, research at IRRI on iron-biofortified rice began to follow two parallel paths – based on the use of first, conventional plant breeding and second, transgenic techniques. This development suggested that the choice facing decision-makers was between the objective merits of two technologies; obscuring the fact that the critical decision had already been made. In both cases, research would follow a genetic-led strategy focusing on centralised targets based on calculations of 'impact' in relation to generic 'populations at risk'. This shared understanding of the choices ahead enabled plant geneticists to define the parameters of engagement with other disciplines, including human nutrition.[25]

Nowhere was this more apparent than in an encounter between plant breeders and nutritionists over the setting of programme-wide breeding targets. With HarvestPlus framed as a strategy in which 'agriculture would be an instrument for human health' (Graham 2002), these targets were to be set at a level that would achieve a significant health impact. However, it soon became clear that such targets would be difficult to achieve within the first phase of the programme. Plant breeders proposed they work towards 'intermediate targets', as is consistent with the common practice of 'breeding up', and releasing a series of improved products over time, 'like Honda cars'.[26] But to the nutritionists, this made no sense: 'you either have the level for biological impact or you don't.'[27] The plant breeders won the argument and intermediate targets were adopted. For the nutritionists, this was a turning point which demonstrated that HarvestPlus remained, first and foremost, a crop improvement programme. As one nutritionist remarked; 'whenever nutrition throws up a challenge, [plant breeders] move the goalposts!'[28]

With the changes accompanying the transition from the ADB-funded project to the global HarvestPlus programme, including the interdisciplinary contestation outlined above, a key lesson from the IR68144/MS13 experience failed to attract attention. When MS13 was released in 2003, members of the 'research family' anticipated a positive response from farmers and consumers, mindful of governmental initiatives to support fortification of staple foods with essential nutrients.[29] However, the release coincided with the launch of a major subsidy programme for hybrid rice producers in the year leading up to the 'International Year of Rice' (PhilRice 2006). Thus the high-iron rice project was but a short chapter in a more complex story of science, policy and politics in the Philippines, in which a narrative of rice self-sufficiency remains as emotive and powerful as it was at the height of the Green Revolution (Brooks 2011b). When asked what was the most important lesson to be drawn from the experience of IR68144/MS13, one participant in the varietal assessment process put it succinctly: 'national priorities matter'.[30]

The shift to zinc: genetic or agronomic biofortification? (2007–10)

By 2007 another series of shifts was under way. The HarvestPlus team had succeeded in securing funding for a second phase. The Challenge Program structure was being questioned during discussions then taking place in the CGIAR around a series of 'mega-programmes'. Meanwhile, those steering rice biofortification research at IRRI recognised that the prospects of meeting HarvestPlus targets using conventional plant breeding alone were increasingly unlikely. Nevertheless, during the first phase of HarvestPlus, plant breeders at IRRI had been screening known rice cultivars for both iron and zinc grain content. A key factor was the exact location of these nutrients within the grain. While a substantial amount of grain iron content is concentrated in the aleurone layer, which is removed in the milling process (so that levels dropped below target levels in white rice – as had been discovered in preparations for the feeding trials), milling had a relatively small effect on grain zinc content (Johnson-Beebout et al 2010). The decision was taken, therefore, to proceed with conventional plant breeding for zinc and transgenic research with respect to iron.

The shift to zinc created new spaces for the development of a different culture of interdisciplinary enquiry at IRRI. This collaboration was prompted by plant breeders' and soil scientists' shared sense of curiosity and puzzlement that neither had been able, from their own disciplinary perspective, to explain observed G × E interaction in grain zinc concentration. Encouraged by managerial changes supportive of interdisciplinary collaboration, a new cohort of young scientists has begun to explore new avenues of research. Importantly, this transformation has taken place, not according to an *a priori* plan, but through an evolutionary process that has followed the formation of lateral relationships between scientists, through serendipitous events, informal connections and friendship. As one scientist commented; 'it helped that we are all women about the same age, and we communicate more easily than the larger group which included mostly men, and mostly more senior scientists'.[31]

From late 2006 onwards, this group continued to meet as a 'cross-disciplinary group of zinc researchers within IRRI' to discuss their work, while continuing to design their own experiments in the normal way. Soil experiments were designed around a range of variables but utilised only one or two genotypes and were therefore 'only moderately interesting to breeders'. Similarly, breeders carried out multi-location trials from which they collected data via 'routine soil tests', which was of little use to soil scientists attempting to interpret the G × E results as the data did not relate to zinc availability. As one scientist explained, 'it took us a long time to realise how differently we understood G × E effects in different disciplines'.[32] A turning point came when funding was secured to recruit a post-doctoral researcher for the project and, instead of an additional plant breeder or agronomist, a plant physiologist was appointed. This individual proved to be the vital link in the interdisciplinary web, able to explain to plant breeders and soil chemists why specific rice varieties perform differently in different environments. These interdisciplinary discussions, enabled as much by personal relationships as any organisational plan, led to the design of a specific set of experiments to answer each other's questions. By early 2011, the group were planning 'plant breeding experiments in strategic locations' representing varying zinc availability, thus enabling the simultaneous collection of plant physiology and soil-related data.

In parallel with these developments at IRRI, however, a new global project has been launched under the auspices of HarvestPlus, based on a different type of agronomy optimising the use of zinc fertiliser technology. Tellingly, this project incorporates scalability assumptions comparable with those of genetics-led biofortification under the first phase of HarvestPlus. In this case, a global mining industry in search of new ways to demonstrate corporate social responsibility and 'mineral stewardship' by promoting zinc as a product that is uniquely 'natural, essential, durable and recyclable' (Green et al 2010) is emerging as a powerful new actor. Initiatives to date have included a high-profile 'Zinc Saves Kids' supplementation campaign (in partnership with UNICEF[33]), and now the industry-sponsored 'HarvestPlus Global Zinc Fertilizer Project'.[34] The latter involves widespread application of zinc fertiliser as a 'short-term' solution to serve as a stop-gap until 'genetic biofortification' (still the 'optimum' strategy) produces its long-awaited results:

> Application of Zn fertilizers or Zn-enriched NPK fertilizers (e.g. argronomic biofortification) offers a rapid solution to the problem, and represents [a] useful complementary approach to on-going breeding programs.
>
> *(Cakmak 2008: 1)*

This view of zinc fertiliser as a 'silver bullet' is contested by agronomists working in the field. The initial success stories of zinc fertiliser-induced biofortification involved only wheat (Cakmak et al 2010; Erenoglu et al 2010). These studies demonstrated the effectiveness of both soil and foliar applications of zinc in increasing grain zinc content, in at least some Zn-deficient environments. However, rice is different from wheat in two important respects. First, it is grown in flooded soils and 'flooding the soil changes everything' (Johnson-Beebout et al 2010). In particular, soil-applied zinc fertiliser sometimes becomes rapidly unavailable to plants after the soil has been flooded (Johnson-Beebout et al 2009). Second, zinc applied on the foliage is not as easily moved into the grain in rice as it is in wheat, due to fundamental physiological differences between the two species (Jiang et al 2007; Stomph et al 2009); although there is still debate about the level of genetic variation within rice varieties for this trait. Wissuwa et al (2008) have therefore cautioned against the use of zinc fertiliser as a generic solution, highlighting results showing 'native soil Zn status' as the dominant factor determining grain Zn concentrations 'followed by genotype and fertilizer'. They argue that it is 'not possible to simply compensate for low soil Zn availability by fertilizer applications' (Wissuwa et al 2008: 37). Plant breeders, however, have contested this, arguing that the genotypes used in the study did not include sufficient genetic variability to support such a conclusion.

Thus biofortification remains a site of contested agronomy. At IRRI, contestation is confined to technical feasibility questions debated among crop scientists. Meanwhile, nutrition studies are conducted elsewhere, with research partners in Bangladesh, with whom, under current organisational arrangements, IRRI crop scientists have little interaction. Similarly, wider issues of effectiveness and appropriateness, such as whether poorer farmers will ultimately be able to afford zinc fertilisers, are 'dealt with' elsewhere within an increasingly dispersed global network.

Conclusions

This chapter takes biofortification research as a case study in contested agronomy, in which a body of knowledge about complex interactions between genotypes, soils, human bodies and populations has evolved over time, in ways that have both reflected and reinforced particular sets of interdisciplinary and interinstitutional relations. In the process, certain types of knowledge have presided over others, with the result that some dimensions of this complex, multidimensional project have been contested, while others have not. Research in each phase has been both groundbreaking and partial – something is always left out – with the consequences of blind spots inherent in one phase being carried over to the next. In this context, biofortification has been an arena of continual contestation, nourished by a succession of 'new paradigms', inflated claims and counterclaims, and never quite resolved.

These dynamics have been examined through the lens of interdisciplinary relations and contests that have characterised different stages of the research. Specifically, the chapter has traced efforts centred at IRRI to develop rice cultivars enriched with the trace minerals iron and zinc. This analysis has shown that the 'software' of interdisciplinary collaboration – built on collegial relations that are difficult to cultivate at a distance – is as important as the hardware that can be drawn on an organisation chart. In particular, a crucial element of fruitful interdisciplinary exchange has been the formation of lateral connections between early career scientists (not yet constrained by imperatives to simplify results and secure future funding) – who have been motivated to learn more about the function of each others' disciplines. Nevertheless, these have tended to be islands of beneficial interdisciplinary contestation and learning that have emerged at particular moments, through serendipitous connections, informal relations and friendship, which have not, thus far, been institutionalised. As a result, interdisciplinary collaboration throughout 15 years of biofortifciation research at IRRI has been variable, inconsistent and partial; and opportunities for institutional learning have been elusive.

The globalisation of biofortification research is predicated on the principle of interdisciplinary collaborative research. In practice, however, the research is increasingly compartmentalised, with specialised components of research dispersed throughout global, heterogeneous networks of institutions and individuals. This effectively closes spaces for contestation, often when and where it is most needed. This chapter has highlighted the inherent challenges in widening (rather than narrowing, as is the current trend) interdisciplinary exchange to incorporate broader issues – political as well as technical – that will ultimately have the greatest influence on the effectiveness of biofortification as a real-world intervention. With zinc-biofortified rice now identified as a 'product line' within the Global Rice Science Partnership (GRiSP, formerly the Rice Crop 'Mega program') (IRRI et al 2010), this would be an appropriate time to review the lessons highlighted by this chapter and consider their implications for research design and practice.

Notes

1 In Chapter 1 of this volume, agronomy is defined as 'the application of plant and soil science to crop production'; however, in this chapter we use the term agronomy as understood at IRRI, where there is a clear organisational division between the constituent activities (and related disciplines) of crop improvement (genetics), crop management (agronomy), and grain quality (cereal chemistry and post-harvest/agricultural engineering) [interviews, Institute of Human Nutrition and Food (IHNF) and IRRI, June 2006; www.harvestplus.org].

2 For example, a recent meta-analysis of community-based studies of the nutritional impact of QPM generated results that were encouraging, but not conclusive (Gunaratna et al 2009).

3 Interview, HarvestPlus, 31 January 2006.

4 Interview, former CGIAR director, 20 January 2006.

5 The term 'bioavailability' refers to the proportion of nutrient the body can extract from food items and make available for utilisation.

6 Interview, Cornell, 19 January 2006.

7 'The potential economic returns on research aimed at helping Turkish farmers on zinc-deficient lands reduce their seeding rate are tremendous', says Braun [of CIMMYT's Wheat Programme]. 'A reduction of 80 kg/ha could save about 400,000 tons of seed a year, with an estimated value of US$80 million' (CIMMYT 1995).

8 Interview, IRRI scientist, 9 June 2006.

9 The full name of the variety, normally abbreviated to IR68144.

10 Parts per million (sometimes expressed as µg/g).

11 Interview, IHNF, 26 May 2006.

12 Interview, HarvestPlus, 27 January 2006.

13 Interview, IRRI scientist, 16 December 2006.

14 Discussions with 'family members' en route to visit participating convents, 21 December 2006.

15 Interview, PhilRice, 7 June 2006.

16 Interview, PhilRice, 30 May 2006, original emphasis.

17 Interview, IFPRI, 17 January 2006.

18 Interviews, IHNF and IRRI, June 2006.

19 www.harvestplus.org

20 Interview, BMGF, 30 November 2005.

21 Interviews, HarvestPlus, January 2006.

22 Interviews, IRRI, November and December 2006.

23 This view solidified following publication of research showing that the bioavailability of iron in ferritin, the proposed source material, compared favourably with ferrous sulphate, a common fortificant (Davila-Hicks et al 2004).

24 Interview, IRRI, 2 June 2006.

25 Interview, HarvestPlus, 31 January 2006.

26 Interview, IRRI scientist, 30 May 2006.

27 Interview, nutritionist, HarvestPlus, 16 February 2006.

28 Ibid.

29 Food Fortification Law (2000).

30 Interview, Rice Variety Improvement Group member, PhilRice campus, Nueva Ecija, 17 January 2007.

31 Ibid.

32 Interview, IRRI scientist, 25 November 2010.

33 www.zincsaveskids.org

34 www.zinc-crops.org/publications/HarvestPlus_Zinc_Project.pdf

References

Anderson, R.S., Levy, E. and Morrison, B.M. (1991) *Rice Science and Development Politics: Research Strategies and IRRI's Technologies Confront Asian Diversity (1950–1980)*. Oxford: Clarendon Press.

Bouis, H. (1995a) 'F.A.S. Public Interest Report: Breeding for Nutrition', *Journal of the Federation of American Scientists*, 1: 8–16.

——(1995b) 'Enrichment of food staples through plant breeding: a new strategy for fighting micronutrient malnutrition', *SCN News*, 12: 1519.

——(1996) 'Enrichment of food staples through plant breeding: a new strategy for fighting micronutrient malnutrition', *Nutrition Reviews*, 54(5): 131–37.

Bouis, H.E., Graham, R.D. and Welch, R.M. (1999) 'The CGIAR Micronutrients Project: justification, history, objectives and summary of findings', paper presented at 'Improving Human Nutrition through Agriculture: The Role of International Agricultural Research', IRRI, Los Baños, the Philippines.

von Braun, J., Fan, S., Meinzen-Dick, R., Rosegrant, M.W. and Nin Pratt, A. (2008) *Agricultural Research for Food Security, Poverty Reduction and the Environment: What to Expect from Scaling up CGIAR Investments and "Best Bet" Programmes*, IFPRI Issue Brief No. 53. Washington, DC: International Food Policy Research Institute.

Brooks, S. (2010) *Rice Biofortification: Lessons for Global Science and Development*. London: Earthscan.

——(2011a) 'Is international agricultural research a global public good? The case of rice biofortification', *Journal of Peasant Studies*, 38(1): 67–80.

——(2011b) 'Living with materiality or confronting Asian diversity? The case of iron-biofortified rice research in the Philippines', *East Asian Science, Technology and Society (EASTS)*, 5(2): 173–88.

Cakmak, I. (1996) 'Zinc deficiency as a critical constraint in plant and human nutrition in Turkey', *Micronutrients and Agriculture*, 1(1): 13–14.

——(2008) 'Enrichment of cereal grains with zinc: agronomic or genetic biofortification?', *Plant and Soil*, 302: 1–17.

Cakmak, I., Pfeiffer, W.H. and McClafferty, B. (2010) 'Biofortification of durum wheat with zinc and iron', *Journal of Cereal Chemistry*, 87(1): 10–20.

CIAT and IFPRI (2002) 'Biofortified crops for improved human nutrition': Challenge Programme proposal presented by CIAT and IFPRI to CGIAR Science Council. Washington, DC and Cali, Colombia: International Centre for Tropical Agriculture and International Food Policy Research Institute.

CIMMYT (1995) *Tackling Zinc Deficiency in Turkey*. Mexico: International Maize and Wheat Improvement Centre.

Combs, G.F., Welch, R.M., Duxbury, J.M., Uphoff, N.T. and Nesheim, M.C. (1996) *Food-based Approaches to Preventing Micronutrient Malnutrition: An International Research Agenda*. Ithaca, NY: Cornell International Institute for Food, Agriculture and Development (CIIFAD), Cornell University.

Corpuz-Arocena, E.R., Abilgos-Ramos, R.G., Luciano, V.P., Justo, J.E., Manaois, R.V., Garcia, G.dG., Escubio, S.S.P., Julaton, Ma.C.N., Alfonso, A.A., Padolina, T.F., Sebastian, L. S., Tabien, R.E., Cruz, R.T. and dela Cruz Jr, H.C. (2004) 'Breeding for micronutrient-dense rice in the Philippines', *PhilRice Technical Bulletin*, 8(2): 11.

Dalrymple, D.G. (2008) 'International agricultural research as a global public good: concepts, the CGIAR experience, and policy issues', *Journal of International Development*, 20: 347–79.

Davila-Hicks, P., Theil, E.C. and Lonnerdal, B. (2004) 'Iron in ferritin or in salts (ferrous sulphate) is equally bioavailable in nonanemic women', *American Journal of Clinical Nutrition*, 80: 936–40.

De Groote, H., Gunaratna, N., Ergano, K. and Friesen, D. (2010) 'Extension and adoption of biofortified crops: quality protein maize in East Africa', Joint 3rd African Association of Agricultural Economists (AAAE) and 48th Agricultural Economists Association of South Africa (AEASA) Conference, Cape Town, South Africa.

Del Mundo, A.M. (2003) 'Closing remarks', paper presented at Feedback Seminar to Rice Feeding Study Participants, 5 October 2003, Pasay City, the Philippines.

Erenoglu, E.B., Kutman, U.B., Ceylan, Y., Yildiz, B. and Cakmak, I. (2011) 'Improved nitrogen nutrition enhances root uptake, root-to-shoot translocation and remobilization of zinc (65Zn) in wheat', *New Phytologist*, 189(2): 438–48.

Gichuki, S., Hagenimana, V., Kabira, J., Kinyae, P., Low, J. and Oyunga, M.A. (1997) 'Combating vitamin A deficiency through the use of sweet potato', results from phase I of an action research project in South Nyanza, Kenya. Lima, Peru: CIP/KARI.

Gieryn, T.F. (1999) *Cultural Boundaries of Science: Credibility on the Line*. Chicago, IL: University of Chicago Press.

Gillespie, S., McLachlan, M. and Shrimpton, R. (2004) *Combating Nutrition: Time to Act*. Washington, DC: World Bank.

Graham, R.D. (2002) 'A proposal for IRRI to establish a grain quality and nutrition research centre', Discussion Paper No. 44. Manila, the Philippines: International Rice Research Institute.

Graham, R.D. and Welch, R.M. (1996) *Breeding for Staple Food Crops with High Micronutrient Density*, Working Papers on Agricultural Strategies for Micronutrients. Washington, DC: International Food Policy Research Institute.

Graham, R., Senadhira, D., Beebe, S., Iglesias, C. and Monasterio, I. (1999) 'Breeding for micronutrient density in edible portions of staple food crops: conventional approaches', *Field Crops Research*, 60: 57–80.

Green, A., Brady, K. and Florin, H. (2010) 'Zinc for life', *Mining Environmental Management*, April: 24–25.

Gregorio, G.B., Senadhira, D., Htut, H. and Graham, R.D. (2000) 'Breeding for trace mineral density in rice', *Food and Nutrition Bulletin*, 21(4): 382–86.

Gregorio, G.B., Sison, C.B., Mendoza, R.D., Adorada, D.L., Francisco, A.S., Escote, M.M. and Macabenta, J.T. (2003) 'Final report on production, milling and cooking trials to assess the Fe and Zn content of IR68144 and PSBRc28'. Los Baños, the Philippines: Plant Breeding, Genetics and Biochemistry Division, International Rice Research Institute.

Gunaratna, N.S., De Groote, H., Nestel, P., Pixley, K.V. and McCabe, G.P. (2009) 'A meta-analysis of community-based studies on quality protein maize', *Food Policy*, 35(3): 202–10.

Haas, J.D., del Mundo, A.M. and Beard, J.L. (2000) 'A human feeding trial of iron-enhanced rice', *Food and Nutrition Bulletin*, 21(4): 440–44.

Haas, J.D., Beard, J.L., Murray-Kolb, L.E., Mundo, A.M., Felix, A. and Gregorio, G.B. (2005) 'Iron-biofortified rice improves the iron stores of non-anaemic Filipino women', *Journal of Nutrition*, 135: 2823–30.

Hagenimama, V., Low, J., Anyango, M., Kurz, K.M., Gichuki, S.T. and Kabira, J. (2001) 'Enhancing vitamin A intake in young children in Western Kenya: orange-fleshed sweet potato can serve as key entry points', *Food and Nutrition Bulletin*, 22(4): 376–87.

Hellin, J. and Erenstein, O. (2009) 'Maize–poultry value chains in India: implications for research and development', *Journal of New Seeds*, 10(4): 245–63.

IRRI, AfricaRice and CIAT (2010) 'Global Rice Science Partnership (GRiSP): CGIAR Thematic Area 3: Sustainable crop productivity increase for global food security', CGIAR Research Program on Rice-Based Production Systems. Manila, Cotonou and Cali: IRRI, AfricaRice and CIAT.

Jasanoff, S. (2005) '"Let them eat cake": GM foods and the democratic imagination', in Leach, M., Scoones, I. and Wynne, B. (eds) *Science and Citizens: Globalisation and the Challenge of Engagement*. London: Zed Books.

Jiang, W., Struik, P.C., Lingna, J., Van Keulen, H., Ming, Z. and Stomph, T.J. (2007) 'Uptake and distribution of root-applied or foliar-applied 65Zn after flowering in aerobic rice', *Annals of Applied Biology*, 150(3): 383–91.

Johns, T. and Sthapit, B.R. (2004) 'Biocultural diversity in the sustainability of developing-country food systems', *Food and Nutrition Bulletin*, 25(2): 143–55.

Johnson-Beebout, S.E., Lauren, J.G. and Duxbury, J.M. (2009) 'Immobilization of zinc fertilizer in flooded soils monitored by adapted DTPA soil test', *Communications in Plant and Soil Analysis*, 40(11): 1842–61.

Johnson-Beebout, S.E., Rubianes, F.H.C., Grewal, D. and Virk, P.S. (2010) 'Improving human zinc nutrition through a combination of crop management and plant breeding for rice', presented at Symposium – Better Nutrition Through Seed Composition during the

Annual Meeting of the American Society of Agronomy, the Crop Science Society of America, and the Soil Science Society of America, 31 October–3 November 2010, Long Beach, CA.

Latham, M. (2010) 'The great vitamin A fiasco', *Journal of the World Public Health Nutrition Association*, 1(1), www.wphna.org/wn_commentary.asp

Long, N. (2001) *Development Sociology: Actor Perspectives*. London: Routledge.

Low, J., Walker, T. and Hijmans, R. (2001) 'The potential impact of orange-fleshed sweet potatoes on vitamin A intake in Sub-Saharan Africa', paper presented at Regional Workshop on Food Based Approaches to Human Nutritional Deficiencies, The VITAA Project, Vitamin A and Orange-fleshed Sweet Potatoes in Sub-Saharan Africa, 9–11 May 2001, Nairobi, Kenya.

Low, J.W., Arimond, M., Osman, N., Cunguara, B., Zano, F. and Tschirley, D. (2007) 'A food-based approach introducing orange-fleshed sweet potatoes increased vitamin A intake and serum retinol concentrations in young children in rural Mozambique', *Journal of Nutrition*, 137(5): 1320–27.

Mertz, E.T. (1997) 'Thirty years of *opaque2* maize', in Larkins B.A. and Mertz, E.T. (eds) *Quality Protein Maize: 1964–1994*. Lafayette, LA: Purdue University Press.

Mertz, E.T., Bates, L.S. and Nelson, O.E. (1964) 'Mutant gene that changes protein composition and increases lysine content of maize endosperm', *Science*, 145(3629): 279–80.

Nestel, P., Bouis, H.E., Meenakshi, J.V. and Pfeiffer, W. (2006) 'Biofortification of staple food crops', *Journal of Nutrition*, 136(4): 1064–67.

Padolina, T., Corpuz, E.R., Abilgos, R.G., Manaois, R.V., Escubio, S.S.P., Garcia, G.dG., Luciano, V.P., Sebastian, L.S., Tabien, R.E., de Leon, J.C., Gregorio, G.B. and Sison, C. B. (2003) *MS13, A Conventionally Bred Rice Line with Enhanced Micronutrient Content*. Nueva Ecija, the Philippines: Philippine Rice Research Institute.

PhilRice (2006) *Hybrid Rice. Vol. 01, Questions and Answers*. Nueva Ecija, the Philippines: Philippine Rice Research Institute.

Prasanna, B. M., Vasal, S.K., Kassahun, B. and Singh, N.N. (2001) 'Review article: Quality protein maize', *Current Science*, 81(10): 1308–19.

Schön, D.A. and Rein, M. (1994) *Frame Reflection: Towards the Resolution of Intractable Policy Controversies*. London: Basic Books/Harper Collins.

Science Council (2006). *Summary Report on System Priorities for CGIAR Research 2005–2015*. Rome: Science Council Secretariat, FAO.

Simmonds, N.W. (1991) 'Selection for local adaptation in a plant breeding programme', *Theoretical and Applied Genetics*, 82: 363–67.

Stein, A.J., Meenakshi, J.V., Qaim, M., Nestel, P., Sachdev, H.P.S. and Bhutta, Z.A. (2005) *Analysing the Health Benefits of Biofortified Staple Crops by Means for the Disability-Adjusted Life Years Approach: A Handbook Focusing on Iron, Zinc and Vitamin A*, HarvestPlus Technical Monographs Vol. 4. Washington, DC and Cali, Colombia: International Centre for Tropical Agriculture and International Food Policy Research Institute.

Stomph, T., Jiang, W. and Struik, P.C. (2009) 'Zinc biofortification of cereals: rice differs from wheat and barley', *Trends in Plant Science*, 14(3): 123–24.

Sumberg, J., Thompson, J. and Woodhouse, P. (2012) 'Contested agronomy: the politics of agricultural research in a changing world', in Sumberg, J. and Thompson, J. (eds) *Contested Agronomy: The Politics of Agricultural Research in a Changing World*. London: Earthscan.

Taverne, R. (2007) 'The real GM food scandal', *Prospect*, 140: 24–27.

Welch, R.M. and Graham, R.D. (2004) 'Breeding for micronutrients in staple crops from a human nutrition perspective', *Journal of Experimental Botany*, 55(396): 353–64.

Wissuwa, W., Ismail, A.M. and Graham, R.D. (2008) 'Rice grain zinc concentrations as affected by genotype, native soil-zinc availability, and zinc fertilization', *Plant and Soil*, 306: 37–38.

6

WATER IN AFRICAN AGRONOMY

Philip Woodhouse

Introduction: the water constraint in African agriculture

Water availability effectively defines the growing season for most of sub-Saharan Africa, and, for the semi-arid and sub-humid climatic zones that comprise most of the region, this includes a highly seasonal pattern of rainfall distribution. However, it is not seasonality or even total annual rainfall that constitutes the main water constraint to African agriculture, but the variability and unreliability of rainfall, giving rise to dry spells during the growing season that cause serious reductions in yield ('agricultural drought'); and longer dry spells interrupting the growing season one year in every four or five, resulting in total crop failure (Rockstrom et al 2010). Even in the relatively humid zone of coastal West Africa, with annual rainfall averaging 2000 mm and above, agricultural production is limited by a four-month dry period, the beginning and end of which are marked by particularly high rainfall uncertainty, translating into high risks of crop loss at planting and harvest time (Richards 1985). It is thus fair to summarise that neither average annual rainfall nor average length of rainy season is a good guide to the extent to which (lack of) moisture availability may constrain crop growth in Africa, or to the need for water management to form a central part of agronomic strategy.

African agriculture is characterised by water management strategies that seek to reduce the risks associated with rainfall uncertainty. These include spreading planted areas among different topographical sites including low-lying wetter locations and higher, better-drained sites. In drier years the 'wetland' fields would be expected to provide a crop even if upland plantings failed, while in wetter years good yields on upland sites would compensate losses due to excess water in valley bottoms. In addition, a variety of techniques involve varying intensity of investment in water management, such as planting crops in pits or basins and building stone lines or earth bunds to trap or harvest rainwater flowing across the soil surface (Reij et al 1996).

Historically, such investments reached very substantial levels in some cases, such as the 'terrace-builders of Nyanga' in north-east Zimbabwe in the sixteenth to nineteenth centuries (Soper 2006) or canal irrigation systems in hilly terrain in East Africa (Adams 1992). Modern variants of such investment in water management infrastructure are exemplified by African farmers' construction of irrigation furrows in Kajiado District, Kenya (Southgate and Hulme 2000); by the bench terrace systems in Machakos, Kenya (Tiffen et al 1994; Murton 1999); and by combinations of bench-terracing and irrigation furrows in Manica Province, Mozambique (Bolding et al 2010). Although the extent of water 'control' varies considerably in these instances, from capturing and conserving rainfall in the soil ('green' water) to diversion of flowing streams ('blue' water), in each case water management constitutes a key organising factor for agriculture, reducing risk and hence increasing the likelihood of positive returns to investments of labour and other production inputs.

Yet such patterns of water management might be regarded as exceptions in a subcontinent frequently characterised by underinvestment, low agricultural productivity and rural poverty. How are we to understand this situation, and what has been the role of agronomic research in fostering it? In the sections that follow, I first trace the trajectories of intervention in agricultural water management in sub-Saharan Africa. I separate these into two periods, overlapping in the 1970s. The first was dominated by a drive towards agricultural modernisation, fostered by colonial government agencies and their post-independence successors. The second, a reaction to the first, has deployed environmental conservation arguments to support 'indigenous' technologies of soil and water management. The chapter then argues that both of these tendencies can be found in current discourses of agricultural water management in Africa, but polarised to a degree that makes it unlikely that agronomic research will engage in ways that address opportunities and constraints in actually existing rural economies. This point is illustrated by identifying examples of investment in water management by farmers, often 'out of sight' of government agencies and with little or no support from agronomic research. In conclusion, I suggest that the water constraint has been inadequately addressed by agronomic research in Africa, for two reasons. The first is the tendency of agronomists to leave agricultural water management to either engineers or environmentalists, with the consequence that agricultural (and livelihood) goals become subordinated to those of engineering design or resource conservation. The second, linked, reason is that engineering/modernisation and conservation/traditional approaches to agriculture are framed by powerful narratives of African rural society and possible development trajectories. To the extent that agronomists' understanding of rural society is bounded by those narratives, they will struggle to engage with the current social dynamics of African agriculture and continue to lack impact on agricultural productivity.

Agricultural modernisation: large-scale irrigation (1930s–1980s)

What is today regarded as formal water management for agriculture – large-scale irrigated agriculture – was started by colonial governments seeking to develop commercial production for export to Europe. Both the Gezira scheme built on the Nile in Sudan in the 1920s, and the Office du Niger in Mali begun a decade later, were originally intended to produce cotton. In the latter decades of colonial administration, these commercial goals of irrigation development were overlain by social objectives, and irrigation projects were designed to provide the economic basis of rural resettlement projects, as in the case of Mwea in Kenya. These schemes established a pattern of publicly funded and government-managed large-scale irrigation that was continued by post-independence African states. It followed a model of state-led development that took shape in the economic recession and war economy of the 1930s and 1940s, notably in the United States, where government funding for major water infra-structure projects such as the Hoover Dam and the Central Valley project in California was prominent (Reisner 1993). The apparent success of such state investment in delivering an affluent society – not least in that leading exemplar of irrigated agriculture, California – lent credibility to its use as a model for development elsewhere.

In Africa, however, productivity on large-scale irrigation schemes proved disappointing. Despite a major stimulus to new irrigation investment in the 1970s, in response to a rainfall reduction of about 30 per cent in much of the West African savannah that began with a severe drought in 1972–73, development of formal irrigation in Africa made little headway compared with developments in countries such as India and Bangladesh. Irrigated agriculture is estimated to account for less than 5 per cent of African agriculture, compared with nearly 40 per cent in South Asia (UNDP 2006: 177). Consequently, although agriculture accounts for 85 per cent of all water withdrawals for economic activity in Africa, this represents only 2–3 per cent of African internal renewable water resources, compared with 25–35 per cent in South Asia (FAO 2011).

Part of the explanation for the poor performance of irrigation in Africa is found in reviews undertaken in the 1980s, which make clear that state-managed irrigation systems, in which African cultivators were typically tenants of the state, suffered from a number of specific design problems. These included engineering design failures, such as cost-cutting measures that omitted adequate drainage and led to waterlogging and salinisation after the schemes were put into operation, and inappropriate dimensions of reservoirs or pumping stations due to designs based on inadequate river flow records. Other problems resulted from inadequate budgets for supporting infrastructure such as roads, resulting in poor market access, or for compensating and resettling populations displaced from sites of reservoirs or new irrigation areas (Moris and Thom 1985; Hocombe et al 1986; Adams 1992). Efforts to sustain the model by reducing the scale of the designs during the 1970s and 1980s proved unsuccessful, as costs (per hectare) appeared just as high on small- as on large-scale schemes (Moris and Thom 1985).

This crisis for state-funded water development was made all the more acute in the context of the Sahel drought of the 1970s and the Ethiopian drought in the 1980s, which brought the water constraint to the fore. Growing disillusion with formal irrigation schemes prompted a retreat from irrigation investment by development funders during the 1980s. Estimates made in the mid-1980s put formal irrigation in sub-Saharan Africa at 2.64 million ha (Hocombe et al 1986). By 1994, this had almost doubled to 5 million ha, but had only risen to 6 million a decade later (FAO 2005).

It should be noted that these irrigation statistics relate to 'areas equipped for irrigation' through water storage and distribution infrastructure. In many cases, lack of maintenance and limited operational budgets resulted in low proportions of these areas being used. Thus, while in Mali cropping intensity figures of 171 per cent indicated that the irrigated area was not only fully cultivated, but much of it was cultivated with more than two crops per year, in contrast in Senegal only 73 per cent of the 'equipped' irrigation area was actually used. Elsewhere, even lower rates of usage of irrigation infrastructure are recorded, such as 43 per cent in Sudan and 11 per cent in Congo (FAO 2005). These data underline the poor performance of formal irrigation in many parts of Africa, and are consistent with a substantial slowing of investment in formal irrigation in the 1990s. In part this reflects a decade-long halt to public investment in irrigation in Africa from the mid-1980s, but also a broader decline in the importance of agriculture in development funders' policies. Lending for agricultural development slipped from 30 per cent of World Bank loans in 1980 to 7 per cent in 2000, only rising to 12 per cent in 2010 as a result of the rise in food prices in 2007–08 (IPS 2010). These trends bore particularly heavily on irrigation, and some sources estimate that loans for irrigation and drainage in Africa were lower in 2002–05 than they had been in 1978–81 (CAWMA 2007: 73).

This retreat from investment in formal irrigation was informed by two critiques that, while not mutually compatible in every respect, reinforced one another in important ways. The first, neoliberal, critique argued that bureaucratic (state) irrigation agencies were inherently inefficient and would be more efficient if governed by 'market disciplines' and accountable to 'clients' or 'water users'. Thus neoliberal policy sought the divestiture of state-owned irrigation assets to private service providers (infrastructure operation and maintenance, input supply, crop processing and marketing) and associations of farmers or water users, with the latter responsible for paying the former at market rates ('*responsabilisation paysanne*' in the terms of Senegal's New Agricultural Policy in 1984). For the most part, the technical design of formal irrigation schemes was not the focus of neoliberal criticism, but was the target of the second critique, which, following Paul Richards (1985), I term 'populist'.

'Populist' agronomy and the conservation agenda

Richards' seminal work *Indigenous Agricultural Revolution* (1985) used evidence from small-scale cultivation in Sierra Leone to argue that African farmers actively engaged in their own crop improvement and experimented with land and water management in order to optimise productivity in valley-bottom lands with seasonally varying water levels. Richards' empirical cases showed such indigenous approaches compared favourably with failed efforts to introduce 'modern' irrigation designs and mechanised cultivation to swamplands and seasonally-flooded valleys. The work provided ammunition for a broader critique of contemporary agricultural research under the banner of 'farmer first' (Chambers et al 1989). This argued that the main product of mid-twentieth-century agronomic research – 'Green Revolution' technology, including crop varieties adapted to irrigation and high fertiliser application – was inappropriate for the needs of poorer farmers and for less favourable ecological conditions (without reliable rainfall or irrigation). Such arguments also tapped into environmental concerns over the impacts of monocrop farming using high levels of fertiliser and pesticide, such as evidence of heightened crop vulnerability to pest damage following the widespread planting of Green Revolution rice in Indonesia in the 1970s.

In contrast, it was argued that 'indigenous technology' was more attuned to local ecologies and less likely to provoke radical and destructive disturbance of natural systems of environmental regulation. As a consequence, 'indigenous agricultural technology' quickly became associated with soil and water conservation, and became the object of both support and expectations of the burgeoning sustainable development movement in the 1990s. From the point of view of agricultural water management, two distinct themes characterise the populist critique of formal irrigation schemes in Africa. On one hand, the threat of drought in semi-arid areas was rethought in ecological, rather than engineering, terms, and instead of irrigation, development agencies favoured indigenous options including rainwater harvesting or other techniques for retaining and conserving rainfall, such as terraces, pits, contour ridges and stone lines (Reij et al 1996; Rockstrom et al 2003). The environmental associations of such approaches were often made explicitly, as in the title *More People, Less Erosion* given to the account of terracing of hillsides in Machakos, Kenya (Tiffin et al 1994), and *Sustaining the Soil: Indigenous Soil and Water Conservation in Africa* (Reij et al 1996).

A second theme of populist critique was a recognition of, and interest in, 'informal' or indigenous irrigation among African farmers (Underhill 1984; Hocombe et al 1986). Subsequently, data for irrigation in Africa discriminated between a 'formal' irrigation sector, equipped for full or partial water control, and 'informal' or 'non-equipped' cultivation of lowland areas. 'Formal' irrigation is typically state-funded and uses standard engineering structures (dams, canals, pumps) to store and distribute water on the floodplains of major river systems. 'Informal' or 'non-equipped' lowland cultivation typically uses indigenous technology to achieve a measure of water management, for example through stream diversion into irrigation furrows, drainage of wetlands, or planting crops following a receding flood. Taken together, these categories have been estimated to total 15.4 million ha of 'areas under water management' in Africa (FAO 2005), of which nearly half is in North Africa and Madagascar. The remaining 8 million ha in sub-Saharan Africa are split between some 6 million ha of formal irrigation and 2 million ha of areas under informal water management.

Figures for informal irrigation (and even formal irrigation, given the extent of underexploitation noted above) are unlikely to be accurate, and the area cultivated will in any case vary considerably from year to year according to varying rainfall and/or flooding. However, FAO data cited by Moris and Thom (1985: 3) showed a number of countries, notably Nigeria, Tanzania, Guinea and Sierra Leone, in which 'informal' irrigation constituted between 70 and 95 per cent of the total recorded irrigated area. This testifies to the importance accorded to indigenous water management, but we can note that these data omit any mention of 'dryland' water management, such as is widely used in drier savannas. As a consequence, the data must evidently underestimate the extent of water management used in African agriculture and perpetuate a discrimination between 'irrigated'/wetland and 'rainfed'/dryland agriculture, implying different scientific disciplines and (almost invariably) separate institutional and organisational structures at the level of both governments (ministries) and research organisations (including CGIAR) (Morardet et al 2005; Rockstrom et al 2010).

Within this framework, in which water management has been delegated to irrigation and soil engineers, agronomic research has been confined to 'in-field' water management. This has focused on questions of planting date, tillage methods, mulching, etc. that could increase infiltration of rainfall into the crop root zone, a 'fine tuning' of the conditions for growing the improved varieties developed by plant breeders. Conversely, crop variety improvement took account of water constraints by trialling new varieties in different agroclimatic zones (of which 'irrigated areas' was one). That is, the approach is to incorporate as much environmental adaptation as possible into the crop genetic material. This emphasis continues in the hopes attached to the use of genetic engineering to generate 'drought-resistant' crops. Interestingly, this is considered unlikely to materialise as a 'solution' to low productivity, according to the Comprehensive Assessment of Water Management in Agriculture (CAWMA 2007: 291). The overall effect has been for field crop agronomists to work with a fairly narrow range of interventions to manage soil moisture within determined agro-ecological expectations, leaving the dichotomy between irrigated/wetland and rainfed/dryland largely unchallenged.

Has the 'populist turn' had an impact among scientists working in these parallel disciplines? In the case of irrigation/wetland agriculture, significant effort went into making irrigation technology more accessible to farmers. One notable success in the 1980s was the introduction of the use of water jets to bore shallow wells in densely populated, low-lying *fadama* lands in northern Nigeria (Carter et al 1983; Carter 1985). Water withdrawn from these wells by small petrol pumps (the maintenance requirements of which could be met by local motorcycle mechanics) was used to irrigate expanded, but still small-scale vegetable production for sale in local urban and peri-urban markets. More broadly, however, despite considerable interest and effort among irrigation engineers to address the shortcomings of irrigation design, exemplified by 33 papers presented at a workshop on 'Design for sustainable farmer-managed irrigation schemes in sub-Saharan Africa', organised in 1990 by Wageningen University's Department of Irrigation and Soil and Water Conservation, there has been no widespread acceleration in the use of irrigation in African agriculture.

At least part of the explanation seems to lie in the failure of researchers to escape the confines of disciplinary boundaries. In their review of irrigation in Africa, Moris and Thom (1985) commented that study of indigenous agricultural water management in Africa had barely begun: 'It is another case where, because the system differs from full irrigation and rainfed arable farming, it is simply ignored by scientists' (p. 35). As an example of indigenous management systems that appeared to defy conventional disciplines of scientific research, they note:

> The valley-bottom 'vertisols' represent some of the best agricultural land available provided they are intelligently used with suitable technologies. The division

between 'irrigation' and 'rainfed' cultivation is here also arbitrary, since what usually occurs is not full irrigation, but rather a combination of drainage, impoundment (for 'wet' rice), and some supplemental water to extend the soil moisture regime.

(Moris and Thom 1985: 71)

This observation remains relevant 25 years later. While the most recent inter-institutional policy document (World Bank 2008) speaks of 'agricultural water management' that embraces both 'irrigation' and 'in-field' water management, it still identifies 'irrigated farming systems' as a separate 'agro-ecological zone' among 14 others defined by rainfall. More fundamentally, perhaps, there is a failure by researchers to overcome their fixation with technology (and its adoption, or not, by 'farmers') and pay serious attention to social and economic context. Moris and Thom (1985: 48) state that the 'largest single error' in economic evaluation of irrigation plans had been the discounting of the cost of family labour, thus effectively ignoring the opportunity cost of any other livelihood activities of the 'beneficiaries' of the irrigation. This point emerged forcefully from Diemer and Vincent's (1992) review of four 'irrigation sector' reports published by development agencies in the late 1980s. In a wide-ranging and detailed critique of irrigation engineering practice in Africa, they state:

> Predictions of farming activities and local incomes are rarely based on the actual strategies pursued by the various categories of farmers that the government has designated as beneficiaries. Key elements of misrepresentation include the failure to include activities in rainfed farming, livestock herding and off-farm employment. This is linked to the view that somehow all income will be generated from agriculture undertaken within the irrigated plot.
>
> *(Diemer and Vincent 1992: 138)*

To this must be added that livelihoods change as a result of investments in irrigation. The altered possibilities of production arising from water management set in train changing social relations that extinguish and create property rights and potential income streams (Southgate and Hulme 2000; Woodhouse et al 2000; Woodhouse 2003). The highly contextual nature of such changes and their repercussions for the operation of 'modern' irrigation are illustrated in some detail by Robertson's (1987) account of informal sharecropping arrangements between plotholders and immigrants in the Gezira scheme in Sudan.

In the case of rainfed/dryland agriculture, scientists have perhaps been more aware of the importance of understanding the logic of African land use. The 'indigeneity' of techniques such as terraces, stone lines and pits to increase rainfall infiltration was an important element of their appeal as possible low-cost, 'farmer-led' alternatives that would alleviate the water constraint in African agriculture. The extensive collection of case studies published by Reij et al (1996) certainly includes some very positive examples, including one from Niger, where recuperation of unproductive land by digging large numbers of planting pits (*tassa*) proved so financially profitable that a market in 'degraded land' became established, and some 6000 ha of previously uncultivable land were brought under cultivation in five years (Hassan 1996). Yet CAWMA (2007) observes that overall adoption of such methods has been slow. It nonetheless regards them as the basis for raising agricultural productivity in African savannah environments, in what it refers to as 'upgraded' rainfed agriculture, particularly by using small-scale water-harvesting to provide supplemental irrigation at critical periods of crop growth during dry spells in the growing season (Rockstrom et al 2010).

Yet, even here, where scientific research is committed to building on indigenous technology, there is a sense that 'at issue is not what engineers recommend, but the topics they ignore' (Jon Moris, cited in Diemer and Vincent 1992). Thus, even though the excellent introductory chapter in Reij et al (1996) abjures us to 'be wary of simple solutions to complex problems', and to 'recognise that technology exists not just as engineering design but in a social and economic context', the book provides instances that raise questions about the social and economic significance of the technologies being described. In particular, the relatively high labour demand of 'improved indigenous' methods used in the Sahel to bring 'degraded' soils back into cultivation – between 40 and 80 work-days per hectare treated with *tassa* or *zwai* pits – will evidently strongly favour those capable of hiring labour. Similar conclusions apply to mulch application in Burkina Faso, which was undertaken only by households with at least two active working adults, thereby excluding almost half the households in the area studied (Slingerland and Masdewel 1996). A more recent review (Barry et al 2008) confirms the importance of differential access to labour, along with insecurity of land tenure, as key barriers to wider adoption of these techniques. This raises the question of whether an emphasis on conserving soil and water as a means of increasing production has obscured an understanding of how that increased production might affect livelihoods.

A continuing dichotomy of scientists' social understanding: modernisation versus conservation

It is important to observe that agricultural scientists' failure to understand local social and economic contexts does not mean that their thinking is not informed by social and economic considerations. All engineering design embodies within it a social model of how it is to be used, and thus, implicitly, a set of assumptions about how society and economy work. Social understanding informing agricultural science in Africa may be identified as largely falling within one of two camps: modernisation and conservation. In some ways this should not be surprising, for the tension between modernisation and conservation of tradition in African society has marked government policy since early in the colonial period, and thus might be expected to have influenced the encounter of science with African agriculture.

Modernisation through application of engineering not only marked the introduction of irrigation in the Gezira in the 1920s, but increasingly informed colonial adminis-tration, particularly in the British settler colonies of eastern and southern Africa. Thus mechanisation was seen as a means of introducing soil conservation measures, such as contour bunds, or even of reproducing certain beneficial indigenous cultivation methods, such as tied ridges. However, the modernisation perspective also prohibited other indigenous water management practices, such as cultivation of wetland and stream banks, on the grounds that these were informed by ignorance and caused degradation of the resources. The transformation of African farming to a 'modern' commercial small-farm model was the basis for most of the heavily intrusive soil and water conservation work associated with 'Native Land Husbandry Act' and 'Betterment' schemes of British-administered southern and Eastern Africa (Scoones et al 1996).

In the contemporary modernisation discourse, engineering has been largely supplanted by the Green Revolution model of technological improvement, but the basic social model remains the same: unproductive and environmentally destructive traditional farming must be transformed by modern technology to enable rural households to develop from a 'subsistence' mentality to a more commercial outlook, thus increasing overall marketed output and raising rural incomes. Within this social model, commercially oriented 'family farms' are expected to be competitive with, or to draw support (e.g. through input supply markets and smallholder outgrower schemes), from larger-scale capitalist agricultural enterprises. This vision, captured perhaps most eloquently by the term 'emerging farmers' used in post-apartheid South Africa, but running throughout the African Union's Comprehensive Africa Agriculture Development Programme (CAADP 2003) and the 'farming as business' discourse of the Alliance for a Green Revolution in Africa (AGRA 2009), entrenches an expectation of linear progress through stages from traditional to modern that is the essence of modernisation thinking. In terms of social relations, family farms are expected to have free access to family labour, the economic activity of women and young adults being assimilated under unitary decision-making of the head of household. Similarly, pressures for changes in access to land are to be negotiated through a land market and tradeable land titles. Although it is acknowledged that more efficient family farms will grow at the expense of others, who are assumed to find employment in the growing non-farm rural economy, it is generally only implicit that further modernisation stages will see an increasing (more highly capitalised) scale of agriculture.

This social model ignores evidence of rather different actually existing social relations. These include a large literature on intra-household gender relations, at least some of which documents women's conflicts with men over access to land, labour and agricultural income (Whitehead and Tsikata 2003), not least as a result of modern irrigation investment (Carney 1988). A further literature on young men's efforts to develop farming independently of their older male relatives documents instances where increasing inter-generational conflict has fuelled wider armed conflict (Chauveau and Richards 2008; Amanor 2010; Kouame 2010). In addition to these gaps, the 'modern family farm' version of African rural society also makes little mention of labour markets or diversified livelihoods that frequently involve seasonal or longer-term migration of young adult members of farming households.

For those whose vision of rural society is informed by a conservationist, rather than modernisation, perspective, there is often a stronger sense of social and economic context because they give explicit attention to analysing local agricultural practice, past and present, and to understanding its underlying logic, for example in terms of labour constraints. Yet, as observed earlier, the relatively large labour investments required for 'improved indigenous technology' advocated by soil and water conservation (SWC) approaches, and the evidence that these are beyond the means of substantial numbers of rural households, seem to generate comparatively little discussion of the social implications of their adoption. Moreover, where technological change is framed by the lexicon of 'resilience', one needs to ask what, in specific social contexts, is envisaged for the future? And to what extent does successful environmental conservation accommodate social change, particularly where it involves radical change in land and water use? There is evidence that some SWC researchers are probing these boundaries. Rockstrom et al (2010), for example, acknowledge the limited potential of dryland SWC efforts so far to move beyond assuring crop survival to significantly raise output and incomes. To achieve this, they advocate abandoning the current divide between rainfed and irrigated agriculture in order to explore how supplemental irrigation can be supported by water management at a larger scale than that of the individual farm, but at a smaller scale than the river basin at which most water sector and irrigation planning operates. This they propose as a 'catchment', or landscape, scale of planning, usually no larger than 1000 km^2, arguing that this would enable a much wider range of water management options, from fully irrigated to fully rainfed. They acknowledge that this would involve interventions in terms of funding and construction of infrastructure, with many associated institutional (political) implications involving government agencies, farmers' organisations and capital investors. This begins to sounds like a response to the criticisms made by Moris and Thom nearly 20 years earlier, but it remains to be seen whether the 'new paradigm' will be able to 'see' the instances in which such developments have already been under way in many parts of Africa, often with little or no formal input from water engineers or agronomists.

Indigenous development of water management: where there are no agronomists?

I have argued that agricultural scientists' assumptions about African rural society may be summarised in terms of either conservationist/'traditional' forms of organisation assumed to be of long historical provenance, or modernising family farming units on the path from subsistence to commercial systems of production. I have suggested that such assumptions are unlikely to hold in many rural contexts, and are likely to undermine scientists' capacity to engage their technical skills with the needs and aspirations of the rural people they wish to serve. Here I wish to illustrate the proposition that there are likely to be many instances of dynamic (and productive) innovation in water management by African cultivators. To be understood, these need to be framed by an understanding that draws not only on a 'new paradigm' of water management, but also a willingness to question the nature and trajectory of African rural societies.

   One obvious starting point for a consideration of dynamic agricultural water use is in the peri-urban areas of Africa's large cities, where market gardening to supply fresh fruit and vegetables to the growing urban markets has provided a strong stimulus to intensify land and water use to achieve year-round production. Such areas are characterised by large influxes of people; competition for, and investment in, land and water; and highly commercial orientation of production, usually by individuals (especially women) operating their own businesses. Relatively few studies of such production systems have been published, but that by Baglioni (2009) in the Niayes outside Dakar conveys a sense of the rapid social and economic changes taking place in such highly productive agricultural contexts.

The high value of horticultural production also provided the stimulus for the development of furrow irrigation in the arid conditions of Kajiado district in southern Kenya. It is an area that colonial planners had deemed unsuitable for human settlement, let alone commercial agriculture. Yet initial experiments by Maasai during drought years in the 1930s successfully diverted water from streams flowing down the foothills of Kilimanjaro into furrows to water subsistence crops. During the 1960s and 1970s, irrigation to produce cash crops was developed by immigrants, notably Kikuyu and Chagga, and by the late 1990s, some 560 farmers, a majority of them immigrants, were using furrow irrigation for commercial production of tomatoes and onions on about 180 ha for the Nairobi and Mombasa markets (Southgate and Hulme 2000). A similar set of dynamics saw local communities in the Sourou river valley in southern Mali clear about 6000 ha of riverine forest to plant rice – a crop not previously cultivated in the area – in a valley that had become flooded as a result of a dam constructed downstream in Burkina Faso. In the mid-1990s, in addition to providing a major contribution to local staple cereal consumption, just under half of the overall crop of about 5200 tons was sold, constituting the most important source of income for two-thirds of those cultivating rice. Again, immigrants formed a key part of those clearing and cultivating rice fields (Woodhouse et al 2000).

A final example is provided by the development of an area estimated at between 5000 and 10,000 ha of irrigation in the hills of Penhalonga, in Manica Province, Mozambique, close to the frontier with Zimbabwe (Bolding et al 2010). A network of irrigation furrows, some dating from the early twentieth century, have been greatly extended as a result of investment over the past decade, made possible by a combination of cheap labour in the form of people (some Zimbabweans, some Mozambicans previously resident in Zimbabwe) moving across from the Zimbabwean side of the frontier, and the erratic but significant generation of capital from gold panning. Irrigation is used for maize, beans, wheat and vegetables, as well as spices such as turmeric and ginger. The detailed study of three furrows suggests the area irrigated has more than doubled between 1991 and 2008, and competition for land, together with the availability of labour, has prompted construction of stone-walled terraces to improve soil and water management. In addition to irrigation, furrows provide water to power grain mills, feed fishponds and support brick-making and livestock watering.

A number of observations on these empirical cases are relevant to this chapter. Firstly, in none of these examples, particularly the latter three, has the development of water management or agronomic practice been planned or managed by scientifically trained staff or, indeed, government officials or planners of any kind. Some infrastructural investment (improvement of weirs and canal structures) has been received in the case of Penhalonga and some irrigation extension input in Kajiado, but in each case only after the system had been established. This is not to argue that such scientific input is not needed. In the Sourou case, the viability of rice cultivation proved relatively short-lived, compromised by, among other things, the lack of an adequate technology to control the rapid spread of perennial weeds in rice fields. Rather, the cases demonstrate that agricultural water management obeys social and economic dynamics other than those ordained by development planners. In relation to the latter point, it is worth noting that annual rainfall in Penhalonga averages 1200 mm, placing it fairly low on a list of sites for irrigation development according to conventional planning criteria.

A second observation is that immigration is a significant feature of the social context, with particular significance for the introduction of skills and technical innovation, as well as providing a supply of cheap labour. This also has significance for markets in labour and land. In such contexts, where immigrants form a significant proportion – and in Kajiado the majority – of the population, assumptions about family units and family labour are clearly unhelpful. Similarly, in all these cases informal land markets, whether purchase or rental/sharecropping, operate, although governed by local customary authority. This situation, which I have referred to elsewhere as a 'vernacular' land market (Chimhowu and Woodhouse 2006), often involves a degree of ambiguity and insecurity over the rights being acquired, as well as instances of contestation and reinvention of what constitutes 'custom'. Issues of local power relations and their legality and legitimacy are evidently central to any understanding of how land and water management can be governed in such contexts. My final point is that dynamic agriculture in Africa is not necessarily found in places or in forms that scientists or planners expect. Indeed, it is arguable that such cases are relatively dynamic because they are not subject to planning controls. The broader challenge for agronomic science is, then, to establish both how to engage with such dynamic agricultural contexts, and perhaps more importantly, why.

Conclusion: 'framing' the water constraint

In this chapter I trace the failure of irrigation in particular, and agricultural water management more generally, to address the problem of rainfall uncertainty and risk in African agriculture. Part of the reason lies in the separation between 'irrigated' and 'rainfed' agriculture and the professional and institutional boundaries that entrench this separation. I argue that beyond the analytical blind spots created by such a structure to scientific thinking there lie further problems arising from the capacity of scientists to 'see' African rural society. The predominance of modernisation and conservationist framings of rural society mean that scientists are liable to see farming activity either in terms of family farms on a linear path of transition from subsistence to commercial production, or as custodians of natural resources to be made 'resilient' to change. When compared with instances of dynamic agriculture in African contexts, which invariably include elements of agricultural water management, such framings appear inadequate as a guide to how and why agronomists should engage with actually existing agricultural production in specific contexts. Despite evidence of willingness among some to abandon the rainfed/irrigated boundary and seek a 'new paradigm' of agricultural water management, there remains, therefore, a challenge to agricultural scientists to test their understanding of rural society against empirical evidence. Certainly, as a minimum, any technical design for agricultural water management should state explicitly what sets of social assumptions it incorporates, including property and power issues that come into focus whenever land and water management (or any natural resources) are managed collectively, so that these may be evaluated, not least by those who are to benefit from the design's implementation.

References

Adams, W. (1992) *Wasting the Rain: Rivers, People and Planning in Africa*. Minneapolis, MN: University of Minnesota Press.

AGRA (2009) Alliance for a Green Revolution in Africa, www.agra-alliance.org/section/about/agrastrategy

Amanor, K. (2010) 'Land sales, family values and commodification: the dynamics of agrarian change in southeastern Ghana', *Africa*, 80(1): 104–25.

Baglioni, E. (2009) 'Fresh fruit and vegetable exports from Senegal, capital, land, and labour issues in the Niayes area', PhD thesis, University of Bologna.

Barry, B., Olaleye, A., Zougmoré, R. and Fatonji, D. (2008) *Rainwater Harvesting Technologies in the Sahelian Zone of West Africa and the Potential for Outscaling*, Working Paper 126. Colombo: International Water Management Institute.

Bolding, A., Post Uiterweer, N. and Schippers, J. (2010) 'The fluid nature of hydraulic property: a case study of Mukudu, Maira and Penha Longa irrigation furrows in the upper Revue river, Manica District', in P. van der Zaag (ed.) *What Role of Law in Promoting and Protecting the Productive Uses of Water by Smallholder Farmers in Mozambique?* CGIAR Challenge Programme on Water and Food.

CAADP (2003) Comprehensive Africa Agriculture Development Programme, www.caadp.net/about-caadp.php#Aim

Carney, J. (1988) 'Struggles over crop rights and labour within farming households in a Gambian irrigated rice project', *Journal of Peasant Studies*, 15(3): 334–49.

Carter, R., Carr, M and Kay, M (1983) 'Policies and prospects in Nigerian irrigation', *Outlook on Agriculture*, 12(3): 73–76.

Carter, R. (1985) 'Groundwater development using jetted boreholes', *Waterlines*, 3(3).

CAWMA (2007) *Comprehensive Assessment of Water Management in Agriculture*. Colombo/London: International Water Management Institute and Earthscan.

Chambers, R., Pacey, A. and Thrupp, L.-A. (1989) *Farmer First: Farmer Innovation and Agricultural Research*. London: IT Publications.

Chauveau, J.-P. and Richards, P. (2008) 'West African insurgencies in agrarian perspective: Côte d'Ivoire and Sierra Leone compared', *Journal of Agrarian Change*, 8(4): 515–52.

Chimhowu, A. and Woodhouse, P. (2006) 'Customary vs private property rights? Dynamics and trajectories of vernacular land markets in sub-Saharan Africa', *Journal of Agrarian Change*, 6(3): 346–71.

Diemer, G. and Vincent, L. (1992) 'Irrigation in Africa: the failure of collective memory and collective understanding', *Development Policy Review*, 10: 131–54.

FAO (2005) *Irrigation in Africa in Figures – Aquastat Survey 2005*. Rome: Food and Agriculture Organization of the UN.

FAO (2011) *AQUASTAT: Countries, Regions, Transboundary River Basins*. Rome: Food and Agriculture Organization of the UN, www.fao.org/nr/water/aquastat/countries_regions/index.stm

Hassan, A. (1996) 'Improved traditional planting pits in the Tahoua Department (Niger): an example of rapid adoption by farmers', in Reij, C., Scoones, I. and Toulmin, C. (eds) *Sustaining the Soil, Indigenous Soil and Water Conservation in Africa*. London: Earthscan.

Hocombe, S., Kidane, P., Jazayeri, A. and Gadelle, M. (1986) 'Irrigation in Africa south of the Sahara', Technical Paper No 5. Rome: Food and Agricultural Organisation of the United Nations, FAO Investment Centre.

IPS (2010) 'World Bank boosts Ag Lending ahead of MDG Meet', Inter Press Service News Agency, www.ipsnews.net/news.asp?idnews=52815

Kouame, G. (2010) 'Intra-family and socio-political dimensions of land markets and land conflicts: the case of the Abure, Cote d'Ivoire', *Africa*, 80(1): 126–46.

Morardet, S., Merrey, D., Seshoka, J. and Sally, H. (2005) *Improving Irrigation Project Planning and Implementation Processes in Sub-Saharan Africa: Diagnosis and Recommendations*, Working Paper 99. Colombo: International Water Management Institute.

Moris, J. and Thom, D. (1985) *African Irrigation Overview*, Water Management Synthesis-II Project Report 37. Logan, UT: Utah State University.

Murton, J. (1999) 'Population growth and poverty in Machakos District, Kenya', *Geographical Journal*, 165(1): 37–46.

Reij, C., Scoones, I. and Toulmin, C. (eds) (1996) *Sustaining the Soil, Indigenous Soil and Water Conservation in Africa*. London: Earthscan.

Reisner, C. (1993) *Cadillac Desert, the American West and its Disappearing Water*. London: Pimlico.

Richards, P. (1985) *Indigenous Agricultural Revolution. Ecology and Food Production in West Africa*. London: Hutchinson.

Robertson, A. (1987) *The Dynamics of Productive Relationships. African Share Contracts in Comparative Perspective*. Cambridge: Cambridge University Press.

Rockstrom, J., Barron, J. and Fox, P. (2003) 'Water productivity in rain-fed agriculture: challenges and opportunities for smallholder farmers in drought-prone tropical agroecosystems', in Kijne, J., Barker, R. and Molden, D. (eds) *Water Productivity in Agriculture: Limits and Opportunities for Improvement*. Wallingford, UK: CAB International.

Rockstrom, J., Karlberg, L., Wani, S., Barron, J., Hatibu, N., Oweis, T., Bruggeman, A., Farahani, J. and Qiang, Z. (2010) 'Managing water in rainfed agriculture – the need for a paradigm shift', *Agricultural Water Management*, 97: 543–50.

Scoones, I, Reij, C. and Toulmin, C. (1996) 'Indigenous soil and water conservation in Africa', in Reij, C., Scoones, I. and Toulmin, C. (eds) *Sustaining the Soil. Indigenous Soil and Water Conservation in Africa*. London: Earthscan.

Slingerland, M. and Masdewel, M. (1996) 'Mulching on the Central Plateau of Burkina Faso', in Reij, C., Scoones, I. and Toulmin, C. (eds) *Sustaining the Soil. Indigenous Soil and Water Conservation in Africa*. London: Earthscan.

Soper, R. (2006) *The Terrace Builders of Nyanga*. Harare: Weaver Press.

Southgate, C. and Hulme, D. (2000) 'Uncommon property: the scramble for wetland in Southern Kenya,' in Woodhouse, P., Bernstein, H. and Hulme, D. (eds) *African Enclosures? The Social Dynamics of Wetlands in Drylands*. Oxford: James Currey.

Tiffen, M., Mortimore, M. and Gichuki, F. (1994) *More People, Less Erosion: Environmental Recovery in Kenya*. Chichester, UK: Wiley.

Underhill, H. (1984) *Small-scale Irrigation in Africa in the Context of Rural Development*. Rome: FAO.

UNDP (2006) *Beyond Scarcity*, Human Development Report 2006. New York: United Nations Development Programme.

Whitehead, A. and Tsikata, D. (2003) 'Policy discourses on women's land rights in sub-Saharan Africa: the implications of the re-turn to the customary', *Journal of Agrarian Change*, 3(1/2): 67–112.

Woodhouse, P, Trench, P. and Tessougué, M. (2000) 'A very decentralised development', in Woodhouse, P., Bernstein, H. and Hulme, D., *African Enclosures? The Social Dynamics of Wetlands in Drylands*. Oxford: James Currey.

Woodhouse, P. (2003) 'African enclosures: a default mode of development', *World Development*, 31(10): 1719–33.

World Bank (2008) *Investment in Agricultural Water for Poverty Reduction and Economic Growth. A Collaborative Program of AFDB, FAO, IFAD, IWMI and the World Bank*, Synthesis Report, www.fanrpan.org/documents/d00508/1-agric_water_investments_World_Bank.pdf

7

UNDERSTANDING AGRICULTURAL INTENSIFICATION ON A FOREST FRONTIER IN MADAGASCAR

Elements of a Malthusian/Boserupian synthesis

Jacques Pollini

Introduction

Slash–and–burn cultivation, a land use that consists of clearing and burning vegetation on a piece of land, planting and harvesting crops, and repeating these operations after a fallow period of varying length, has been practised in many regions of the world since the beginning of agriculture. It is still practised today, mostly in low-income tropical countries (Palm et al 2005). It is a sustainable land use when the fallow is sufficiently long to reconstitute significant biomass and nutrient stocks, but often leads to land degradation when the population density is incompatible with long fallowing (Palm et al 2005). Since the Earth Summit held at Rio in 1992, the search for alternatives to slash–and–burn has become prominent among organisations supporting agricultural development and environmental conservation. The Global Environment Facility, for instance, funded an ambitious international, collaborative effort – the Alternative to Slash–and–Burn (ASB) Programme – coordinated by the World Agroforestry Centre and launched in 1991.

One of the implicit premises of such programmes is that, in order to escape a Malthusian crisis, scientists need to design alternative cropping systems that will provide higher yields while not depleting soil fertility. This approach has been criticised for overlooking the political economy of land degradation and deforestation (Pollini 2009), and it is also open to critique in relation to the work of Ester Boserup (1965). This author describes an historical sequence of agricultural intensification that goes from long fallow to short fallow, and then to annual and multi-cropping systems. The transition from one stage to the next is triggered by population growth. The key variable that discriminates between each stage is the frequency of cropping, which goes from once every 20–25 years when a long fallow is practised, to several times per year in a multi-cropping system. The key constraint to intensification is labour availability, with the new systems demanding more labour input for the same output, as a way to compensate for the loss of natural capital (lower biomass, biodiversity and fertility) as a consequence of shorter fallow. Boserup's emphasis on the frequency of cropping and on labour availability contrasts starkly with mainstream approaches to agricultural intensification, where yield and soil fertility are regarded as the key variables.

This chapter tests these Boserupian assumptions in Beforona, a rural municipality located on a forest frontier in eastern Madagascar. If these assumptions were verified, population control and crop yield increase – two key strategies adopted by rural development projects working in this area, as well as by most agronomists working in similar areas – would be of secondary importance when searching for alternatives to slash-and-burn.

I start by describing the slash-and-burn cultivation systems of Beforona, the other cropping systems that farmers have developed or use in the area, and the constraints to land-use change. I show that slash-and-burn cultivation has always been combined with other cropping systems, particularly paddy fields and home gardens, but that the respective importance of these systems in the local economy has varied over time and space, through successive phases of intensification and extensification, as a consequence of changing economic and policy contexts and differentiated access to markets. I conclude that the Boserup-versus-Malthus controversy makes little sense once the epistemology that sustains it is questioned, and persists mostly because of political bias in the production of knowledge. Both authors refer to processes that exist in the real world, but that interact in a dialectical way, with often unpredictable outcomes.

Data collection took place between 2001 and 2007. In 2001, I lived for six months in Ambodilaingo, a village in the municipality of Beforona. From 2001 to 2007, I made frequent visits in Ambodilaingo and to other villages of the municipality to collect additional data and monitor a rural development project implemented by a small NGO (*Zanaky ny Ala*), which I created with a Malagasy colleague. Data collection was primarily through informal discussions while touring the area, or during meals and other social gatherings. A snowball sampling strategy was used that resulted in more than 100 persons being interviewed in the area, although only a selection of these interviews inform this chapter.

Beforona and Ambodilaingo

The rural municipality of Beforona is located 160 km east of Antananarivo, in the Moramanga District of Mangoro–Alaotra Region. Beforona is the centre of the municipality, where the town hall, health centre, junior high school, several shops and a weekly market are located. Ambodilaingo is a village of about 130 households (in 2003) that is a 16 km walk south from the National Road 2 (NR2), which passes through Beforona.

The area experiences a tropical wet climate, with an average annual rainfall of 2757 mm at the nearby Marolafo Research Station (Nambena 2007). Rains occur throughout the year but primarily take the form of light drizzle from June to November. Cyclones can strike the area from February to May, when winds of more than 100 km per hour can destroy crops and provoke flooding and landslides. The hydrographic network is dense, with water running all year round in rivers and most streams. The average temperature ranges from about 16°C in July to 26°C in January.

The topography shows a regular pattern of small valleys formed by low hills with steep slopes. The altitude ranges from 500–700 m except for a north–south escarpment that reaches 1300 m on the western edge. This escarpment is the only part of the landscape that is still forested (Vohidrazana forest). Many families live near to the forest boundary in order to find more fertile soils to cultivate, but forest clearing essentially stopped in 2002, when the government and its international partners conducted an aggressive campaign against the use of fire and slash-and-burn cultivation (Pollini 2007, 2011).

With the exception of any recently cleared land, forest and bottom-land soils are ferralitic and strongly desaturated. The main soil constraints to cultivation are low phosphorus availability and aluminium toxicity. Neither sheet nor gully erosion is prominent: the most dramatic cause of erosion is landslides associated with cyclones (Brand and Rakotovao 1997).

Farmers live in dispersed settlements in order to remain close to their fields. The economy has long been based on agriculture, and *tavy*, the local form of slash-and-burn cultivation, is the dominant land use, although more intensive systems are also present. Logging produces a significant complementary income for families living close to the forest, including most people in Ambodilaingo, who sell their labour to transport boards to the road, where they are collected. This activity has been in decline since about 2006. Mining (corundum in Ambodilaingo, gold in a few other villages) also plays a marginal role in the economy.

Tavy cultivation in Ambodilaingo

In 2001, a farmer from Ambodilaingo described *tavy* as follows:

> When we clear the primary forest, we first grow rice and then plant sweet potato on part of the plot when the rice is 30 cm high. Clearing the forest is the basis of our way of life. We cultivate the land a second time after 3–4 years, again with rice and sweet potato, but we also add cassava. We do not wait longer because we lack area to cultivate due to population increase. After that, we wait six years before cultivating again, because the soil is not very fertile. The fallow period after this third cultivation cycle will have to be still longer. […]
>
> We plant beans, maize and *tsidimy* [*Phaseolus lunatus* L.] with the rice. The rice is sown first. Maize grows better in the first cycle. We do not stop cultivating until the land is invaded by *tenina* [*Imperata cylindrical* (L.) Raeusch.] and *rangotra* [*Pteridium aquilinum* (L.) Kuhn]. This usually occurs at the fifth cultivation cycle, but these plants can disappear if we wait about 20 years. *Tenina* can also invade from the third cultivation cycle. For the fourth cycle of cultivation, we usually wait 8–10 years because the soil is not fertile. We sow one vat [20 kg] of rice and harvest 8–20 vat [400 kilograms] …

This description is consistent with other interviews and with descriptions found in various reports about the area (Projet Terre-Tany/BEMA 1997, 1998; Messerli 2003;

Nambena 2004), although there is some local variation in the duration of the fallow periods, crop rotations and associations. It suggests that slash-and-burn already faces its agro-ecological limits, as revealed by the practice of short fallow and invasion by the weed *Imperata cylindrica*. Primary forest remains that could be cleared to make more land available and increase the fallow period, but the analysis of local maps shows that it is located at relatively high altitude (above 800 m), where the risks of heavy rain, cold temperatures and low harvests are higher. The ban on forest-clearing instituted by the government, although loosely enforced, also explains the reluctance to clear, as we will see. The quantity of rice that is sown and harvested varies greatly from one family to another. The amount sown ranges from 1–5 kg, resulting in harvests of 0.3–1.0 tons[1]; harvests beyond 1 ton per household being exceptional. Considering that an average family (two adults plus four children) requires about 800 kg of rice per year (rice is the staple food), most households are short of home-produced rice for three to nine months per year. During this period, the diet shifts to cassava and bananas unless income can be generated to buy rice, usually by transporting boards to the road.

Variation in the area dedicated to *tavy* is also explained by competition with other land uses. Irrigated rice, which is a more intensive system in the sense that the same land can be cultivated many years without fallowing, is also practised. As a consequence, the working calendar is full (farmers do not have time to grow more crops), which is consistent with the fact that household food production is insufficient:

> We sow *tavy* first, in October–November and we sow rice in paddy fields later, in November–December–January. We can sow in paddy fields at different seasons because there is no problem of water. Ploughing the paddy is in January, at the same time as weeding in *tavy*. We always lack time. We also lack time for watching over paddy fields and *tavy* in the same time.
>
> *(a farmer from Ambodilaingo 2001)*

Paddy rice production seems to have played a more prominent role in the past, as did other agricultural activities including cattle and perennial crops. We will now see that there have been successive phases of intensification and extensification that can be explained by economic and policy factors as well as labour availability. This will provide arguments both for and against Boserup's model.

Intensification and extensification in Ambodilaingo

Tavy has played a significant role in the local economy since as far back as people remember, but was always combined with irrigated rice cultivation, perennial crops and cattle. According to some informants, the first paddy fields were created in the period 1914–18. Villagers even claim that their ancestors are Bezanozano (Rakotoarijaona Razafimbelo 2005), a people whose way of life and culture have many similarities with those of the Merina. Like the Merina, the Bezanozano's main land use is irrigated rice cultivation. But the families who moved to the Ambodilaingo area adopted the Betsimisiraka way of life, which centres on the practice of *tavy*, although paddy fields also play a role in their livelihood (Le Bourdiec 1974). In effect, they became Betsimisaraka.

Regarding cattle husbandry, this activity was of great economic importance in the 1950s:

> About half of the families had big cattle in 1959. Those who had animals had many: 15 to 30, sometimes more. Those who did not have animals borrowed them from others. They did not refuse because people had good relations at that time. Those who had large herds hired people to watch over animals and paid them by giving calves. Usually the herds were all put together to avoid being lost ... There was much area available for grazing ... The animals were put in corrals during the night, but only during the cultivation season, in order to avoid damage to the crops ... Animals had good care and were visited by veterinarians ... They were used to earn money and for sacrifices [rituals]. More animals were sacrificed than sold.
>
> *(an elder from Ambodilaingo 2001)*

Beyond revealing the importance of cattle, this excerpt shows that the state provided some services, and that non-market based exchanges and rituals – manifestations of social capital – might have played a significant role in the economy.

Cattle were also part of farmers' 'physical capital', an agricultural 'tool' used to puddle the soil in paddy fields, thereby relaxing the labour constraint to intensification:

> There was a time when paddy fields covered more area than now, because people had many more cattle. The animals were used for treading [puddling] the land before sowing.
>
> *(an elder from Ambodilaingo 2001)*

Today, only a handful of families in Ambodilaingo have cattle, and the situation is similar all over the region. The main direct cause of the decline seems to have been increasing conflict between cattle and cropping, and the resulting shortage of feed:

> There has been a big decrease in cattle since the 1970s. The main reason is that the people started to be bad and asked penalties when cattle damaged their crops ... These damages mainly concerned cassava, sweet potatoes and coffee in the bottom land and in the lower part of the slopes. As a consequence, cattle started to lack access to pastures. People did not build fences because agriculture officers told the herders to care for their herds. In ancient times, damage was limited because there were fewer crops in bottom lands and people were not so bad.
>
> *(an elder from Ambodilaingo 2001)*

Another reason for the decrease in cattle is because they were sold due to poverty and for sacrifices ... Cattle also died because of diseases: some people bought cattle from other regions, and this brought the disease. The animals quickly became thin and died. The liver is full of small animals and cannot be eaten. This disease developed around 1983 and still exists.

(an elder from Ambodilaingo 2001)

The loss of cattle provoked a decline in irrigated rice cultivation because of their role in soil preparation:

Cattle were used to tread paddy fields before sowing. My father had 50 head. He had a paddy field because treading was easy. Paddy rice was a big activity in ancient times because people had many cattle.

(an elder from Ambodilaingo 2001)

If we do not have cattle, we can only cultivate small areas of paddy fields.

(an elder from Ambodilaingo 2001)

A tentative systemic explanation can thus be drawn: the development of agricultural activities, probably as a consequence of population growth, led to increasing tensions between cattle and cultivation, a reduction of land available for grazing, feed shortages and livestock disease, reduction of herds, difficulty in preparing paddy fields, abandonment of paddy rice and sale of most remaining animals in time of hardship. In other words, increased population density could have induced agricultural extensification, a trajectory that appears to contradict Boserup's model. Farmers apparently failed to create new institutions to manage new problems (conflicts between cattle and cultivation) arising out of higher population density. They also seem to have failed to develop new ways to feed their animals in a context of dwindling grazing resources, or new tools and techniques with which to prepare paddy land without cattle.

This lack of social and technical innovation, however, could be explained by external disruption (like the possibly misguided advice of agricultural officers reported in the citation above, which might have distracted people from building fences); by erosion of the social and human capital (people becoming 'bad' and selfish, assertions that were frequently made); or by the reduction of state support (veterinarians stopping visiting the area). These could themselves reflect the overall economic decline that Madagascar experienced at that time. If these explanations hold, some or all of the processes described by Boserup may indeed have been operating, although not leading to the expected outcomes as a consequence of macro-economic constraints.

Macro-economic constraints to land-use changes

The period during which paddy rice and cattle husbandry declined corresponded with the change from relative economic prosperity in the 1960s to the deep economic and political crises of the 1980s. This change in economic and political context was a consequence of the degradation of the terms of trade and the failure of Madagascar's 'socialist revolution'. People in Ambodilaingo were deeply affected by these changes, and often refer to them with very concrete figures:

> Coffee cultivation developed around 1950, under the authorities of the *contremaitre*.[2] Coffee generated higher income at that time. One kilogram was sold for 150 francs, while one kilogram of rice cost 30 francs. Today, one kilogram of coffee is sold for 2500 francs, and one kilogram of rice costs about 2000 francs.
>
> *(an elder from Ambodilaingo 2001)*

A corollary of the economic crisis was the decline in government support for the development and maintenance of irrigation. In the 1950s and 1960s, several dams were built in the municipality of Beforona, including at least one in Ambodilaingo, with support from government. But since the mid-1970s nothing has been provided for their maintenance and they have been progressively degraded by cyclones and heavy rains. Basic public services have also been eroded; today the most educated villagers are those who received their education during the colonial period or just after independence in 1960. People in remote villages were left to fend for themselves, which reduced their communication with the outside world and the range of options available to them.

The Malagasy economy started to recover during the 1990s, when it opened up to foreign investment and received increased financial support from the international community. The renovation of NR2 in the late 1980s led to significant changes in the villages located near it. Many farmers moved into cash crops (mostly ginger and bananas), which triggered investment in permanent cultivation and the expansion of home gardens. They created irrigation systems and experimented with ploughing, crop rotation and the application of manure (Messerli 2003; Nambena 2004; Pollini 2007), processes that are consistent with Boserup's model and that cannot be explained by project intervention.[3] But many people living in more remote areas such as Ambodilaingo never experienced this economic recovery. Indeed, farmers in Ambodilaingo are unanimous in presenting the period since the 1970s as one of continuous degradation of their livelihoods. As they put it, 'we are always becoming poorer'.[4] The technical changes that occurred in villages located close to the road did not reach them, except during a few years when ginger could be sold at a high price. The level of poverty is now dramatic, resulting in limited investment capacity, risk-avoiding strategies, the persistence of extensive cultivation systems, increasing individualism, and further erosion of all forms of capital (Pollini 2007).

In sum, the 1970s and 1980s were a period of financial, physical and human capital decline that was reversed in the late 1980s in villages located near NR2, but not in Ambodilaingo, where the crisis persisted. Hence Boserupian outcomes were observed on NR2 but not in Ambodilaingo.

Policy constraints to land-use changes

Beside the lack of technical and institutional innovation and the overall economic decline, policy changes in relation to forest clearance and the practice of *tavy* also help explain the failure to intensify and the abandonment of paddy rice. A ban on the practice of *tavy* existed during the 1950s, but was lifted soon after independence:

> The main period concerning prohibition of clearing was after the visit of Mr Abraham and the forest guards in 1954 … Restrictions mainly concerned the upper part of the slopes. People clearing forest at that time were sent to jail, but this did not occur any more after independence.
>
> *(an elder from Ambodilaingo 2001)*

Extensification since the 1970s could thus have been the consequence of a reduction of population pressure following the reopening of the forest frontier. However, this explanation contradicts the 'induced extensification' thesis outlined previously (the idea that less land leads to a cattle crisis that forces the abandonment of paddy fields and a return to extensive cultivation systems). If this thesis was correct, a lowering of population pressure should have favoured the redevelopment of animal husbandry and a return to the paddy fields, neither of which occurred. One could argue that relaxing the ban on forest clearing did not make enough difference to reverse the dynamic of extensification because not enough suitable additional land (that is, forest land at low altitude) was available for clearing. But then, the extensification pathway could not be explained by policy change either. In sum, the fact that relaxing the ban on forest clearing did not bring the cattle back suggests that economic rather that policy drivers had a greater influence on land-use change.

Policy change, however, could have affected the economy in another way: by sending contradictory and unexpected signals regarding the availability of forest biomass. It is well known that variation in crop price creates uncertainties that constrain long-term investments among risk-averse farmers. The same might apply to policies relating to resource access. At the time when most of these interviews were conducted (2001), the fear of government intervention did not appear to be elevated, and some families, usually those with many children to feed and abundant labour, cleared primary forests. The situation changed in 2002, when the government initiated its repressive campaign to enforce the ban on forest clearing, and then changed again a few years later when the authorities relaxed this policy because of its excessive social and political cost. In such an unstable policy environment, farmers cannot readily adjust their strategies. Creating paddy fields and rebuilding herds obviously requires time and effort that makes such endeavours worthwhile only over the long term: the same is also true in relation to the appropriation of natural capital when control is relaxed.

Discussion and conclusion

More research is required to tease apart the various causes of the failure to intensify. But the picture that emerges here is one of progressive erosion of the various forms of capital that could have facilitated a shift to more intensive land use. If irrigation schemes had been maintained and multiplied, and if appropriate tools, such as ploughs or ards, had been available, paddy cultivation could have expanded and substituted for *tavy*. If stables and fences had been built in order to reduce crop damage, and if veterinarians had continued to visit the area, more cattle could have been raised to puddle paddy fields, pull ards or ploughs, and provide manure to fields. Endogenous innovation might have been more effective if human and social capital had not been eroded, if the economic and policy environment had been more stable, and if vulnerability and risk aversion had not increased. In other words, the chances of successful intensification would have been higher if the price of coffee had not declined and if the government had not been bankrupt. Maintaining a ban on forest clearing, by limiting the land available for cultivation, would also have favoured the transition. It would have stimulated intensification in the same manner as population growth, while the absence of regulation might have contributed to the return to more extensive systems. But sporadic and brutal enforcement of the ban, as in 2002, proved ineffective because alternative land uses were not supported (Pollini 2007, 2011) and economic constraints remained in place.

The case study also shows that issues are more complex than they appear at first sight, and that the 'Malthusian argument of the impoverishing effects of population growth' and the 'Boserupian argument of induced intensification and resource improvement' (Pender 1998) can both be valid. On one hand, farmers in Ambodilaingo faced the ecological limits of their systems, which helped propel them into an economic crisis. Population increase led to a reduction in fallow periods, which reduced the productivity of *tavy* and increased conflicts between cultivation and cattle keeping, and in the process added new constraints to intensification. On the other hand, farmers had developed more intensive cropping systems (alternatives to slash-and-burn) and used them when the economic environment was favourable. They were encouraged to do so by increasing population density and the closure of the forest frontier, although these also created new constraints.

This conclusion is consistent with recent literature around Boserup's model (Morrison 1996; Brookfield 2001), and with the findings of other case studies in Côte d'Ivoire (Demont et al 2007) and Bangladesh (Turner and Shajaat Ali 1996). According to Turner and Shajaat Ali (1996: 14990), Malthus and Boserup:

> share various assumptions about the relationships among population, technology, and resource use but differ primarily in their views of the origins of technology. Malthus implies that technology is exogenous in the sense that its development is not necessarily linked into the population–resource condition. Boserup, in contrast, grounds this development directly into that condition; technological change is endogenous to it.

Boserupian statements can indeed be found in the writings of Malthus, for example when he states that the population dynamic:

> keeps the inhabitants of the earth always fully up to the level of the means of subsistence; and is constantly acting upon man as a powerful stimulus, urging

him to the further cultivation of the earth, and to enable it, consequently, to support a more extended population.

(Malthus 1992 [1798]: 281)

Why is it, then, that the Boserup versus Malthus controversy has fuelled so much heated debate (Hunt 2000; Stone 2001) and remains unsettled? I see two reasons for this. One is epistemological and the other is political, but both are intimately inter-twined. Understanding these reasons is one of the core tasks of political agronomy analysis, so I will dedicate the final sections of the chapter to this understanding.

The contradictory nature of the debate can be explained by the confusion between what Roy Bhaskar (1979) called the domain of the real and the domain of the actual. The domain of the real is the ontological domain within which natural laws operate. These natural laws are the consequence of structures located in the real world, and their effects are expressed by powers, or tendencies, that are universal and can only lead to certain outcomes. The fact that these outcomes are not always realised does not refute the universality of these laws. One can easily understand this by considering a metallic ball suspended in air by a magnetic field – despite its mass, the ball does not fall. The law of gravity operates on the ball, but does not lead to the expected outcome (the fall) because it does not operate in isolation (the magnetic field operates as well).

Patterns of events, on the other hand, constitute the ontological domain of the actual. They are the regularities observed in the real world, like the fact that most objects fall to the ground when they are not supported. They are generated by nat-ural laws, but are not universal, because natural laws never operate alone – they combine in unpredictable ways in the real world. Their universality is claimed only when they are confused with the laws that generate them, that is, when the domain of the real and the domain of the actual are conflated ontologically.

Humans tend to confuse these two domains. First, they are interested in predicting events, and can more easily pretend to make such predictions when patterns of events are mistakenly considered to be universal (like the laws that generate them). Second, the purpose of science is the discovery of natural laws, but only patterns of events can be observed and discovered; natural laws can only be inferred from them. When a scientist pretends to test a natural law, he/she only attempts to observe a known pattern of events. Any pattern that is observed is indeed the outcome of a combina-tion of laws whose effects can never be completely isolated, because real objects can never be completely isolated from the world to which they belong. Facing this lim-itation, many scientists conflate the non-universal patterns they observe with the universal laws they are searching for.

Coming back to Boserup, she was right to argue that population pressure creates a tendency toward intensification. She did not prove this law, but she discovered patterns of events (such as correlations between frequency of cropping and population densities), through her many travels around the world, that could more easily be explained by this law than by anything else. Beyond these patterns of events, the solidity of her theory can be evaluated in the light of common-sense arguments, also elaborated from the observation of other patterns of events that might have nothing to do with agriculture intensification. Why, for instance, would someone under any sort of pressure not try to find a solution to reduce this pressure? Why would farmers facing resource (land) scarcity not try to use more of another resource (labour, ingenuity) in order to sustain their livelihood? Boserup's model might indeed simply be the expression of a more encompassing law that is at the foundation of economic thinking: the tendency of economic actors to substitute a resource for another when it becomes scarce, and to increase the efficiency with which they transform inputs into outputs. This finding is consistent with the fact that farmers tend to maximize their output in relation to their scarcest production factor, a mechanism described in detail by Chayanov (1986 [1922]), discussed again by Dufumier (1996) and Mazoyer and Roudart (2006), and which is now part of 'textbook knowledge' (see for instance Norton et al 2010). The literature dealing with induced innovation in the industrial world (Ruttan 2001) is also consistent with this finding. The substitution of one resource for another in a context of scarcity might indeed be a universal tendency explaining the failure of sustainability strategies that attempt to keep all resources at a constant level. It might reflect humans' will to satisfy their needs no matter what happens, combined with their capacity to design new things, institutions and processes.

What we need to do now is to define the conditions within which expected outcomes such as induced innovation are realised. As we have already seen in the case of Beforona and Ambodilaingo, the economic and policy environments are critical. If population pressure is the law of gravity, then policy and economic shocks represent unstable magnetic fields that can give the ball a new trajectory. While these fields need to be understood, unfortunately, more detailed analysis will be difficult, for two reasons. First, tendencies can only be imperfectly isolated from each other, because real-world objects cannot be easily isolated. They can be only disconnected virtually, in the abstract models that represent them, which exposes any analysis to the risk of reification. Second, there is a great temptation to look only at the tendencies that generate outcomes that are compatible with a given incomplete theory, or with a political agenda, which further encourages reification. This leads us to the second reason why the Boserup versus Malthus controversy fuelled so much debate: the political biases in science and the production of 'convenient' knowledge.

The biases surrounding the production of knowledge about the environment have been extensively analyzed in the political and ecology literature with some of the most influential work being that of Leach and Mearns (1996), Fairhead and Leach (1998) and Peet and Watts (2004). Very briefly summarised, the argument is that the will of elites to capture resources, which is embedded in social and political structures, favours knowledge that justifies taking control over resources, to the detriment of local people whose land use is conveniently labelled as 'unsustainable' and whose innovations are ignored or disregarded. In the case of the debate that concerns us here, this political bias favours the Malthusian view, which considers that technological innovation is mostly exogenous. The consequence is never-ending research and extension efforts aimed at designing and promoting new technologies (alley cropping, improved fallows, contour-line hedgerows, no tilling, cover crops, slash-and-mulch, composting, the System of Rice Intensification (SRI), fish farming, etc.) that farmers rarely adopt (Pollini 2007). Since the rise of climate change mitigation in the international environmental agenda, carbon has become the resource to be captured, which has created a new political bias in favour of techniques that maximise biomass production and restrict the use of fire (Fairhead et al 2012).

This political economy analysis of the production of knowledge, however, is incomplete, as the critique might also carry its own biases, which justifies a critique of the critique (Pollini 2010). One such bias, which is symmetrical to the one analysed above, is the tendency to idealise the behaviour of smallholder farmers and to consider that their decisions always lead to harmonious nature/society relationships and optimal output/input ratios, if no external social, economic or political disturbances occur. Such harmony might be the exception rather than the rule. Empirical observations show that relative social/ecological balances can be achieved over long periods, but that biodiversity is usually not part of the calculus of these balances. Farmers, through successive resource substitutions, convert primary ecosystems into anthropogenic ones that provide most of the ecological and economic functions they need. At least in the short term, a fraction of the initial biodiversity is sufficient to provide these services: the rest is sacrificed through regimes that reduce the number of available ecological niches. Late-successional species, for instance, fail to establish with short fallow periods.

A second bias of the political ecology literature is the anti-essentialist critique and its corollary, the argument of particularism, or localism, visible in the work of Brookfield (2001) and in Morrison's (1996) critique of Boserup. These authors emphasise the need to contextualise local situations, and see Boserup's model as being overly universalist. Much of the literature engaging with Boserup falls into this line, by showing that intensification is not the only response to increasing population pressure. The most frequently mentioned alternatives are extensification (occupation of new land), which we observed in the case of Ambodilaingo; diversification by the development of off-farm activities (trade, handicraft and wage labour), also observed in Ambodilaingo in the form of the transportation of boards; out-migration (settlement in other regions), which is observed in many regions of Madagascar; the protection of the land from outside intrusion, also frequent in Madagascar; and fertility control.

But even if these alternatives played a prominent role, they do not falsify Boserup's model. They just show that institutional innovation, in addition to technological innovation, is also induced by population pressure. In fact, Boserup herself showed that population growth can also trigger institutional innovations, such as the evolution of property regimes toward more individual ownership. We can criticize her on the fact that she did not analyse the whole range of processes listed above, but the reason might simply be that she did what most scientists do when they want to discover a pattern of events: she created a *ceteris paribus* model (Stone 2001). She isolated the causal relationship between population density and agricultural intensification from other mechanisms that could interfere with it, in order to identify the generative mechanism (the 'natural law') that creates the tendency toward intensification.

This brings us back to the epistemological discussion above. Universalist claims represent a danger when they are applied to pattern of events, but are legitimate when dealing with natural laws, which otherwise should not even be called laws. If knowledge is not to fall into relativist traps, and if policy-makers are to take decisions at a reasonable cost (with moderate knowledge inputs), general tendencies (that is, the elementary structures of the way the world works) have to be discovered. Malthus and Boserup probably discovered some of those general structures, which is why both the universality of their models (as generators of tendencies) and the contingency of their outcomes (the patterns of events they conjointly generate) need to be recognised.

In sum, this case study shows that reality needs to be investigated holistically if some sense is to be made out of it. Rather than being 'investigated', it might even need to be fully experienced through an involvement of all human intellectual skills and faculties (perception, reason, emotion and intuition). If science is to answer the sustainability issues faced by humanity today, it might need to reach a third stage in the production of knowledge. Bhaskar (1979) called this stage transcendental realism. Beyond the empirical observation of patterns of events, the inference of abstract models from these patterns, and the reification of these models (by both classical empiricists and their idealist critiques), scientists could proceed to the empirical testing of models that would be the outcome of their imaginary power, nurtured by their observations, but also by their life experience, their common sense and their values. Producing and testing such holistic and open imaginaries might be the remedy to reductionism and could help counter some of the political forces that bear on the practice of agronomic science. They could also help shift the Malthus versus Boserup debate toward more practical and constructive questions, such as how to maximise the chances that induced innovation succeeds; and how to minimise the risk that Malthusian crises occur? These are two formulations of the same question, and a contested agronomy analysis, beyond helping achieving this reformulation, might play a key role in finding practical answers.

Notes

1 Based on a questionnaire passed to all 135 families living in Ambodilaingo, in 2003.
2 Staff from the colonial agriculture services.
3 Rural development projects working in the area reject the techniques developed by farmers, such as the ploughing of hillsides to plant ginger or the expansion of 'messy' home gardens, and propose instead techniques that farmers do not adopt, such as agroforestry, cover crops and SRI (an extremely intensive mode of rice cultivation). See Pollini (2007) for details.
4 This statement was made frequently during enquiries, and contrasts with the situation in villages close to the road, where some villagers assert that their situation improved during the past decades due to increasing opportunities to market products, mostly ginger and bananas.

References

Bhaskar, R. (1979) *A Realist Theory of Science*. Hassocks, UK: Harvester Press.
Boserup, E. (1965) *The Conditions of Agricultural Growth: The Economics of Agrarian Change Under Population Pressure*. London: Earthscan.
Brand, J. and Rakotovao, W. (1997) *Dégradation des sols*, Cahier Terre Tany no. 6, Antananarivo-Berne, FOFIFA–GDE/GIUB, pp. 19–33.
Brookfield, H. (2001) *Exploring Agrodiversity*. New York: Columbia University Press.
Chayanov, A. (1986 [1922]) *The Theory of Peasant Economy*. Madison, WI: University of Wisconsin Press.

Demont, M., Jouve, P., Stessens, J. and Tollens, E. (2007) 'Boserup versus Malthus revisited: evolution of farming systems in northern Cote d'Ivoire', *Agricultural Systems*, 93: 215–28.

Dufumier, M. (1996) *Les Projets de Developpement Agricole: manuel d'expertise*. Paris: Karthala.

Fairhead, J. and Leach, M. (1998) *Reframing Deforestation: Global Analysis and Local Realities*. London and New York: Routledge.

Fairhead, J., Leach, M. and Amanor, K. (2012) 'Anthropogenic Dark Earths and Africa: a political agronomy of research disjunctures', in Sumberg, J. and Thompson, J. (eds), *Contested Agronomy: Agricultural Research in a Changing World*. London: Earthscan.

Hunt, R. (2000) 'Labor productivity and agricultural development: Boserup revisited', *Human Ecology*, 28(2): 251–77.

Leach, M. and Mearns, R. (1996) *The Lie of the Land*. Portsmouth, NH: Heinemann.

Le Bourdiec, F. (1974) *Hommes et Paysages du Riz à Madagascar*. Antananarivo: Etude de Géographie Humaine, Imprimerie FTM.

Malthus, T. (1992 [1798]) *An Essay on the Principle of Population*. Cambridge: Cambridge University Press.

Mazoyer, M. and Roudart, L. (2006) *A History of World Agriculture: From the Neolithic to the Current Crisis*. New York: Monthly Review Press.

Messerli, P. (2003) 'Alternatives à la culture sur brûlis sur la falaise est de Madagascar: stratégies en vue d'une gestion plus durable des terres', PhD dissertation, Université de Berne.

Morrison, K.D. (1996) 'Typological schemes and agricultural change: beyond Boserup in precolonial South India', *Current Anthropology*, 37(4): 583–608.

Nambena, J. (2004) 'Analyse de la subsistance paysanne dans un système de production en crise et identification participative de stratégies durables d'adaptation: cas de Beforona, versant oriental de Madagascar', PhD dissertation, Université de Heidelberg.

Nambena, S. (2007) 'Régionalisation de l'utilisation des ressources naturelles à partir du cas de Beforona', PhD dissertation, Université d'Antananarivo.

Norton, G.W., Alwang, J. and Masters, W.A. (2010) *Economics of Agricultural Development: World Food Systems and Resource Use*. London and New York: Routledge.

Ostrom, E. (2005) *Understanding Institutional Diversity*. Princeton, NJ: Princeton University Press.

Palm, C.A., Vosti, S.A., Sanchez, P.A. and Ericksen, P.J. (2005) *Slash-and-Burn Agriculture: The Search for Alternatives*. New York: Columbia University Press.

Peet, R. and Watts, M. (2004) *Liberation Ecologies: Environment, Development, Social Movements*, 2nd edn. London and New York: Routledge.

Pender, J.L. (1998) 'Population growth, agricultural intensification, induced innovation and natural resource sustainability: An application of neoclassical growth theory', *Agricultural Economics*, 19: 99–112.

Pollini, J. (2011) 'The difficult reconciliation of conservation and development objectives: the case of the Malagasy Environmental Action Plan', *Human Organizations*, 70(1): 74–87.

——(2010) 'Environmental degradation narratives in Madagascar: From colonial hegemonies to humanist revisionism', *Geoforum*, 41(5): 711–22.

——(2009) 'Agroforestry and the search for alternative to slash-and-burn cultivation: From technological optimism to a political economy of deforestation', *Agriculture, Ecosystems and Environment*, 133: 48–60.

——(2007) 'Deforestation and slash-and-burn cultivation in Madagascar: representations and realities', PhD thesis, Department of Natural Resources, Cornell University, New York.

Projet Terre-Tany/BEMA (1997) 'Un système Agro-Ecologique Dominé par le Tavy: la Région de Béforona, Falaise Est de Madagascar', *Cahier Terre-Tany*, 6, CDE/GIUB and FOFIFA, Antananarivo.

——(1998) 'Les Stratégies endogènes et la gestion des ressources naturelles dans la région de Beforona: les résultats des recherches pluridisciplinaires de la phase 1995–98', *Cahiers Terre-Tany*, 8, CDE/GIUB and FOFIFA, Antananarivo.

Rakotoarijaona Razafimbelo, N.M. (2005) 'Intégration des Paysans dans un Projet de Développement dans le Fokontany d'Ambodilaingo, Commune Rurale de Beforona, District de Moramanga', Master's thesis, Département d'Histoire, Université d'Antananarivo, Antananarivo.

Ruttan, V.W. (2001) *Technology, Growth, and Development: An Induced Innovation Perspective.* Oxford: Oxford University Press.

Stone, G.D. (2001) 'Theory of the square chicken: advances in agricultural intensification theory', *Asia Pacific Viewpoint*, 42(2/3): 163–80.

Turner, B.L. and Shajaat Ali, A.M. (1996) 'Induced intensification: agricultural change in Bangladesh with implications for Malthus and Boserup', *Proceedings of the National Academy of Science*, 93: 14984–91.

8

ALTERNATIVE CONFIGURATIONS OF AGRONOMIC EXPERIMENTATION

Harro Maat and Dominic Glover

Introduction

The emergence and spread of the System of Rice Intensification (SRI) have stimulated heated controversy among rice scientists and development workers. SRI is a method of rice cultivation that is said to produce high yields while also conserving natural resources, especially water. Claims that dramatically increased yields can be achieved with SRI, in some cases exceeding what plant physiologists consider to be the yield ceiling for rice, triggered hostile responses from some scientists. Promoters of SRI argue that it is superior to existing cultivation practices, and has particular advantages over the technology packages associated with the Green Revolution. Many within the rice research establishment dismiss SRI as a combination of well established 'good management' practices and some extraordinary claims that cannot be substantiated or replicated. Proponents of SRI insist that remarkable results are being achieved in farmers' fields, and point to the enthusiasm of both farmers and non-governmental organisations in using and spreading SRI to rice-growing regions around the world (Berkhout and Glover 2011; Glover 2011).

Until recently, the SRI dispute has been conducted largely as an argument about the best methods for cultivating rice. In this chapter we take a different tack and argue that the controversy surrounding SRI exemplifies a more general and fundamental disagreement about how agronomic research on rice should be organised and pursued.

To develop our argument, we examine the nature of experiments in agronomy. The design and conduct of agronomic experiments serve to configure the relationship between the worlds of scientific research and agricultural practice. This relationship is fundamentally concerned with the generation and transmission of information, knowledge and techniques. In principle, these can flow in both directions – from the laboratory and field station to farmers' fields and *vice versa*.

The relationship between formal science and farming practice can be configured in different ways, however. Here we examine the historical processes that have led to the evolution of particular configurations of this relationship, which are associated with a bifurcated division of labour in agronomic science between researchers and agricultural extension agents. As an intrinsic part of this organisational partition, the two branches of the profession developed different methods for structuring their relationships with farmers. We argue that because of this division of labour, in different times and places the relationship has been configured in ways that have tended to privilege the flow of information, knowledge and technology in one direction rather than the other.

We use the example of SRI to show that the discontinuities between the two aspects of professional agronomy and their characteristic methods and approaches continue to exist. These discontinuities helped not only to shape the technical content of SRI, but also to fuel the passionate disputes that surround it. We show that SRI emerged in relative social isolation from the international mainstream of rice agronomy. Consequently, it was developed using a particular style of scientific practice, which helped to produce a distinctive set of rice cultivation methods. In particular, we draw attention to the organisation of the field-level activities and practices that led to the development of SRI methods, including the social and institutional setting within which those developments occurred.

Experiments in agronomy

Most agronomists would agree that an essential feature of agronomic science and expertise is their applied and practical nature. Agronomy is not just about biological, chemical and physical processes and relationships, but is integrally concerned with farming practice, skill and technique. For agronomists, foundational research on topics such as soil chemistry, plant physiology and crop growth modelling is valuable only when outputs are tested, monitored, evaluated and applied in real production conditions.

Experimentation plays a crucial role in connecting the academic discipline of agronomy with agricultural practice. Historically, there is a strong argument for considering 'experimental turns' in two antecedent disciplines, organic chemistry and biology, as key moments in the development of agronomy as a distinct discipline. For organic chemistry, this goes back to the work of Justus von Liebig, whose experimental approach, developed in Germany in the 1820s and 1830s, gave impetus to the work of agricultural research stations worldwide (Rossiter 1975). A few decades later, Charles Darwin's work forged an experimental connection between biology and agriculture. Darwin himself pointed out that plant and animal breeding mimicked evolutionary processes, and his theory of evolution provided a scientific basis for experimental research in plant breeding and plant physiology (Kimmelman 1987; Cittadino 1990).

Agronomists and other agricultural scientists generally draw a distinction between experiments and demonstrations. Experiments are usually seen as having an objective to discover facts or principles, generate data, test hypotheses, determine causes or confirm theories. They are designed by, and primarily for, professional researchers. Experiments are understood as methods for systematically comparing two or (more typically) more 'treatments' or sets of treatments, using designs (including replications, plot sizes, plot arrangements, spatial placement, etc.) that allow systematic data collection and rigorous analysis of the statistical significance of treatment effects and interactions. Many agronomic field experiments are undertaken to provide information that can be fed into the development of new production methods and technologies.

Demonstrations, on the other hand, are usually seen as having an objective to demonstrate, convince or persuade. They typically have a simple format with perhaps only two treatments, a straightforward side-by-side comparison, and often little formal 'analysis'. They are generally conducted by extension officers or company representatives, often with the cooperation of a farmer, for the purpose of disseminating new knowledge and practices that have already been discovered, developed and refined by scientists. This distinction between experimentation and demonstration reflects a specific perception of the relationship between science and practice, a perception that underpins the basic division of labour seen in present-day professional agronomy and the different approaches to field-based activities.

However, it is not at all unusual or misleading to apply the term 'experiment' to pedagogical exercises designed to demonstrate phenomena that are already well known – school science lessons being an obvious example. Studies in the history and sociology of science and technology show the long-standing dual role of experiments – as instruments of scientific discovery and as methods of instruction and persuasion. Experiments as well as demonstrations represent the key means by which science and its publics (including users of scientific knowledge, such as farmers) have been linked.

An early example is given by Steven Shapin (1988), who describes the activities of Royal Society Fellows in seventeenth-century England. To gain acceptance for the observations they made and the theories they developed, it was not enough for these early scientists merely to attend to their instruments and apparatuses. Much of their time and energy was devoted to what is nowadays called social networking, specifically the arrangement of an appropriate audience of influential people before whom, during carefully choreographed social events, they would replicate experiments that they had previously refined in their workshops. The experiments themselves had to be designed, as well as explained, in such a way that they would convince such an audience.

A similar point is made by Bruno Latour in his account of Louis Pasteur's work on the anthrax vaccine. While it was relatively easy to make the vaccine work in the laboratory, the real challenge was to convince veterinarians and livestock farmers of its value. To achieve this, Pasteur organised 'demonstrations' on a farm in France that were designed 'to bring to the still uncertain public a fresh and more grandiosely staged proof of the efficacy of the vaccine' (Latour 1983: 152). In this way, the French veterinarians and farmers were bound together with Pasteur's microbiology laboratory. This connection, Latour argues, is not simply about research results being disseminated to the livestock industry, but is about the creation, by means of an experiment, of a mutual dependency between all the actors involved, creating an 'actor-network' in which the laboratory forms a central node. Within the actor-network, not only Pasteur but also veterinarians and farmers (not to mention livestock, microbes and vaccines) had their roles to play.

The work of Shapin and Latour makes clear that there is only a thin line between experiments designed to test hypotheses and demonstrations designed to convince a selectively targeted audience. For researchers, the key to success lies in mobilising support from a larger set of actors, and experiments (including, for our purposes, demonstrations) play a central role in this effort. It is the type of audience to be convinced that largely determines the design and arrangement of the experiment. Those to be convinced may encompass a wide range, from the scientist's immediate colleagues within a laboratory or institute to a much wider public outside it. Because of its applied nature, agronomic science is not an activity conducted entirely behind the fences of research stations; through experiments and demonstrations, it is also carried out in public view.

Shapin's and Latour's analyses of scientists' activities in the seventeenth and eighteenth centuries apply equally to contemporary scientific practice (Latour 1987). This point is underlined by Levidow and Carr (2010) in their discussion of the way field trials of a controversial technology such as genetically modified crops are amenable to a variety of interpretations by different stakeholders. These trials can be simultaneously demonstrations of the technology's efficacy and safety; tools for identifying risks and hazards; ways of modelling the behaviour of farmers, crops, insects and weeds; and politically charged orchestrations intended to persuade reluctant consumers to accept an unpopular technology. In a similar vein, Glover (2007: 165) found that the staff of a commercial agribusiness company that was attempting to develop a market for genetically modified seeds in India 'did not draw clear distinctions between a trial as a safety assessment for regulatory purposes, as a pre-commercial performance evaluation on a new proprietary crop variety or as a demonstration plot to be used as a marketing tool'.

Experiments and demonstrations help to establish a connection between science and practice through a site-specific process of network building, in which the skilled activities of various actors play crucial roles. One such role is played by professionals who mediate between basic researchers and the eventual end users of their work. In the case described by Latour, it was veterinarians who helped to connect Pasteur to cattle farmers. In agronomy, this role is usually played by agricultural extension officers.

The intermediary role of agricultural extension is not just about disseminating knowledge from the laboratory to the field. In his account of field trials conducted in California, Henke (2000) shows that the quality of the experimental results depended on the skilled work of a variety of different actors, not just scientists. In particular, extension officers played a key role in mediating between scientists, farmers, field technicians, farm labourers and company representatives. Henke also shows that crucial parts of the experimental work were done by Mexican immigrant fieldworkers, whose farming skills were vital in securing the data: 'Through their harvest skills, these fieldworkers not only help advisors [extension officers] make their trials more "lab-like", by standardizing the collection of data, but also more "field-like", by helping them get the right kind of data' (Henke 2000: 500).

Extension officers must work closely with farmers in order to bridge the gap between science and practice. Moreover, farmers themselves have skilled work to do in order to translate scientific information into farming methods that are adapted to their own conditions. An agricultural development project implemented in East Timor illustrates both the involvement of farmers as key actors in the successful generation and dissemination of knowledge and technologies, and the dual nature of on-farm experiments. In the Seeds of Life programme, farmers performed a central role in the management of 'on-farm demonstration trials' – the combination of 'trial' and 'demonstration' is significant – that 'served a double purpose: as a testing ground for seed germplasm performance and, simultaneously, as an agricultural extension strategy whereby the improved seed could be disseminated through local channels' (Shepherd and McWilliam 2011: 204).

Just as agronomists must engage with the world of practice, anthropological studies show that farming practice also involves experimentation. The designers of the Seeds of Life programme drew explicitly on anthropological insights and deliberately enrolled farmers as full participants in the project in order to achieve its goals. The anthropologist Paul Richards (1989a, 1989b) has shown from his studies of rice producers in Sierra Leone that agricultural practice is intrinsically experimental. Other scholars and practitioners have also explored the nature of farmers' experiments and confirmed farmers' capacity to frame research questions, try out interventions and engage with scientists' experimental methods (Sumberg and Okali 1997; van Veldhuizen et al 1997). Examples like these demonstrate the importance of building effective connections between formal science and farming practice. The key challenge is how best to configure those connections.

The emerging gap between science and practice

In the previous section, we cited several examples which show that the social worlds of science and practice may be connected by means of a range or continuum of different field activities – including experiments and demonstrations – which combine knowledge generation and dissemination in locally, historically and topically specific ways. In this respect, agronomy is no different from other science disciplines. The distinction that modern agronomy makes between experiments and demonstrations results from the particular way that this continuum has been divided conceptually, professionally and methodologically. To further develop this argument and to explore how this partitioning occurred, we examine the case of agricultural science in the Netherlands and its former colonies.

During the second half of the nineteenth century, the nascent agricultural sciences in the Netherlands faced a growing demand from below in the form of farmers' associations seeking (and paying for) scientific advice. From above, governments invested in agricultural research and education to stimulate the agricultural sector (Marcus 1985; Maat 2001; Harwood 2007). The emerging agricultural research stations, schools and universities offered support to the farm sector through demonstration plots, school gardens and field experiments. These diverse activities were the main source of information for farmers and researchers alike. Their information needs differed, however: farmers sought reliable information with which to improve their practices, while agronomists sought a reliable basis from which to make appropriate generalisations and provide good advice.

However, researchers soon realised that simply trying a farming method or technology and observing the result during a single season was not appropriate, primarily because of site-to-site and season-to-season variability. By the end of the nineteenth century, many agronomists were aware that replication and inference calculation or statistical significance testing could help solve this problem, but several decades passed before appropriate methods were developed and applied in a standardised format. A professor of statistics was appointed at the Agricultural College in Wageningen in 1913, but for many years there were still no guidelines or handbooks that provided extension officers with agreed methods for the design and analysis of field trials (Gigerenzer et al 1989; Maat 2008).

As they struggled to find the best way to generate reliable information that would meet their respective needs, differences began to open up between agricultural researchers and extension officers. In the early 1910s, for example, the agricultural chemist Joost Hudig criticised Dutch agricultural extension officers for lacking a proper under-standing of the mathematical complexity of experimentation. His main worry was the extension officers' habit of combining experiments from different locations and drawing conclusions based on averages calculated over locations (Hudig 1911, 1912). In a response to Hudig, one extension officer explained that he felt 'morally obliged' to inform farmers about results of trials even if they did not follow the latest scientific norms (Rauwerda 1913).

In the mid-1920s, the Ministry of Agriculture created a committee to develop guidelines for the conduct of field experiments. The committee found that not much had changed since the 1910s. The chairman complained during a conference that field trials were not real experiments but demonstrations, which were not carried out according to 'the new scientific methods of experimenting' (Koeslag 1922). Several extension officers responded to his presentation, emphasising the value of demon-strations which, they argued, helped farmers to get a vivid impression of the effects of particular treatments.

The committee took several years to arrive at an agreed position, which was turned into a manual for agronomic field activities that was published by the ministry. The manual distinguished between five different types of activity: (1) demonstrations of clearly observable differences; (2) observation experiments for disease resistance; (3) exploratory experiments to determine which factors needed more precise testing; (4) experiments where 'yield was the decisive element'; and (5) 'institute experi-ments' to be conducted at research stations and not suitable for farmers' fields (Landbouwvoorlichtingsdienst 1934).

The manual's five categories are remarkable because they reflect the committee's perception that there should be a range of activities in the space between the worlds of science and practice. However, while the committee had been deliberating, research stations and extension services had grown in size and, despite the central coordination exercised by the Ministry of Agriculture, evolved into different kinds of institution, each with its own organisational features. It was this organisational differentiation, together with the adoption of particular methodologies for different types of field activities, that helped to entrench the distinction between experiments and demonstrations which has persisted to the present day.

Guided by the work of Ronald Fisher and other statisticians, professional agronomic researchers in the Netherlands, like their counterparts elsewhere, increasingly understood that the meaning and significance of experimental results could became apparent only through the application of controlled and randomised experimental designs and the use of sophisticated mathematical techniques (Gigerenzer et al 1989). Such designs and analytical methods not only made it possible to be much more confident that an observed result could be attributed to a given treatment, they also allowed researchers to identify subtle effects and interactions that were not visible to the naked eye.

Extension officers, on the other hand, knew that farmers were most likely to be convinced by vivid demonstrations, whether these could be directly observed in the field or in easily grasped numbers. Over-elaborate experiments might alienate the very farmers who were supposed to benefit from them, while subtle or invisible effects might not be very persuasive. Over the years, extension officers have become increasingly preoccupied not with the rigour of experimental designs as such, but with identifying effective methods of communication, measuring the impact of extension systems, promoting knowledge exchanges and stimulating innovation processes (Leeuwis and van den Ban 2004).

The emerging division of labour between research and demonstrations was not accepted by all agronomists, however. A clear example can be found in the activities of Dutch agricultural officers in colonial Indonesia.

By and large, the graduates who were employed as agricultural extensionists in the Dutch colonies were agronomists with some training in social science disciplines, primarily agricultural economics (Maat 2001). Extension officers in the Netherlands Indies faced the challenge of setting up extension activities for a type of agriculture with which they were not familiar. Establishing a basic understanding of agricultural practice in the region was a core element of their activities.

In 1947 one of these Dutch extension officers, W. J. Timmer, proposed an integrated methodology for agricultural research and extension based on empirically driven field research incorporating both plant and social sciences. Timmer called this model 'social agronomy' and argued that its foundation should be a detailed appraisal of the rural area: 'the principle "know your district" is a crucial requirement for every social agronomist and, if this is not met, appropriate extension is out of the question' (Timmer 1947: 176).

Timmer proposed a step-wise procedure: after collection and analysis of information, research topics were to be prioritised, after which cultivation practices, treatments or techniques would be tested and disseminated. In practice, advisors were occupied primarily with the last phase – testing and promotion. Research institutes put pressure on the extension service to disseminate their findings and as a result extension officers had little time for an elaborate exploratory phase. Timmer complained that this meant the introduction of new cultivation methods or technologies was often based on little more than 'a good guess' (Timmer 1947: 182). In place of this, Timmer wanted to make agronomy speak to the locally specific conditions of farmers, not by intensifying the downstream flow of information, but by creating a broad and integrated exchange of information between the field and research institutes.

Timmer's interest in social agronomy was not unique. The importance of empirical field research was stressed by other colonial agronomists, such as Pierre De Schlippe in central Africa (Richards 1989a) and Jean-Paul Dobelmann in Madagascar (Dobelmann 1961). Even earlier, René Dumont (1935) in Vietnam realised that farmers themselves needed to carry out their own experiments in order to work out locally adapted farming methods. The concerns of these colonial-era agronomists resurfaced in later decades, perhaps most prominently in the form of farmer participatory research and participatory plant breeding and varietal selection (Okali et al 1994; Almekinders and Elings 2001).

More recently, some scholars have proposed new institutional and methodological arrangements that would involve an even more profound rebalancing of the relationship between farmers' experiments and the experimental practices of agricultural scientists, while enlarging the base from which knowledge can be generated and disseminated. As we noted above, the Seeds of Life programme in East Timor deliberately harnessed the knowledge, experimental behaviour and social networks of farmers in both seed selection and the dissemination of improved, locally adapted seed varieties (Shepherd and McWilliam 2011). Richards et al (2009) have taken this kind of design to a new level, with a proposal to exploit the power of 'unsupervised learning' among a large number of farmers, modelled on artificial neural networks. In a similar vein, van Etten (2011) has offered detailed proposals for exploiting the potential of 'crowdsourcing' in crop improvement programmes.

These proposals seek to mobilise the knowledge, skills and experimental behaviour of farmers themselves, in order to achieve outcomes that are both meaningful to science and readily applicable in farmer practice. In doing so, they seek to broaden the locus of knowledge generation and transform the flow of technology dissemination, by acknowledging farmers as crucial partners in both of these activities. Although we do not have space here to describe the proposals in detail, we simply note that they seek to accomplish these objectives by deliberately blending different approaches to experimentation and technology dissemination. They also accept that institutional separation of research and extension is a historically contingent fact rather than an intrinsic feature of agronomic science, and seek therefore to rethink the division of labour between researchers and agricultural extension officers.

In the next sections, we consider the case of SRI as an illustration of our argument. Both SRI and the controversy that surrounds it serve to illustrate the continuing disconnection between formal agricultural research, extension and farming practice. The case of SRI also illustrates our argument that agronomic science, technological innovation and changes in farming practice occur through historically situated and contingent engagements between farmers, extension officers and scientists, where the experimentation and demonstration functions are not neatly separated.

The emergence of SRI

SRI is a method of rice cultivation which involves a number of principles or practices that can be concisely summarised as follows: the transplanting of single, very young, widely spaced seedlings; irrigation using very limited amounts of water during the vegetative growth period, sometimes including short periods when the soil is allowed to dry; and careful control of weeds, ideally by disturbing the soil so as to increase aeration. Application of substantial quantities of organic fertiliser is encouraged in order to stimulate microbial activity in the soil.

These principles are said to allow rice plants to achieve significantly higher levels of growth and grain yield, while consuming much less water. SRI's advocates position it as an agro-ecological, low external-input farming method, which is peculiarly accessible to resource-poor farmers since it does not require the adoption of new rice varieties or expensive chemical inputs (Uphoff 1999, 2003, 2007; Stoop et al 2002; Mishra et al 2006).

SRI was first elaborated by Father Henri de Laulanié, a French missionary of the Catholic Jesuit order who earned a diploma in agronomy from the National Agronomic Research Institute (INRA) in Paris. When he was sent to Madagascar in 1961, de Laulanié was unfamiliar with rice and therefore depended heavily on his own observations and the handful of manuals and handbooks available to him. He examined rice plants closely, studied their growth patterns in detail, and paid attention to the cultivation methods he saw being used by Malagasy farmers, including atypical practices he observed in certain locations. One year, he observed something remarkable that was not explained by the information available in his handbooks: rice seedlings transplanted at only 15 days old (a strategy to cope with an early season drought) seemed to grow with surprising vigour, leading to a higher grain yield.

Unfortunately, in the Madagascar of the 1970s and 1980s, de Laulanié was largely cut off from any agricultural research or extension system that could either provide him with scientific advice or incorporate his observations and experiences into existing research programmes. He seized upon the few sources of scientific information that came his way and, in the absence of more systematic support, he relied heavily on the simple trial-and-error experiments carried out by students in his own training fields. His professional judgements were informed not only by his agronomic training, but also by his experience and intentions as a development worker. The local success of his inductive scientific methods depended on close engagement with small-scale Malagasy farmers and on his combined status as scientist and priest (Berkhout and Glover 2011; Glover 2011).

SRI as contested agronomy

The disconnection between de Laulanié's inductive scientific practice in the Madagascar highlands and formal agricultural research helps to explain not only the nature of the rice production system he devised, but also the controversy that surrounds it today.

Since de Laulanié had based SRI partly on field manuals and on the physiological characteristics of rice, it is not surprising that some of the practices he advocated resemble aspects of 'best management practices' recommended by rice science institutions such as the International Rice Research Institute (IRRI). At the same time, because de Laulanié's scientific method was inductive, and because SRI was based on farmers' existing practices and optimised for a particular agro-ecological setting and community of farmers, it is also not surprising that SRI is somewhat distinct from the recommendations of mainstream rice science. Under the Green Revolution regime, international rice research and development were organised in line with a single, standardising template for rice improvement that took relatively little account of diverse local variations in growing conditions (Harwood 2009; Smith 2009). In contrast, the distinctive features of SRI reflect the special characteristics of the time and place in which it emerged, as well as the subjective judgements of the individual who played a dominant role in its development (Berkhout and Glover 2011; Glover 2011).

Together, these similarities and differences help to explain why SRI received a hostile reception from mainstream rice scientists when it began to spread beyond Madagascar in the late 1990s. How, they must have asked, could a missionary based in the Madagascar highlands have developed a method of rice cultivation that was superior to the systems recommended by the foremost national and international centres of rice research? The fact that SRI combined well established good management practices (such as the application of organic fertiliser) with unorthodox elements made this question all the more explosive.

The arguments for and against SRI published in agronomic journals confirm that the controversy is partly about rice biology and physiology, and partly about the proper organisation and conduct of agronomic research. Scientists associated with IRRI have dismissed SRI as a delusion based on mistaken theory and inaccurate measurement. Some of their most trenchant critiques of SRI have taken the form of theoretical and modelling analyses, using estimates based on existing scientific knowledge, which have led them to conclude that the claims made on behalf of SRI were implausible because they breached the known physiological limits of rice growth and productivity. The authors of these papers insisted that SRI had nothing to offer in the quest to increase the yield potential of rice, which, in their view, would require advanced biotechnology-based breeding methods (Dobermann 2004; Sheehy et al 2004).

In response, supporters of SRI argued that it was inappropriate to use scientific theory to dismiss remarkable empirical observations from farmers' fields; instead, it should be the role of agronomic science to investigate and explain these surprising field observations. Second, they challenged the IRRI scientists' implicit assumption that increasing rice yields should be the primary goal of rice research. They pointed out that what poor and marginal farmers really need is locally adapted and accessible cultivation methods based on the intensification of labour, rather than standardised high-yielding technology packages that depend on expensive external inputs. Indeed, SRI proponents have argued that it is spreading spontaneously from farmer to farmer and country to country precisely because of its intrinsic attractiveness and accessibility to resource-poor farmers (Stoop and Kassam 2005; Uphoff 2007). Third, SRI's proponents argue that conventional methods of evaluation are inadequate for assessing a technology whose most powerful effects are produced, they believe, through synergetic interactions among several different practices. They believe that these synergetic relationships extend the physiological potential of the rice plant, which explains why spectacular yield increases have been reported in farmers' fields (Uphoff 1999; Stoop et al 2002; Uphoff et al 2008). It is interesting to note that, with the latter two arguments, SRI advocates assert both that yield should not be the exclusive centre of attention, and that SRI can unlock a higher yield potential compared with conventional methods.

Although statistical techniques developed for field experiments typically test for effects within a single set of treatments (e.g. different rice varieties), depending on the experimental design, the interactions between different sets of treatments such as varieties and N fertiliser can also be analysed. Some of the data cited by SRI proponents to support their claims have been derived from rather simple side-by-side comparisons of rice performance under SRI and an alternative management practice. Unless such comparisons are designed and replicated very carefully, the interactions among variables and the benefits or disadvantages of particular practices or combinations of practices are impossible to discern (Berkhout and Glover 2011).

SRI's proponents take a different view, arguing that SRI represents a particular type of field-level innovation, discovered and developed through practical experience and grounded empiricism rather than formal scientific experimentation. They also suggest that the impact of SRI is crucially related to it having been grounded in situated farming practice, because it exploits the cumulative effects of a steady improvement in soil quality through the addition of organic fertilisers and altered water management practices. They argue that these features of SRI are liable to be systematically underestimated by short-term field trials carried out on research stations (Stoop and Kassam 2005).

By focusing on the practical experiences of farmers in this way, the advocates of SRI draw attention to the visibility of its effects as a key factor in its development and spread. While the impacts of SRI methods on yield and productivity continue to be disputed, one consistent observation is that SRI typically produces significant changes in the growth and morphology of individual rice plants, which are visible to the naked eye. The plants generally produce more luxuriant vegetative growth and often a large number of panicles. When the plants are pulled out of the ground, they often reveal long and visibly healthy root systems (Berkhout and Glover 2011).

In farmers' fields, this dramatic demonstration of the impact of SRI can create a powerful impression. Numerous photographs showing side-by-side comparisons of rice fields and rice plants grown under SRI and conventional management have circulated in cyberspace, creating a vivid impression of the difference between the two. Rice scientists pose questions about such images, however. They point out that the rapid and vigorous growth of rice plants grown under SRI does not necessarily or consistently lead to a higher grain yield. In particular, it has often been observed that there is a trade-off between planting density and the size and productivity of individual plants. For instance, when planted at low densities, individual rice plants tend to produce a large number of panicles per plant, but the number of panicles per square metre may not be any greater than with more densely spaced plants, even if these densely packed plants are visibly less productive on an individual basis (Angladette 1966).

Instead of having an impact on yield (land productivity), the most attractive effects of SRI may be a substantial increase in the productivity of other inputs, including seeds, water and even labour. Such benefits may be extremely attractive to poor rice farmers, perhaps even more so than an absolute increase in yield. However, these productivity effects may be subtle and apparent only at the end of the season, after reflection, measurement and calculation. To demonstrate such subtle effects, sophisticated experimental designs and statistical methods may be required; few of the studies published to date have met these standards (Berkhout and Glover 2011; Glover 2011).

Compared with such methods, the visual impression created by comparing obvious differences between two fields, plots or plants can be much more immediate and powerful. These visible differences appear to play a role in helping SRI to spread, often through the arrangement of demonstrations designed to show farmers that the system makes a clear, beneficial difference to the growth of individual rice plants. Such demonstrations work in the same way as the original observation of the growth patterns of young transplants that led Henri de Laulanié to develop SRI in the first place. In both cases, empirical observation of a striking phenomenon stimulates action.

A factor that makes the case of SRI particularly interesting is the extended network of organisations and individuals promoting it. In the cases typically analysed in the field of science and technology studies, network building is an activity generally initiated by scientists, laboratories and research institutes, while other actors such as entrepreneurs, companies and governments also play important roles. In the SRI case, a strong lateral network has emerged within and between countries and regions, involving not only research scientists, but also farmers' associations, non-governmental organisations and civil society groups, philanthropic agencies and others. SRI can thus be 'understood not merely as a set of crop management principles but as the fruit of a distinctive socio-technical system of knowledge and innovation that has operated, at least partly, outside the mainstream circuits of the international agricultural research system' (Berkhout and Glover 2011: 137).

This institutional characteristic of the SRI phenomenon may be one important reason for the dismissive responses of some scientists and research institutes. The bifurcation of professional agronomy into separate groups of research scientists and extension officers, the evolution of extension towards information dissemination and input distribution, and the establishment of the international agricultural research institutes in the 1950s and 1960s disrupted the channels for the upward flow of information from the field to the research station and the laboratory. The substantial stream of information generated by the SRI network thus confronted national and international research institutes with a difficult and unfamiliar task: how could this new information be related to their own knowledge and research practice?

Conclusion

Experiments and demonstrations of various kinds play a central role in agronomy, because they serve to configure the relationship between the worlds of scientific research and agricultural practice. Field experiments and demonstrations should both be understood as events conducted in specific historical, social and institutional settings, through which the knowledge and skills of various actors are mobilised and combined. Historically, however, different norms and standards have been adopted for experiments and demonstrations. True experiments are considered 'science-only' events for the generation or validation of new agronomic knowledge, practices and technologies. Demonstrations – which can include some kinds of field trials that have an avowedly investigative character – are seen primarily as mechanisms for promoting and disseminating these scientific products to farmers.

This division of labour and its linear, top-down information flow emerged from efforts to solve the practical problem of connecting agronomic research with farmers' practice. It became a standard institutional model, which was entrenched through choices made in the formal organisation of agricultural research institutes and extension organisations. Dissatisfaction with this model led some individuals and organisations to propose new ways of incorporating information and innovation generated at farm level, including social agronomy, participatory plant breeding and participatory varietal selection, crowdsourcing and unsupervised learning. However, these developed (or are now being proposed) only on the margins of mainstream agronomy.

The controversy over SRI demonstrates some of the continuing effects of the disconnection between formal agronomic research and field-level technology development and promotion. Our analysis suggests that a resolution of the SRI controversy will require the interests and activities of farmers to be connected to, and balanced with, the scientific requirements of researchers. The principal spaces where this is likely to happen are experimental and demonstration plots. It is here that the knowledge and practices of laboratory scientists, technicians, extension officers, field technicians, labourers and farmers can be combined and coordinated to improve the connections between scientific agronomy and farming practice.

References

Almekinders, C.J.M. and Elings, A. (2001) 'Collaboration of farmers and breeders: participatory crop improvement in perspective', *Euphytica*, 122(3): 425–38.

Angladette, A. (1966) *Le Riz* [Rice]. Paris: G.-P. Maisonneuve & Larose.

Berkhout, E. and Glover, D. (2011) *The Evolution of the System of Rice Intensification as a Socio-technical Phenomenon: A Report to the Bill and Melinda Gates Foundation*. Wageningen, the Netherlands: Wageningen University and Research Centre.

Cittadino, E. (1990) *Nature as the Laboratory: Darwinian Plant Ecology in the German Empire 1800–1900*. Cambridge: Cambridge University Press.

Dobelmann, J.-P. (1961) *Manuel de Riziculture Améliorée à l'usage des Conseillers ruraux* [Manual of Improved Rice Cultivation for Use by Rural Advisors], publisher not stated, Tananarive (Antananarivo), Madagascar.

Dobermann, A. (2004) 'A critical assessment of the system of rice intensification (SRI)', *Agricultural Systems*, 79(3): 261–81.

Dumont, R. (1935) *La Culture du Riz dans le Delta du Tonkin; Étude et Propositions d'amélioration de Techniques traditionelles de Rizicultures tropicale* [The Cultivation of Rice in the Tokin Delta: Study and Proposals for the Improvement of Traditional Techniques of Tropical Rice Cultivation]. Paris: Société d'Editions Geographiques, Maritimes et Coloniales

van Etten, J. (2011) 'Crowdsourcing crop improvement in sub-Saharan Africa: a proposal for a scalable and inclusive approach to food security', *IDS Bulletin*, 42(4): 102–10.

Gigerenzer,G., Swijtinck, Z., Porter, T., Daston, L., Beatty, J. and Krüger, L. (1989) *The Empire of Chance. How Probability Changed Science and Everyday Life.* Cambridge: Cambridge University Press.

Glover, D. (2007) 'The role of the private sector in modern biotechnology and rural development: the case of the Monsanto smallholder programme', PhD thesis, Institute of Development Studies at the University of Sussex, Brighton, UK.

——(2011) 'A system designed for rice? Materiality and the invention/discovery of the System of Rice Intensification', *Journal of East Asian Science, Technology and Society*, 5(2): 217–37

Harwood, J. (2007) *Technology's Dilemma: Agricultural Colleges between Science and Practice in Germany 1860–1934.* New York: Peter Lang.

——(2009) 'Peasant friendly plant breeding and the early years of the Green Revolution in Mexico', *Agricultural History*, 83(3): 384–410.

Henke, C. R. (2000) 'Making a place for science: the field trial', *Social Studies of Science*, 30(4): 483–511.

Hudig, J. (1911) '*De betrouwbaarheid van landbouwkundige proeven*' ['The reliability of agronomic trials'], *Landbouwkundig Tijdschrift*, 23: 543–44.

——(1912) '*Nog eens de beteekenis der "waarschijnlijke fout" berekening bij het landbouwkundig onderzoek*' ['Once again the importance of calculating the "probable error" in agronomic research'], *Landbouwkundig Tijdschrift*, 24: 355–57.

Kimmelman, B.A. (1987) *A Progressive Era Discipline: Genetics at American Agricultural Colleges and Experiment Stations 1900–1920.* Ann Arbor, MI: University of Michigan.

Koeslag, J. D. (1922) '*Het proefveldwezen in Nederland in vergelijking met het buitenland*' ['The conduct of field trials in the Netherlands compared to foreign countries'], *Verslag van het 74e Landhuishoudkundig Congres te Leeuwarden* [Proceedings of the 74th Land Management Science Congress, Leeuwarden], pp. 32–53.

Landbouwvoorlichtingsdienst [Agricultural Extension Service] (1934) *Handleiding voor veldproeven* [Field Trials Handbook]. Den Haag: Ministry of Agriculture and Fisheries.

Latour, B. (1983) 'Give me a laboratory and I will raise the world', in Knorr-Cetina, K. and Mulkay, M. (eds) *Science Observed: Perspectives on the Social Study of Science.* London: Sage.

Latour, B. (1987) *Science in Action: How to Follow Scientists and Engineers Through Society.* Cambridge, MA: Harvard University Press.

Leeuwis, C. with van den Ban, A. (2004), *Communication for Rural Innovation: Rethinking Agricultural Extension* (3rd edn). Oxford: Blackwell.

Levidow, L. and Carr, S. (2010) *GM Food on Trial: Testing European Democracy.* New York: Routledge.

Maat, H. (2001) *Science Cultivating Practice: A History of Agricultural Science in the Netherlands and Its Colonies 1863–1986.* Dordrecht, the Netherlands: Kluwer Academic.

Maat, H. (2008) 'Statistics and field experiments in agriculture: the emerging discipline of inferential statistics', in P. M. M. Klep, J. G. S. J. van Maarseveen and I. H. Stamhuis (eds) *The Statistical Mind in Modern Society. The Netherlands 1850–1940* (Vol. 2). Amsterdam: Aksant.

Marcus, A.I. (1985) *Agricultural Science and the Quest for Legitimacy; Farmers, Agricultural Colleges, and Experiment Stations 1870–1890.* Ames, IA: Iowa State University Press.

Mishra, A., Whitten, M., Ketelaar, J.W. and Salokhe, V.M., (2006) 'The System of Rice Intensification (SRI): a challenge for science, and an opportunity for farmer empowerment towards sustainable agriculture', *International Journal of Agricultural Sustainability*, 4(3): 193–212.

Okali, C., Sumberg, J. and Farrington, J. (1994) *Farmer Participatory Research: Rhetoric and Reality.* London: Intermediate Technology Publications.

Rauwerda, A. (1913) '*Wetenschappelijk onderzoek en voorlichting van den practischen landbouwer*' ['Scientific research and extension advice for the practical farmer'], *Landbouwkundig Tijdschrift*, 25: 18–23.

Richards, P. (1989a) 'Agriculture as a performance', in R. Chambers, A. Pacey and L. A. Thrupp (eds) *Farmer First. Farmer Innovation and Agricultural Research*. London: Intermediate Technology Publications.

Richards, P. (1989b) 'Farmers also experiment: a neglected intellectual resource in African science', *Discovery and Innovation*, 1(1): 19–25.

Richards, P., de Bruin-Hoekzema, M., Hughes, S.G., Kudadjie-Freeman, C., Offei, S.K., Struik, P.C. and Zannou, A. (2009) 'Seed systems for African food security: linking molecular genetic analysis and cultivator knowledge in West Africa', *International Journal of Technology Management*, 45(1–2): 196–214.

Rossiter, M.W. (1975) *The Emergence of Agricultural Science: Justus Liebig and the Americans 1840–1880*. New Haven, CT: Yale University Press.

Shapin, S. (1988) 'The house of experiment in seventeenth-century England', *Isis*, 79(3): 373–404.

Sheehy, J.E., Peng, S., Dobermann, A., Mitchell, P.L., Ferrer, A., Jianchang Yang, Yingbin Zou, Xuhua Zhong and Huang, J. (2004) 'Fantastic yields in the system of rice intensification: fact or fallacy?', *Field Crops Research*, 88(1): 1–8.

Shepherd, C. and McWilliam, A. (2011) 'Ethnography, agency and materiality: anthropological perspectives on rice development in East Timor', *Journal of East Asian Science, Technology and Society*, 5(2): 189–215.

Smith, E. (2009) 'Imaginaries of development: the Rockefeller Foundation and rice research', *Science as Culture*, 18(4): 461–82.

Stoop, W., Uphoff, N. and Kassam, A. (2002) 'A review of agricultural research issues raised by the system of rice intensification (SRI) from Madagascar: opportunities for improving farming systems for resource-poor farmers', *Agricultural Systems*, 71(3): 249–74.

Stoop, W. and Kassam, A. (2005) 'The SRI controversy: a response', *Field Crops Research*, 91(2–3): 357–60.

Sumberg, J. and Okali, C. (1997) *Farmers' Experiments: Creating Local Knowledge*. Boulder, CO: Lynne Rienner.

Timmer, W. J. (1947) *Object en Methode der Sociale Agronomie* [*The Object and Method of Social Agronomy*]. Wageningen, the Netherlands: Veenman.

Uphoff, N. (1999) 'Agroecological implications of the System of Rice Intensification (SRI) in Madagascar', *Environment, Development and Sustainability*, 1(3–4): 297–313.

Uphoff, N. (2003) 'Higher yields with fewer external inputs? The system of rice intensification and potential contributions to agricultural sustainability', *International Journal of Agricultural Sustainability*, 1(1): 38–50.

Uphoff, N. (2007) 'Agroecological alternatives: capitalising on existing genetic potentials', *Journal of Development Studies*, 43(1): 218–36.

Uphoff, N., Kassam, A. and Stoop, W. (2008) 'A critical assessment of a desk study comparing crop production systems: the example of the "system of rice intensification" versus "best management practice"', *Field Crops Research*, 108(1): 109–14.

van Veldhuizen, L., Waters-Bayer, A., Ramírez, R., Johnson, D. A. and Thompson, J. (eds) (1997) *Farmers' Research in Practice: Lessons from the Field*. London: Intermediate Technology Publications.

9

'THIS FIELD IS OUR CHURCH'

The social and agronomic challenges of knowledge generation in a participatory soil fertility management project

Joshua Ramisch

Contesting the ubiquitous 'participatory' label

Certain types of participation have gained legitimacy among agronomists in national and international research centres, such as 'farmer field schools' and other group-based experimentation or demonstration approaches, and participatory ranking exercises for identifying constraints or evaluating new crop varieties. In addressing the participation imperative, on-farm research engages twin – social and agronomic – objectives: 'empowerment', knowledge sharing, and improved social capital on the one hand, and more effective technology development and promotion on the other, visible as improved crop performance and yields, soil fertility, etc. (Okali et al 1994). However, it is not clear that the research products and data gained from these activities are effectively advancing either farmers' welfare or agronomy.

As participatory, on-farm research has become accepted as 'mainstream' (van Asten et al 2008) and a 'new orthodoxy' (Leeuwis et al 1998), even its proponents remain critical that it has failed to live up to its promised potential (Rola et al 2002; Orr 2003; Nederlof and Dangbégnon 2007). It is indeed worth contesting the 'participatory' label when it is so widely applied, especially where it is used without evident reflection to describe a diversity of practices (or mere rituals?) in nearly every branch of agricultural research (Simpson and Owens 2002). More sceptical observers might consider that, in its ubiquity, the participatory designation is now applied only to give a donor-friendly gloss to business-as-usual.

However, even if institutions and governments are rhetorically committed to participatory research, a project such as the one described in this chapter, which made 'rigorous', participatory research central to its efforts to improve soil fertility management practice, is clearly still at the margins of agricultural research (at least in terms of budgets and staffing). Critics of the project, and by extension participatory research more generally, contended that the complexity of on-farm conditions made the generation of useful (or publishable) data difficult, and that the social challenges of conducting and understanding the research products were 'too time consuming' and 'too complicated' for an agricultural research institute with a finite budget (TSBF–CIAT 2008: 7:25–28; see also Lightfoot and Barker 1988; Davis 2006; Kamau 2007; Braun and Duveskog 2008).

This chapter applies a political agronomy framework to primary material from the author's own experience with participatory, on-farm research in western Kenya. The Folk Ecology Initiative (FEI) was a community-based soil fertility management project that ran from 2001 to 2008, and that explicitly sought to bridge the episte-mological and power differences between scientists and local communities through participatory learning and action. This chapter investigates to what extent the FEI was able to: (i) balance the competing social and scientific demands inherent to a group-based approach; and (ii) generate data and new knowledge useful to both local communities (farmers) and outsiders (agronomists, soil and social scientists, etc.). It is written explicitly from the perspective of a researcher who promoted and defended a participatory project, against both biophysical scientists who felt that on-farm research was a costly way to produce ultimately unusable data, and social scientists who challenged the rigour and depth of the participatory process. The chapter begins by introducing some of the debates relating to group-based approaches to on-farm technology development, such as farmer field schools (FFS). The following sections then introduce the FEI, the politics and implications of its implementation, and the challenges of generating and interpreting data from collective and individual experimentation within the FEI.

A context for group-based, participatory soil fertility management research in Africa

Even in the colonial era, extension agents knew to 'start where farmers are, with what they have, to help them help themselves' (Semana 2002: 1). The effectiveness of contemporary participatory approaches is, however, undermined by a lack of social science capacity in most national (and now many international) agricultural research organisations, which should guide the formulation and implementation of such activities and also analyse their social dimensions and impacts (Johnson et al 2003; German et al 2010). A direct consequence is that most agronomists and other biophysical scientists conducting participatory research are compelled to become 'generalists', learning the skills of facilitation or participatory appraisal on the job and without the benefit of a grounding in broader social scientific literatures or debates (Isubikalu 2007; van Asten et al 2008). It also means that participatory research is often reduced to a limited set of the most popular or accessible 'tools': group-based extension and experimentation in FFS, wealth ranking, participatory varietal appraisals, etc. (Kamau 2007).

The starting point of most extension approaches is that researchers have knowledge or technologies that farmers 'need' to acquire. The assumption is that farmers who then acquire this knowledge will benefit from it, and that others in the same situation will actively seek it out once its utility becomes known (Hagmann et al 1999; Gallagher 2003). Whereas conventional dissemination or extension methods fill this perceived knowledge gap with a unidirectional flow of information (researcher → extension → farmer), there is an element of participation inasmuch as farmers disinterested in the knowledge or technologies on offer will either ignore them, opt out (cf. Misiko 2010), or try to adapt them to their own uses.

However, advocates of participatory on-farm research suggest that the unidirectionality of conventional extension approaches (such as Training and Visit, T&V) limits the effectiveness of knowledge transmission. When the identification and conceptualisation of knowledge 'gaps' as researchable problems begins with researchers' own priorities and interests, or their own understanding of farmers' contexts, these are likely to correspond only partially (if at all) to the problems or 'gaps' identified by farmers. For example, if a research organisation has expertise in a given crop (e.g. maize), it is entirely reasonable to assume that its technical solutions will address ways to overcome the constraints limiting maize yields. However, the importance of maize within the livelihood or food security context might not justify farmers investing time, energy or other scarce resources in making even marginal improvements in their maize yields (cf. Orr 2003).

Finally, if problems are considered rooted in 'ignorance', then the logical solution is 'more extension teaching' (Chambers 1983), with 'increased adoption' an expected indicator of that teaching having produced learning.[1] Group-based extension strategies can actually play into this flawed thinking: if previous approaches failed because they did not train a 'critical mass' of farmers (Witt et al n.d.), then working with groups rather than individual 'contact farmers' can seem a seductively cost-effective way of accelerating dissemination (cf. Youdeowei 2003; Karungi et al 2005). Even if approaches such as FFS emphasise 'adult education' and 'co-learning' by researchers and farmers, they are structured around curricula that are developed first and foremost by research teams, not by the communities themselves (Nederlof 2006). This is not to say that there is something intrinsic to either researchers or extension agents that predisposes them to 'lecturing'. But the premise of FFS is that there is a great deal that farmers in particular need to learn about the invisible worlds of plant ecology or soil nutrients (and indeed about experimental methods) before they can begin to effectively manipulate and innovate with either their current practices or new technologies that are introduced to them. It is easy, therefore, for farmer groups associated with participatory research projects to become conduits for 'more extension teaching' and technology promotion, whether these knowledge 'gaps' have been identified by researchers or the farmers themselves (Isubikalu 2007).[2] It also becomes easy for the success of the FFS to be evaluated by the degree to which participants have acquired detailed knowledge about, or adopted, the technologies that were tested (e.g. Bunyatta et al 2006), rather than evaluating whether participants could test and evaluate new problems and solutions on their own after leaving the FFS (Braun et al 2006; Gallagher et al 2006).

The Strengthening Folk Ecology Initiative (FEI)

The FEI ('Strengthening "Folk Ecology": Community-Based Interactive Farmer Learning Processes and their Application to Soil Fertility'), was implemented from 2001 to 2008

FIGURE 9.1 FEI field sites (2001–08).

by the Tropical Soil Biology and Fertility Institute (TSBF–CIAT) with local governmental and non-governmental partners[3] and funding from the International Development Research Centre (IDRC). In its first phase (2001–4) it operated in four sites in western Kenya, and two more sites were added in 2004 (Figure 9.1; Table 9.1). The sites were situated along an agro-ecological and cultural gradient representative of the region's high (but variable) rainfall, low soil fertility (N- and P-depleted), high population density and history of out-migration.

The intention was specifically to 'strengthen' farmers' existing knowledge rather than change specific practices. This might seem a nuance, but it meant that activities focused on disseminating generic scientific principles relating to soil fertility constraints and plant productivity, rather than promoting specific techniques or technology 'packages'. The project employed a number of participatory tools, especially joint farmer–researcher demonstrations, dialogue, and participatory monitoring and evaluation (PM&E) to facilitate exchange of knowledge. This adaptive learning process of dialogue between farmers' local ecological knowledge ('folk ecology') and outside

TABLE 9.1 Overview of study sites and evolution of farmer research groups (2002–08)

Site name (District)	Population density (people km^{-2})	Annual precipitation (mm)	Average residents per household	Average farm size (ha)	Number of farmer groups		
					2002	2005	2008
1 Emuhaya (Vihiga)	1317	1800–2000	4.5	0.34	3	3	6
2 Mabole (Butere-Mumias)	508	1300–2000	n.d.	n.d.	–	5	12
3 Nyabeda (Siaya)	316	1600–1950	n.d.	n.d.	–	6	18
4 Muyafwa (Busia)	359	1270–1790	4.6	1.39	2	3	17
5 Butula (Busia)	462	1270–1790	4.3	0.92	2	4	20
6 Chakol (Teso)	559	760–1015	5.5	1.85	2	5	21
Total					9	26	94

Source: Muruli et al (1999); Republic of Kenya (2001); author's own data, reported in FEI (2009).

knowledge systems was intended to develop a shared, 'dynamic expertise' of soil fertility management (Ramisch et al 2007).

Although FEI came to be known (in the study sites, internally to TSBF–CIAT and within the Kenyan agricultural development research community) for iterative processes of consultation involving both collective and individual on-farm demonstration trials, the adaptive learning component was rooted in a desire to understand indigenous knowledge relating to soil and soil fertility (Otwoma 2004; Mairura 2005; Misiko 2007: ch. 7; Mairura et al 2007, 2008; Ramisch et al 2012). This included both the agro-ecological knowledge of local soil 'experts' as well as the 'common sense' about soil held by the vast majority of people who knew, or only wanted to know, the basic minimum needed to manage their soils. Attention to the social dynamics of groups and group-based learning was also crucial to understanding why certain groups and their research activities thrived (Misiko et al 2011) while others did not (Misiko 2010). Finally, one of the project's explicit objectives was to show that folk knowledge and practice could be strengthened through repeatable, enduring processes rooted in local institutions, actors and processes that were not inherently reliant on a project's presence. If a 'dynamic expertise' relating to soil fertility management could be created and sustained, it would also answer those critics who believed that farmers were agreeing with scientists only to secure short-term benefits (Misiko 2007: 7).

The FEI team and its approach

The core team of the FEI included an anthropologist (Michael Misiko) who was regularly in the field, a Nairobi-based project leader and anthropologist-geographer (Joshua Ramisch), as well as field-based staff: an agronomist (John Mukalama) and an economist (Isaac Ekise), both of whom had worked previously in the FEI sites for a community-development NGO. The team consulted regularly with soil scientists within TSBF–CIAT (especially Bernard Vanlauwe and later Pablo Tittonell). At the community level, pre-existing self-help groups (typically with 15–25 members) helped provide the FEI with strong community ties, local legitimacy and some degree of local leadership. One of the project objectives was to understand better the internal dynamics of farmer groups, and so, with time, the local participants and the scientific team became better versed in identifying and cultivating appropriate leaders (Misiko 2007; Ramisch et al 2007).

The farmer groups operated under a variety of different labels, largely informed by the level of exposure to (and enthusiasm or contempt for) other agricultural development activities in the area. In Emuhaya, for example, previous research activity had organised local groups as farmer field schools, a name that was retained in some cases, or replaced with 'farmer research group'. In other sites, groups retained their existing identities as 'self-help', 'women's', or 'youth' groups, or added the designation 'research group' or 'field school'.

As discussed below, all the participating groups collectively managed at least one central 'demonstration' site over the life of the project. The FEI often referred to these sites as the 'mother' trials and to individual experiments as 'baby' trials, reflecting the dominance of the 'mother–baby' model for collaborative farmer–scientist experimentation (Snapp et al 2002). This model, whose name was coined by a farmer, originated in Malawi for participatory plant breeding, where data collected on crop performance under the researcher-controlled 'mother' trial could be compared with the results of the same technologies on satellite 'baby' trials on adjacent farms under farmer-managed conditions. The 'mother–baby' model persists in much participatory agricultural research, including situations like the FEI's where the 'mother' trial was jointly designed and controlled by researchers and farmers and was thus not 'pure' researcher-controlled trial. The FEI originally adopted the 'mother–baby' terminology with some trepidation, as it seemed to imply a top-down (or at least vaguely condescending) attitude towards farmer experimentation, which clashed with the project's stated objective of using the learning embodied by individual experimentation to feed back into choices made on the 'mother' trial sites. However, unlike the research team, participating farmers had no issue with the terminology, and even noted that 'babies grow up and have children of their own' (although no-one suggested that children can also teach their mothers …).

Framing the FEI: indigenous soil knowledge beyond ethnopedology

At its inception, the FEI was not contesting agronomic or participatory practices so much as arguing that there was a space in research on indigenous soil knowledge that went beyond ethnopedology (identifying and characterising the local taxonomies of soil types). The initial activities were therefore geared towards broadening the discussion of local soil agro-ecological knowledge to see soil management within its local context. In the terminology of Niemeijer and Mazzucato (2003), identifying and using the 'grammar' (local theories) rather than just the 'sentences' (taxonomies) of local knowledge provides a much clearer insight into how farmers will deal with changing circumstances and new crops than the static way in which local taxonomies are often treated.

The project was furthermore contesting some of the orthodoxies of the day by being explicitly agnostic about possible assumptions relating to local soil knowledge, namely that:

- there are gendered differences in knowledge
- a coherent 'knowledge' of soil exists within a given community
- either there is deep knowledge waiting to be found or that local knowledge will be of limited relevance
- local networks of knowledge generation and sharing exist, and
- these networks can be tapped or enriched with scientific knowledge to 'scale up' the impact of current small-scale projects.

Given the possibility of misrepresentations, these agnosticisms are important when products of different knowledge systems are being 'translated'. As Geertz (1983) has pointed out, fitting local knowledge to our [sic] own frame of reference is a 'translation' in which fundamental things will inevitably get lost or distorted. Applying this notion, an influential study of perceived land degradation in West Africa's forested zone specifically referred to the accumulation of misunderstandings and misrepresentations as *The Lie of the Land* (Leach and Mearns 1996).

The conflict of epistemologies goes even further, as 'scientific' knowledge is often itself deeply contested. Yet scientists continue to see it as their responsibility to help solve the environmental problems they observe, even when many of today's agro-ecological problems stem, in part, from previous science-driven efforts to 'modernise' agriculture (Leeuwis 1999; Mackenzie 2000). A cyclic pattern therefore emerges that whatever the farmer knows or is currently practising is at least partly at odds with the dominant scientific discourse. Examples would be to compare the criticism at Kenyan independence that 'farmers do not use fertilisers' with today's critique that they 'use fertilisers alone without organic inputs' and are therefore depleting their soil's nutrients (Misiko et al 2011). Similarly, we can contrast the facts that farmers were urged to adopt iron hoes and ploughs in western Kenya in the 1940s to increase their labour productivity, while today they are told that such implements cause soil erosion and therefore undermine productivity (Crowley and Carter 2000). Crops that were hailed as modern in the post-independence era, such as maize (especially hybrid varieties) and kale (Kiswahili: *sukuma wiki*), are now blamed for impoverishing farmers and their soils because of 'poor management' (Mango 2002).

Because many farming communities in rural Kenya have only intermittent contact with agricultural researchers, most farmers adopt a highly sceptical attitude towards outsiders' knowledge. Not only do the visitors from outside continually change, but so too do their messages. This mutability (and the sceptical response to it) is reinforced by the political jockeying of local NGOs, who try to win adherents to their projects to demonstrate 'impact' to their donors. In so doing, these outside actors are using polemical presentations of how their message differs from that of 'rival' actors, extolling, for example, the virtues of 'organic' agriculture or agroforestry or farming based on agrochemical inputs as the 'new', 'best' practice. The notion that an existing repertoire of soil fertility management already exists and should be built on does not enter into the equation (Goldberger 2008).

The study sites and their context

Western Kenya was historically neglected by central authorities, and today rural populations contend with poor infrastructure, poor market access, high rates of HIV and AIDS, and widespread, semi-permanent out-migration of young people (predominantly young men) (Crowley and Carter 2000). Agriculture is constrained by both land and labour shortages, while biophysical challenges beyond soil fertility decline include significant climatic variability and widespread crop pests, weeds and diseases.

The FEI involved ethnically distinct communities chosen along an agro-ecological and population density gradient from Vihiga district through Siaya and Butere-Mumias districts to Busia and Teso districts (Figure 9.1; Table 9.1). All six sites had significant, previous engagement with either international or local NGOs working on soil fertility management. However, notwithstanding this long history of project work, research and extension agencies consistently identified these as areas with low adoption rates of new practices such as the use of inorganic fertiliser and improved germplasm (FEI 2009).

Rainfall at the FEI sites is bimodal, with rains falling in the 'long' first season (March–July) and again during the 'short' second season (October–December). Livelihoods are subsistence-based and (as elsewhere in western Kenya) maize is the dominant staple food. Other crops include beans, sweet potatoes, sugarcane (most dominant in Butere-Mumias), bananas, cowpeas, sorghum, millet, cassava, kale and other green vegetables, groundnut (Teso), cotton (Busia and Teso), French beans, green grams and tea (Vihiga).

Implementing the FEI

From its launch, the FEI's scientific team struggled to balance the technical and social dimensions of on-farm experimentation. On the one hand, the activities had to introduce to the communities scientific concepts and technologies of potential utility, in ways that could be meaningfully and rigorously tested by scientists and community members alike. On the other hand, the social motivations for participation in FEI's activities needed to be understood, managed and sustained, even while we followed the evolution of individual and collective knowledge about soils and soil fertility management in the study sites. Since participants learned and mastered concepts at different rates, and consequently made their own decisions about which technologies to use or modify at different stages of the project, a simple yet flexible schedule of activities was needed that could respond to and stimulate the interest of a wide range of participants.

Evolution of activities

The FEI began in 2001 with community interviews held in four sites where TSBF–CIAT had ongoing or recently completed work. These sessions were convened as *barazas* (Kiswahili for official, public meetings called by local authorities) in venues such as churches, community grounds or schools. The interview sessions were designed to establish dialogue between TSBF–CIAT and potentially interested participants about local agricultural opportunities and constraints and soil fertility management, and also to understand – and manage – general expectations relating to outside development actors (Misiko 2007: 8–9). Further meetings discussed farmers' real-life situations to establish personal rapport with representatives from all sections of the community and to build support.

Farmer collaborators clearly expressed a preference for a hands-on, interactive process that would focus on demonstrations and open field events to ensure inclusive participation and plentiful attendance. The scientific team responded by introducing demonstrations relating to the concepts of 'resource quality' (Swift et al 1979; Palm

TABLE 9.2 Number of collective (C) and individual (i) experimental plots within the FEI sites of western Kenya (2002–07)

Technology	2002	2003	2004	2005	2006	2007
Resource quality (maize-bean test crop)	1 C	4 C				
		>30 i	>20 i			
Resource quality (addition to compost)		>20 i	11 i	42 i	60 i	>100 i
Resource quality (local vegetable crops)		6 C				
			8 i			
Inorganic fertiliser (NPK test strips)	1 C	4 C	4 C	4 C	6 C	6 C
'Improved' farmyard manure		3 C				
	6 i	35 i	47 i	80 i	>100 i	>100 i
New legume varieties (soyabean screening)	1 C	4 C			6 C	1 C
		10 i	>60 i	>200 i	>500 i	>1000 i
Legume–cereal rotations		4 C	4 C	4 C	6 C	6 C
			10 i	35 i	>50 i	>60 i
Legume (soyabean)–cereal intercropping			40 i	>100 i	>200 i	>600 i
Legumes for Striga control (legumes, IR maize*)				3 C	4 C	
				15 i	>600 i	>600 i

> Indicates that this count was not exhaustive.
* The seeds of IR (imazapyr-resistant) maize are coated with a Striga-killing herbicide.
Source: Community studies and adapted from Misiko (2007).

et al 2001), which over time developed into testing a wider range of concepts and technologies that responded to local interests (cf. Misiko 2007: 8–10). Table 9.2 shows how rapidly the numbers of participants and research topics grew. Most new topics began on collective experimentation sites ('C') and often spread in subsequent seasons as individual experiments ('i') on private farms.

This table highlights the twin challenges of keeping up with the complexity of research results while meeting the needs of an ever-growing population interested in joining the FEI process. The initial collective trials (in Emuhaya only in 2002, then in Emuhaya, Butula, Muyafwa and Chakol in 2003) were all researcher-designed ideas that responded to the interests raised in the community discussions: the 'resource quality' trials on staple crops to show the relative values of different, locally available organic amendments; the soil nutrient test strips to evaluate the nutrient deficiencies in each site; ways to manage livestock manure in pits better; and the legume–cereal rotation trials to showcase legume-based options for building soil fertility.

The initial participants all built on these concepts (as part of the evolving 'dynamic expertise' of the dialogue between farmers and scientists) with their own individual and new collective experiments, particularly by adapting the 'resource quality' concept (2003–05) and the legume–cereal technologies (2004–08). The first challenge for the scientific team, therefore, was to support these new activities with appropriate technical advice and resources. In applying the 'resource quality' concept to fertilising indigenous vegetables rather than maize, the experimentation process stalled within a few seasons because vegetable seeds were nearly impossible to source in sufficient quantity or quality, and too little was known about how to control the many pests that attacked the trials (especially the fertilised plots). Farmer-to-farmer exchange sustained a longer-term interest in individual experiments that tested the incorporation of different organic materials into compost rather than directly into the soil, but here the scientific team proved unable to provide significant technical support for monitoring or evaluation. The scientific team was best able to support the diverse, individual experiments that adapted the legume–cereal technologies, since multiple actors in the region (public, private and NGO) could provide germplasm, crop husbandry, processing and marketing advice. But even here, there were many technical questions (e.g. about suppression of the parasitic weed *Striga hermonthica*) that were at the limits of scientific knowledge. Farmers' experiments therefore helped highlight new research questions for the scientific team, but in many cases the team's capacity to take these forward was lacking.

While this learning and adaptation was occurring, there were of course new participants attracted by the FEI activities. The second challenge for the project was therefore to continue to welcome and integrate these new participants while still maintaining the interest and enthusiasm of the initial participants. These initial participants quickly determined that the 'resource quality' concept did not need to be continued in the collective demonstrations after 2003, but the legume–cereal trials were maintained in every site from 2003 until the project's end in 2008, even after most participants felt that they had learned its lessons. As one farmer from Butula noted in 2004, 'This field is like a chalkboard. We can take visitors there easily and it holds us all together.' This raises the question, echoed by Braun and Duveskog (2008), of whether the FEI was truly achieving its goal of developing a 'dynamic expertise' of rigorous research skills grounded in the local context or whether the project was merely institutionalizing the outward symbols and forms of research.

Rituals of participatory research: field trials as 'church'

The farmer groups themselves did not hesitate to refer to the symbolic power of their collective activities or the importance of having consistent, ritualistic practices. As an example, farmers in Chakol decided in 2007 to replicate their collective legume–cereal demonstration at a different site 4 km away, an activity which they likened to 'building a church of the same denomination'. According to the local group leader:

> This was part of our scaling-out mission. We decided to preach the same gospel. We liked the trial as designed by TSBF–CIAT because it showed clear

lessons. So we replicated it here for ourselves too, even though many of us already knew the key lessons and some are not practising them.

It is worth noting that the legume–cereal demonstration was copied on this new, collective site in nearly every degree, including the square plots, row planting, the 'control plots' of continuous maize and beans and the fertiliser applications. This despite the fact that group members who had planted legume–cereal combinations on their own farms were typically not using row planting or inorganic fertiliser, or testing their technologies against a formal 'control'.

That farmers in Chakol who already knew the lessons decided not only to repeat the same experiments but also to participate consistently in visits to these trials reflects complex processes of bonding and loyalty that underpin the rituals of most collective action (Bellah 2005). As one farmer put it, 'The presence of a church is a sign of devotion, not salvation.' Like church attendance, participating in the research group activities embodied many social functions, strengthened social networks and facilitated reciprocity beyond the FEI's knowledge exchanges (Misiko et al 2011). Some farmers' irregular participation meant that they missed out on key learning moments and misconstrued the intentions of the project. However, the opportunity of other group members to bring these people 'back to the fold', as one woman put it, 'Gives us the chance to hear the Word [a joking reference to the underlying lessons of the demonstration] again ourselves with fresh ears and perhaps learn something new too.' Learning was thus not a linear process, and the solidarity of the group setting allowed many farmers to revisit their own decisions about technology (non-)use or adaptation. Furthermore, as with many African churches, there were other tangible benefits to participation, including the lunches or sodas provided by researchers, folk arts (songs and dramas prepared by group members), the convivial atmosphere created by host farmers, and contact with interesting visitors.

It could be argued that the scientific team also found a comfortable, even ritualistic focus in the collective trials. The shared history of learning and hardships overcome, the regularity of the field visits for planning, PM&E or dialogue sessions all built more than just 'dynamic expertise' relating to soil fertility management. Visitors to the FEI often remarked on the genuine depth of collaboration and understanding, which was often evident in the 'open days' hosted by the FEI at the collective and individual experiment sites. Follow-up studies showed that many farmers outside the FEI had gained useful messages and ideas from these events, while group members reported feeling re-energised to continue experimenting or using the technologies (FEI 2009; Misiko 2009). By contrast, the field days of FFS elsewhere were reportedly less successful, even seen by their members as a 'funeral' rite to mark the end of the learning process (Isubikalu 2007: 151). Studies in western Kenya (Duveskog et al 2003; Kiptot 2007; Amudavi et al 2009) and elsewhere (Feder et al 2004a, 2004b; Tripp et al 2005; van den Berg and Jiggins 2007) emphasise that learning during field visits and open days relies heavily on good facilitation and follow-up, elements that the FEI had worked hard to institutionalise with both the scientists and communities.

Generating and using data

Although the FEI addressed a wide range of soil fertility-related concepts and technologies (Table 9.2), for simplicity the following sections focus on the project's work with legume–cereal rotations, which involved both collective demonstrations and individual experiments.[4] The legume–cereal work was one of the more complex and long-running elements of the FEI, and became well known in the region and with Kenyan (and Kenya-based) soil scientists. These activities were based on the logic that testing an array of legumes under a range of management regimes would allow farmers to select the most appropriate one(s) for various soil, climate and cropping conditions. The attraction of legumes rests on their multiple potential uses (for food and fodder, biomass incorporation and nitrogen fixation). These potential multiple benefits imply reduced costs for investment in soil fertility, soil structure improvement and erosion control, income generation through marketing and seed production, and the disruption of crop pest and disease cycles (Misiko et al 2008). Western Kenyan farming systems already make use of legumes such as common bean (*Phaseolus vulgaris*), typically intercropped with maize or other cereals. Other legumes that have been promoted in the region include soybean (*Glycine max*) and the inedible cover crop mucuna (*Mucuna pruriens*).

The legume–cereal rotation demonstrations were designed to illustrate two different, new technologies that TSBF–CIAT researchers felt would be useful for improving soil fertility in western Kenya: (i) the potential of legumes (soybean and mucuna, as well as locally known crops such as groundnut) for improving crop yields when grown in rotation with staple cereal crops; and (ii) the optimal use of mineral fertilisers in legume–cereal rotations. While the demonstration approach was considered ideal for showcasing known legume technologies to farmers, since the actual performance of these technologies' under different farm-level circumstances was unknown, an experimental element was unavoidable (Ramisch 2011).

Legume–cereal rotation: collective experimentation

The legume–cereal rotation component of the FEI began with collectively managed demonstrations in each participating community, initiated in the first season (the March–July 'long rains') of 2003. Almost immediately thereafter, individual households began their own experiments, inspired by or adapted from these collectively managed sites.

In each site, the demonstration trials were hosted by farmers whom their groups had identified as popular, well integrated into their communities, and having easily accessible farms representative of local soil types and history of cultivation (e.g. cultivated continually for 20–50 years). As scientists, we had hoped the groups would select sites to demonstrate the new technologies where the soils at least represented the (low) fertility norm in each community. It turned out, however, that many of the participating communities had deliberately selected their most extreme, 'problem soils' (Kiswahili: *udongo tatanishi*), such as fields that were infested with *Striga* or were heavily depleted by decades of continuous cultivation. This might have been because, in this densely settled and intensely cultivated region, these were the only parcels available (at least for free, since the project did not pay to use the land). However, later investigation revealed a local logic that was widespread but initially covert: if potential solutions could be found for such challenging sites, then the new technologies would have proven their ability to solve problems of agricultural productivity on other, less difficult plots (Misiko et al 2011: 30).

Figure 9.2 summarises the design of the legume–cereal rotation trials, which followed the same model at every site. The legume crops tested were planted and fertilised in the 'long rains' of each year. A maize–bean intercrop followed in the second season (the 'short rains'). The design was kept simple so that all four (fertiliser) treatments for a given test legume could be compared on 6 × 6 m contiguous plots. While the pattern of the four cells (no inorganic inputs, N alone, P alone, N+P) was constant across legumes and between sites, the rates of fertiliser application varied depending on the soil fertility status and agronomic recommendation for each site. The phosphorus (triple super-phosphate, TSP) treatments were all on the same (down-slope) side of the path as one walked into the trial. The nitrogen (urea) treatments (alone or with phosphorus) were also always opposite each other on either side of the path for easy comparison. In every site, the first two legumes were the unfamiliar soybean and mucuna, followed by a local legume chosen by the farmer group (e.g. groundnut, yellow gram, green gram or cowpea). The final treatment block was always intercropped maize and common beans, essentially a 'control' treatment equivalent to the standard practice of continuous planting of the region's staple crops in both long and short rains.

While the compact, simple, unreplicated design was at the request of the participating farmers, the decision to put all the phosphorus treatments on the same side reflected the

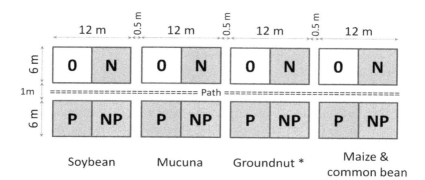

FIGURE 9.2 Layout of the legume–cereal rotation demonstration trial, Butula site, 2004. The legume treatments were planted in the long rain season (see also Figure 9.3a). All sixteen plots were planted with intercropped maize and common beans during the short rain season (Figure 9.3b). Fertiliser treatments were applied at planting in the long rain season: 0, no inputs; N, 45 kg urea ha^{-1}; P, 50 kg TSP ha^{-1}; NP, 45 kg urea and 50 TSP ha^{-1}. *Groundnut was selected by farmer groups as a locally-favoured legume.

FIGURE 9.3 Phosphorus responses of the legume–cereal rotation demonstration trial, Butula site, 2004. (a) Long rains: legume treatments, June 2004; (b) short rains: maize–beans only, October 2004.

scientists' desire to call attention to the fact that soils in the region are quite phosphorus-depleted. The scientists' arguments in favour of phosphorus application (on legumes as well as on the staple crops) were thus bolstered by the dramatic impacts of phosphorus fertilisation visible in both the legume and cereal phases of the rotation (Figure 9.3a and b).

However, it should be noted that farmers drew their own, quite different conclusions about fertilisation from these trials. Although the impacts of phosphorus were noted in the PM&E at crop emergence, and continued through flowering and crop maturation, since legumes were being promoted to farmers as a means of improving soil fertility, a common reaction was that 'a fertiliser should not itself have to be fertilised!'. Indeed, in the sites where the farmer groups had selected groundnuts as their third test legume, the fact that the groundnut (unlike the other legumes or the maize–bean 'control' plots) did *not* respond strongly to phosphorus was taken as a very encouraging sign. 'This is a crop we know very well and can now see is a good one, even under low fertility conditions', a farmer observed in Chakol.

Interpreting the trials: dealing with data

In contrast to a researcher-managed experiment, the demonstration trial plots did not have randomised treatments or replications. The main reason for not including replications was an effort to maintain what farmers and researchers alike considered a clean and easy-to-follow design, a style of demonstration found elsewhere in the region where land is scarce (Mukhwana and Odera 2006). Plots were not randomised for a similar reason, to ensure that all the plots of a legume under different fertiliser treatments could be easily seen and compared side-by-side, rather than scattered within the trial. This was not just the research team's version of a simplified, watered-down or farmer-friendly science (cf. Thrupp 1989), but a layout that was discussed with the participating communities and corresponded to what appeared to be the experimental style typical of the study areas (e.g. unreplicated trials of new treatments immediately beside existing, known practices) (Sumberg and Okali 1997). In the words of the farmers, 'too many plots' (or multiple plots that showed the same treatments) were confusing at best and was-teful of scarce inputs and land at worst. As we were told at a group meeting in Emuhaya, this demonstration was seen as similar to the science experiments that one might conduct at school, 'If these are things that have been proven after decades of research, it is better that we use our little land to demonstrate and learn as many of them as possible.'

One consequence of maximising the number of treatments was that any extra-polation of crop performance from 6 × 6 m plots was very sensitive to error. For example, during the 2004 short rain season, the yield of maize on the 16 plots of the Butula demonstration site (Figure 9.3b) averaged 1.87 kg but ranged from 0.14 to 5.12 kg. To facilitate comparison with performance elsewhere, we would regularly convert these results into yields per hectare, making each 1 kg of biomass or grain yield on the sampled area of the treatment plot (once buffers were excluded this was 22.5 m^2) equal to 444 kg ha^{-1}. However, given the small sizes of most farms in the study sites (see Table 9.1), the largest stand of any given crop is often on the order of 20–30 × 30–50 m, so farmers were not comfortable with thinking in terms of full hectares. Instead, farmers typically assessed their crop production volumetrically, either in '2 kg' cooking oil containers called *gorogoro* or in the bags that would hold 90 kg of shelled maize, and usually for an entire farm season ('last long rains I had 10 bags of maize') rather than at the level of an individual field's productivity.

This meant that PM&E of the demonstration trials was conducted in largely sub-jective terms. The growth characteristics (such as the colour and number of leaves or flowers, plant height or bushiness, number of pods or cobs, etc.) were assessed throughout the season by farmers in weekly group meetings that coincided with weeding or other field tasks (Ramisch et al 2007). Monthly discussions were also organised with the FEI scientific team, which reviewed the concepts behind the demonstration,

FIGURE 9.4 Harvesting a demonstration trial, Emuhaya site, August 2002. (a) Group members count plants in a treatment plot before harvesting; (b) husked maize cobs ready for inspection and weighing.

and whether, how or why those concepts could explain the observed differences in plot performance. Even at harvest, farmers were comparing relatively modest numbers of cobs (Figure 9.4), looking not just at their overall (fresh) weight, but also the size of kernels and the number of rows per cob as indicators of plant vigour.

The use of these local logics for evaluating 'good' results at different points in the growing season proved much more robust than relying solely on the researchers' criteria (Ramisch et al 2007). This is certainly what has been observed elsewhere with more standard 'mother–baby' trials (Snapp et al 2002). While the FEI scientists expected the demonstrations would show tangible effects of mineral P fertiliser (in particular) on legume productivity, the PM&E activities revealed that farmers were not always impressed by these effects. Rather, they commented on the continuing and visible importance of constraints other than soil fertility (e.g. crop diseases like maize streak virus, erratic rainfall and *Striga* infestation), which were also beyond the control of either farmers or researchers.

Without replication or randomisation, the impacts of localised phenomena on crop performance could be amplified in ways that were hard to quantify. While occasionally yields were positively enhanced by 'hotspots' of increased fertility (e.g. from charcoal burning, tree stump clearance, termite mounds or, in one case in Muyafwa in 2003 where cleared weeds had been heaped and burnt on the plots that were meant to be the 'control'), most often the effects were negative. Both the number of plants and their vigour (and ultimate grain or biomass yields) could be undermined by factors such as late and uneven germination (discussed below), seeds being eaten by chickens or wild animals, erosion, hailstones, *Striga* infestation, or attack by crop pests and diseases. Farmers unfamiliar with row planting also often found it difficult (at least at first) to maintain even spacing within rows (e.g. between 17 and 25 holes in a maize planting that should have been 20 holes per row), an error which was not always easily corrected at thinning or weeding given the other sources of potential plant losses mentioned above.

Many of the expected treatment effects were simply overshadowed by this variability, or difficult to discern and often 'taken on faith' pending future seasons' results. The harvest data presented in Table 9.3, from the legume treatment phase grown in Butula during the 2004 long rains (the same plots as in Figures 9.2 and 9.3a), show that the expected pattern of NP > P > N > 'no inputs' is evident only for the grain yields of the continuous maize–bean plots and for the fresh biomass yields of soybeans. For mucuna and groundnuts, the urea-treated plots appeared to have lower yields of biomass and grain than the neighbouring input-free and TSP-only plots. Interpretation of the legume plots was often compromised by the major and unpredictable variation in the numbers of plants surviving until harvest, particularly in the plots where N and P had been combined.

Although the Butula site had been continuously cultivated for 50 years, its conditions and crop performance were not unique. While the high levels of variability, the lack of replication and the difficulty in extrapolating larger-scale performance from a few kilograms of seed or a handful of cobs meant that the research team often left the sites feeling that their technologies were not actually being 'demonstrated', the farmers had more tools at their disposal for interpreting performance. The legume treatment performance in the long rains, and particularly the cereal response in the short rains, were compared with memories of both previous crop (and weed!) yields in the same sites and of equivalent crop stands on local farms. This type of intuitive covariance analysis (Sumberg and Okali 1997: 100) eventually formed the basis for the emerging 'dynamic expertise' of the FEI collaborators through the accumulated experience of multiple seasons of collective experimentation. Indeed, the data from these multi-year trials were eventually even accepted for publication in agronomic journals (e.g. Misiko et al 2008, 2011).The experience of difficult-to-explain variability on the collective sites convinced most FEI participants of the need to repeat the trials either collectively, or modified as individual experiments, to see whether the technology would work under different conditions and also whether over time it would visibly improve the soil or crop performance (particularly on the very degraded sites like those in Butula or Emuhaya).

TABLE 9.3 Harvest characteristics, legume treatment phase, Butula site, long rains (July) 2004

		Soybean		Mucuna		Groundnut		Maize	
		0 N	+ N	0 N	+ N	0 N	+ N	0 N	+ N
0 P	No. plants*	530	497	222	186	494	356	60	85
	Biomass†	0.12	0.88	0.72	0.55	1.21	0.95	0.39	1.19
	Grain‡	0.06	0.44	0.20	0.15	0.43	0.32	0.04	0.25
+ P	No. plants*	626	529	172	170	412	363	120	78
	Biomass†	0.90	1.08	2.63	2.15	2.75	1.67	3.06	3.28
	Grain‡	0.44	0.45	0.88	0.77	1.29	0.53	0.45	1.04

*Number of crop plants harvested within the sample areas (22.5 m^2 for maize, soybean; 24 m^2 for Mucuna; 25.5 m^2 for groundnut).
†Total mass of fresh matter (grain, stems, leaves, pods/haulms/cobs) at harvest in T ha^{-1}.
‡Total dry grain mass at harvest in T ha^{-1}.

Interpreting the trials: scientists as 'not very good farmers'

While some literature on farmer-managed experiments suggests that farmers will 'assist' poorly performing control (or other) plots by secretly fertilising or otherwise tending them, this was not something we observed. Farmers were, however, embarrassed by, or openly critical of, plots with technologies that appeared not to deliver the promised benefits. Echoing our research team's own language of 'validated technologies' or 'best bet options', farmers in Emuhaya told us, 'We are counting on you to bring us new, good things that you have seen elsewhere and that can make a difference for us here.' This assumption that *all* the treatments on display in the demonstrations – including the miserable performance of unfertilised control treatments – were 'good things' inherently worth using had some participants trying to rationalise the outcomes, but left many others initially disappointed with the project (Ramisch 2011):

> When I saw those stems without any cobs, looking so dry, I thought: if [you, the] researchers can't grow maize here – ayi! – what can we do. We were counting on the project for help but even me I can grow better looking maize than that.
>
> *(Female farmer, Emuhaya 2003)*

A more persistent and problematic reason why many farmers (especially those not participating in the FEI) were disappointed by the performance of the demonstrations related to logistical challenges of jointly managed, participatory research. Because of the group-centred approach, all decisions about land preparation and planting required consultation within the groups, and between groups and the scientific team. Mobile telephony (which became widely available even in rural Kenya over the lifetime of the project) greatly assisted in communication, but nevertheless any gathering of community members (to work on the collective plots or to visit them for PM&E) required substantial coordination. Add to this the need for a relatively small project staff to requisition vehicles and drivers from the regional office, to coordinate activities in four (and later six) sites that were as far as 150 km apart, and the institutional bureaucracy of deploying finances to purchase seed or the necessary inputs, and it was little wonder that the demonstration trials were regularly planted several weeks later than the communities (or scientists) considered to be ideal. Frustrations with the late planting (and in several seasons the poor-quality seed that had been acquired by the project team) were always met with vows to do better next time, but were systematically hard to overcome.

Individual experiments: creative complexity

The Kiswahili term for 'experiments' (*majaribio*) means 'things that are tried'. The collectively managed 'demonstrations' were referred to typically as *majaribio ya kuelimisha*, 'things that are tried for purposes of teaching', a special case of the general category of 'things that are tried'. The contrast between this Kiswahili terminology (which was jointly agreed between farmers and researchers) and the English word 'demonstration' is important. In English, we were merely *showing* farmers a range of previously validated technologies (often referred to within TSBF–CIAT project documents as a 'basket of options') with the objective that farmers would choose the most appealing ones. The Kiswahili term belies a deeper level of trying (*kujaribu*) and therefore contingent experimentation. As noted above, these technologies had yet to prove themselves in the local context, and for most participants the collectively managed demonstrations were the first opportunity to see legume–cereal rotations in operation.

However, the process nature of how the experiments were being evaluated can be seen in the shift in group behaviour over the life of the FEI. By 2006, the farmer groups in most sites were combining their routine PM&E visits to the collective demonstrations with visits to experiments that individuals were conducting on their own farms. By the end of the FEI project in 2008, the collective demonstrations still retained the symbolic and instructional roles discussed earlier but the centre of attention had very clearly shifted toward assessing the viability and utility of the technologies on offer in a broader range of 'real-life' contexts over multiple seasons.

These individual experiments played a number of different roles (explored in more depth by Ramisch et al 2007 and Ramisch 2011): (i) 'validating' what had been seen on the collective site, as would be expected from the 'mother–baby' model (Snapp et al 2002); (ii) adapting the technology or concept more comprehensively for use; (iii) exploring new or alternate uses for the technology; and (iv) a more ritualistic use of the technology to symbolically reaffirm 'participation' in the research project. These individual experimental sites also had the virtue of effectively showcasing the performance of the currently most favoured technologies (e.g. the growing popularity of soybean 2006–08), whereas the demonstration sites retained the role of testing and promoting additional new and unfamiliar technologies.

Adapting and innovating with technologies

In a 2006 study, the vast majority of farmer experiments (186 of 201; 93 per cent) were adaptations or new uses of the concepts and technologies from the collective demonstrations (Misiko 2009: 410). For example, the temporal, 'rotation' element of the legume–cereal trials was modified to test spatial, 'intercropping' combinations of the crops. Farmers who had appreciated the benefits of inorganic fertilisers observed that it was more economic to purchase diammonium phosphate (DAP), which combines N and P (18:46:0), than to use urea and the harder-to-locate TSP that the collective demonstration had featured to show the distinct impacts of the nutrients. Finally, many farmers had observed that the new legumes appeared to suppress *Striga* germination on the collective sites, and they developed individual experiments to test this hypothesis.

Figure 9.5 shows the layout of one household's adaptation of the legume–cereal rotation concept in Muyafwa in 2004, the year following the first demonstration. The farmer explained her design as simultaneously testing the following ideas:

Would soybean suppress *Striga*? She noted some *Striga* germinating and dying before flowering in the soybean plot in the long rains season. *Striga* infestation of the maize–bean crop in the short rains appeared to be milder than in 2003, but not reduced by the 75 per cent that had been her target for success.

Could maize and soybean be intercropped? She tried one row of maize planted between three rows of soybean in both seasons of 2004, and found that maize grew without too much competition from the soybean, which also yielded well. In 2005, she and other farmers in the study sites tested two rows maize to two rows of legume, which was promoted by an NGO in the region as the *mbili* (Kiswahili for 'two') system (Tungani et al 2002).

Does DAP improve the performance of maize? In comparison with previous years, the answer appeared to be yes, although the incorporation of soybean residue after the first season harvest was considered to be a contributing factor. For financial reasons, the household did not apply DAP in 2005.

Is it better to plant the maize rotation in the more reliable, long rains (this is the normal, local practice) **or in the short rains** (as had been the case on the demonstration trial)? The harvest of maize after the short rains was noticeably higher than it had been in 2003 (she attributed this to the effects of DAP, soybean, and reduced *Striga*) but less that the yield after the 2003 long rains, which suggested to her that maize is best grown in the longer season.

This experiment (and others like it) stimulated a lot of discussion about inter-cropping versus rotation, about the appropriate timing of a legume in a rotation, and about *Striga* suppression. Farmers made comparisons and drew parallels with their own farms or experiments using only crude quantification. Unlike the demonstration trials, which included a 'control' that was supposed to represent the local farmer

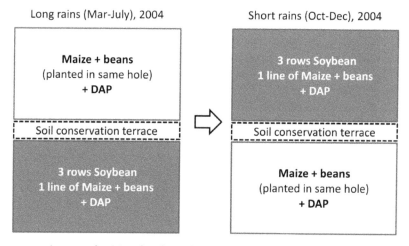

FIGURE 9.5 Layout of a Muyafwa household's individual experiment in the long and short rain seasons of 2004. Both plots (above and below the terrace bund) were roughly 10 m long and 35 m wide. The lower plot was heavily infested with *Striga hermonthica*. DAP = diammonium phosphate (18:46:0) fertiliser applied at planting.

practice, individual experiments only tested the new technologies or concepts and compared their performance against either remembered yields on the same plot in previous season or the crop performance on surrounding farms. As one farmer in Chakol put it, ' … we know control; simply look around if you wish to know the poor plant growth we are trying to reverse'.

The scientific team did its best to follow these individual trials but, as the designs and data collection (if any) did not follow a uniform protocol, this documentation was largely anecdotal. This meant that they were difficult to draw statistical conclusions from to aid the individual farmers or their groups, and even more difficult to publish. Describing a similar situation of diverse, farmer-run experiments, an agronomist working in the Kenya Agricultural Research Institute (KARI) commented, 'If I can't show it at headquarters [because of its non-standard design and lack of quantification], then it doesn't exist.'

Challenges and implications of the FEI experience

The FEI spent over eight years working to foster a 'dynamic expertise' of soil fertility management that incorporated both scientists' and local farmers' knowledge and experience. It did so during the same time period that FFS were promoted by KARI as the favoured model for technology development and promotion throughout Kenya (Bunyatta et al 2006). As a project of an international agricultural research centre within the CGIAR, the FEI addressed the participation imperative of the time (Ashby et al 2000), and was regularly presented as evidence that soil management could be an entry point for participatory research on natural resource issues (e.g. CIAT 2005: 16).

However, as this chapter shows, both participation and research elements of the participatory research had their ambiguities and challenges. While personally and professionally satisfying to the FEI's team (scientists and farmers alike), in terms of broader impact the number of farmers influenced was relatively modest: growing from roughly 200 participants in 2001 to no more than 2500 in 2008. Group-based participatory research is not meant to be a substitute for extension (Davis 2006), but in the absence of a functional national extension service, and with the proliferation of KARI- or NGO-run field schools to both test and promote innovations (Duveskog et al 2003), it was easy for critics to fault the FEI as an expensive way to interact with a small number of communities.

At the same time, despite the groups' language of 'churches' and the ritualised practices, there was enough evidence of both a 'dynamic expertise' of soil fertility management and experimentation and a social cohesion to sustain the groups' activities after the project's end (FEI 2009; Misiko 2009). In other words, the groups were not simply mechanically repeating elements of an outsiders' curriculum (Braun et al 2006; Isubikalu 2007) nor strategically parroting the project's attitudes in the hopes of further patronage (Misiko 2007).

Indeed, the processes of collective and individual experimentation, PM&E and dialogue within the FEI helped both farmers and scientists to adapt their 'normal' experimentation and learning styles towards shared language and practice (Table 9.4). This 'dynamic expertise' relied heavily on site- and season-specific observation and

TABLE 9.4 Experimentation styles in FEI sites compared with 'conventional' experiments designed by researchers or farmers in western Kenya

Characteristic	Conventional, researcher-managed trial	Jointly managed FEI 'demonstration trial'	FEI individual experiment	Typical western Kenyan individual experiment
Number of treatments	Few	Many	Few	Few
Factors tested	One at a time, interactions isolated	One at a time, interactions isolated	All at once, many variables carefully observed	All at once, many variables carefully observed
Plot shape	Square	Square	Irregular	Irregular
Plot size	Small and equal	Small and equal	Variable	Variable
Plot husbandry	Row planting	Row planting	Row or broadcast planting	Row or broadcast planting
Plot basal spraying or fertilisation	Yes (to isolate confounding factors)	No (except to control major pest or weed problems)	No (would be considered a treatment)	No
Replication	Essential (for valid statistical analysis)	No (to make fullest use of space)	No, or perhaps paired with	No (to make fullest use of space)
Numbers (quantification)	Yes (essential for statistical analysis)	Visual analysis as important as quantification	Visual analysis with few numbers	Visual analysis with few numbers
Control plots	Yes (essential for baseline data)	Yes (essential for baseline data)	No (baseline 'known')	No (baseline 'known')
Who is it for?	1 Research team 2 Scientific community	1 Local community 2 Research team	1 That household 2 Local community	That household only
Serendipity	Confounding factors isolated and controlled	Confounding factors monitored and explained	Confounding factors monitored and explained	Confounding factors monitored and explained
Conclusions from	Specific data measurements	Specific data measurements, observation and comparisons	Observation, memory and comparisons	Observation, memory and comparisons

explanation, and the accumulation of (at least partially quantified?) memories of pre-vious seasons' results. In the case of farmers' experiments, these were not rehearsals for future practice – rather, they were being lived in real time and played out with the resources that could actually be managed that season. The FEI's collective experiments became similar, real-time performances that were tied to the seasons and circumstances of each site, with all the messiness of data and interpretation that that entailed (Ramisch 2011). Farmers made decisions to use or reject technologies and concepts that the scientific team often felt were 'hasty', based on very partial or interim results. But even the FEI's more formal interpretations of the collective trials often relied heavily on contextual explanations (e.g. of rotation effects or the impacts of burning or late planting) that farmers did not always find convincing.

In the end, neither participation nor soil science emerged from the FEI unaltered. The social research findings continue to bear fruitful investigation, for example relating to the dynamics of participation (Misiko 2010) or experimentation as per-formance (Ramisch 2011). Elements of the FEI's approach – such as its diagnostic (Chianu et al 2006) and consultative processes (Tittonell et al 2005) – were even applied by non-social scientists within TSBF–CIAT as part of efforts to build 'dynamic expertise' in collaboration with other communities. However, the most cited papers emerging from the FEI remain rather utilitarian ones about using local indicators of soil fertility status (Barrios et al 2006; Mairura et al 2007, 2008) rather than those that discuss the challenge of applying soil scientific procedures to respond to farmers' priorities (e.g. Misiko et al 2008; Misiko 2009). As this chapter shows, the challenge for participatory research projects is not only learning how to listen to farmers, or to learn how to farm (or experiment) like them, but to be able to respond effectively with relevant technologies, inputs and advice. Farmers in the study sites effectively used the rituals of the participatory approach to sustain elements of the FEI and its technology generation process that they believed were worthwhile. The research team, and perhaps even the host institute, were humbled by the difficulty of keeping pace with the enthusiasm of that local participation.

Notes

1 Of course, this is too narrow a metric to explain technology choices. Critics will point out that it is more likely that farmers do not adopt technologies because they are wise, not because they are ignorant (Asiabaka 2002).

2 The culture of deference to extension agents (greeted in Swahili as *Bwana Officer*) is often deeply entrenched, even among younger farmers who did not necessarily live through the colonial or state-run T&V eras (Oniang'o 2002). Active facilitation efforts are needed to transcend such deferential attitudes, but such efforts are easily undermined if the curriculum or the topics identified require long periods of exposition and demonstration of 'education' by outsiders.

3 Partners included African Highlands Initiative (AHI), the Kenyan Agricultural and For-estry Research Institutes (KARI, KEFRI), Ministry of Agriculture (MoA), and local NGOs such as the Appropriate Rural Development Agricultural Programme (ARDAP), Kenya Agricultural Productivity Project (KAPP), Farm Inputs Promotion Services (FIPS), World Neighbours, and the Sustainable Community Based Input Credit Scheme (SCOBICS).

4 For analysis of local knowledge and attitudes towards soil nutrients and inorganic fertilisers, see Misiko et al (2011). For discussion of the local logic of organic resource use, see Ramisch et al (2007) and Misiko (2007: ch 4). For discussion of participatory research and soybean screening in the FEI sites, see Misiko et al (2008).

References

Amudavi, D.M., Khan, Z.R., Wanyama, J.M., Midega, C.A.O., Pittchar, J., Hassanali, A. and Pickett, J.A. (2009) 'Evaluation of farmers' field days as a dissemination tool for push-pull technology in Western Kenya', *Crop Protection*, 28: 225–35.

Ashby, J.A., Braun, A.R., Gracia, T., Guerrero, M.P., Hernandez, L.A., Quiros, C.A. and Roa, J.A. (2000) *Investing in Farmers as Researchers: Experiences with Local Agricultural Research Committees in Latin America.* Cali: CIAT. www.ciat.cgiar.org/downloads/pdf/Investing_farmers.pdf

Asiabaka, C.C. (2002) 'Promoting sustainable extension approaches: farmer field school (FFS) and its role in sustainable agricultural development in Africa', *International Journal of Agriculture and Rural Development*, 3: 46–53.

Barrios, E., Delve, R.J., Bekunda, M., Mowo, J., Agunda, J., Ramisch, J.J., Trejo, M.T. and Thomas, R.J. (2006) 'Indicators of soil quality: a South–South development of a methodological guide for linking local and technical knowledge', *Geoderma*, 135: 248–59.

Bellah, N.R. (2005) 'Durkheim and ritual', in: Alexander, J.C. and Smith, P. (eds) *The Cambridge Companion to Durkheim.* Cambridge: Cambridge University Press, pp. 183–210.

Braun, A. and Duveskog, D. (2008), *The Farmer Field School Approach – History, Global Assessment and Success Stories,* Background Paper for the IFAD Rural Poverty Report 2010. www.ifad.org/rural/rpr2010/background/1.pdf

Braun, A., Jiggins, J., Röling, N., van den Berg, H. and Snijders, P. (2006) *A Global Survey and Review of Farmer Field School Experiences.* Nairobi/Wageningen: International Livestock Research Institute/Endelea. www.share4dev.info/kb/output_view.asp?outputID=1880

Bunyatta, D.K., Mureithi, J.G., Onyango, C.A. and Ngesa, F.U. (2006) 'Farmer field school effectiveness for soil and crop management technologies in Kenya', *Journal of International Agricultural and Extension Education*, 13(3): 47–63.

CIAT (2005) *CIAT in Focus 2004–2005: Getting a Handle on High-value Agriculture,* Annual Report of the Centro Internacional de Agricultura Tropical (CIAT), Cali, Colombia. http://webapp.ciat.cgiar.org/newsroom/pdf/ciat_in_focus_2004_2005_full_color.pdf

Crowley, E.L. and Carter, S.E. (2000) 'Agrarian change and the changing relationships between toil and soil in Maragoli, Western Kenya (1900–994)', *Human Ecology*, 28(3): 383–414.

Chambers, R. (1983). *Rural Development: Putting the Last First.* London: Longman.

Chianu, J., Vanlauwe, B., Mukalama, J., Adesina, A. and Sanginga, N. (2006) 'Farmer evaluation of improved soybean varieties being screened in five locations in Kenya: Implications for research and development', *African Journal of Agricultural Research*, 1(5): 143–50.

Davis, K. (2006) 'Farmer Field Schools: boon or bust for extension in Africa?', *Journal of International Agricultural and Extension Education*, 13(1): 91–97.

Duveskog, D., Mburu, C. and Critchley, W. (2003) 'Harnessing indigenous knowledge and innovation in farmer field schools', in CIP-UPWARD (eds) *Farmer Field Schools (FFS): Emerging Issues and Challenges.* Los Baños, the Philippines: International Potato Centre (CIP) – User Perspectives with Agricultural Research and Development (UPWARD), pp. 197–209.

Feder, G., Murgai, R. and Quizon, J.B. (2004a) 'Sending farmers back to school: the impact of farmer field schools in Indonesia', *Review of Agricultural Economics*, 26: 45–62.

——(2004b) 'The acquisition and diffusion of knowledge: the case of pest management training in farmer field schools, Indonesia', *Journal of Agricultural Economics*, 55(2): 217–39.

FEI [Folk Ecology Initiative] (2009) *Strengthening 'Folk Ecology': Applying Community-based Learning and Communication Strategies to Improve Soil Fertility and Livelihoods in Western Kenya,* Final Technical Report, IDRC Project no. 103081 (February 19), http://idl-bnc.idrc.ca/dspace/handle/10625/41595

Gallagher, K. (2003) 'Fundamental elements of a farmer field school', *LEISA Magazine* (March): 5–6.

Gallagher, K.D., Braun, A. and Duveskog, D. (2006) 'Demystifying farmer field school concepts', paper prepared in response to *Journal of International Agricultural and Extension Education* paper by K. Davis. www.jatropha.pro/PDF%20bestanden/FFS%20demystification.pdf

Geertz, C. (1983) *Local Knowledge: Further Essays in Interpretive Anthropology*. New York: Basic Books.

German, L., Ramisch, J.J. and Verma, R. (2010) 'Agriculture, natural resource management, and "development" beyond the biophysical', in German, L., Ramisch, J.J. and Verma, R. (eds) *Beyond the Biophysical: Knowledge, Culture, and Power in Natural Resource Management*. New York: Springer, pp. 1–21.

Goldberger, J.R. (2008) 'Non-governmental organizations, strategic bridge building, and the "scientization" of organic agriculture in Kenya', *Agriculture and Human Values*, 25(2): 271–89.

Hagmann, J., Chuma, E., Murwira K. and Connolly, M. (1999) *Putting Process into Practice: Operationalizing Participatory Extension*, Network Paper No. 94. London: Overseas Development Institute, Agricultural Research and Extension Network (AGREN). www.odi.org.uk/work/projects/agren/papers/agrenpaper_94.pdf

Isubikalu, P. (2007) 'Stepping-stones to improve upon functioning of participatory agricultural extension programmes: farmer field schools in Uganda', PhD thesis, Wageningen University, the Netherlands.

Johnson, N., Lilja, N. and Ashby, J. (2003) 'Measuring the impact of user participation in agricultural and natural resource management research', *Agricultural Systems*, 78: 287–306.

Kamau, G.M. (2007) 'Researching with farmers: a study of KARI participatory research practices in context', PhD thesis, Wageningen, the Netherlands.

Karungi, J., Isubikalu, P., Nampala, P., Semana, A.R. and Adipala, E. (2005) 'Enhancing university-based outreach through a Farmer Field School's approach: experiences and lessons from Uganda', *African Crop Science Conference Proceedings*, 7: 827–31. www.acss.ws/Upload/XML/Research/620.pdf

Kiptot, E. (2007) 'Seeing beyond fertiliser trees: a case study of a community-based participatory approach to agroforestry research and development in western Kenya', PhD thesis, Wageningen University, the Netherlands.

Leach, M. and Mearns, R. (eds) (1996) *The Lie of the Land: Challenging Received Wisdom on the African Environment*. Oxford: James Currey.

Leeuwis, C. (1999) 'Science and integral design in agriculture and resource management', in Leeuwis, C. (ed.) *Integral Design: Innovation in Agriculture and Resource Management*, Wageningen University, the Netherlands: Mansholt Institute, pp. 1–13.

Leeuwis, C., Röling, N. and Bruin, G. (1998). 'Can the farmer field school replace the T&V system of extension in sub-Saharan Africa?', paper presented at the *15th International Symposium of the Association for Farming Systems Research-Extension*, Pretoria, South Africa, 30 November–4 December, pp. 493–97.

Lightfoot, C. and Barker, R. (1988) 'On-farm trials: a survey of methods', *Agricultural Administration and Extension*, 30: 15–23.

Mackenzie, F.D. (2000) 'Contested ground: colonial narratives and the Kenyan environment 1920–45', *Journal of Southern African Studies*, 26(4): 697–718.

Mairura, F.S. (2005) 'Identification of local plants as indicators of soil quality in the Eastern African region', MSc thesis, Institute of Environmental Sciences (IES), Kenyatta University, Nairobi, Kenya.

Mairura, F.S, Mugendi, D.N., Mwanje, J.I., Ramisch, J.J., Mbugua, P.K. and Chianu, J. (2007) 'Integrating scientific and farmers' evaluation of soil quality indicators in central Kenya', *Geoderma*, 139: 134–43.

Mairura, F.S., Mugendi, D.N., Mwanje, J.I., Ramisch, J.J., Mbugua, P.K. and Chianu, J. (2008) 'Scientific evaluation of smallholder land use knowledge in Central Kenya', *Land Degradation and Environment*, 19: 77–90.

Mango, N.A.R. (2002) 'Husbanding the land: agrarian development and socio-technical change in Luoland, Kenya', PhD thesis, Wageningen University, the Netherlands.

Misiko, M. (2007) 'Fertile ground?: Soil fertility management and the African smallholder', PhD thesis, Wageningen University, the Netherlands.

Misiko, M., Tittonell, P., Ramisch, J.J., Richards, P. and Giller, K.E. (2008) 'Integrating new soybean varieties for soil fertility management in smallholder systems through participatory research: Lessons from western Kenya', *Agricultural Systems*, 97:1–12.

Misiko, M. (2009) 'Collective experimentation: lessons from the field', *Journal of Agricultural Education and Extension*, 15(4): 401–16.

——(2010) '"Opting out": a case study of smallholder rejection of research in western Kenya', in German, L., Ramisch, J.J. and Verma, R. (eds) *Beyond the Biophysical: Knowledge, Culture, and Power in Natural Resource Management*. New York: Springer, pp. 129–48.

Misiko, M., Tittonell, P., Giller, K.E. and Richards, P. (2011) 'Strengthening understanding and perceptions of mineral fertilizer use among smallholder farmers: evidence from collective trials in western Kenya', *Agriculture and Human Values*, 28: 27–38.

Mukhwana, E.J. and Odera, J (2006) 'Best-bet comparison of soil fertility management recommendations in western Kenya: Independent testing by non-governmental organisations', paper presented at the *10th KARI Biennial Scientific Conference*, Nairobi, Kenya 12–17 November 2006. www.kari.org/fileadmin/publications/10thproceedings/Volone/BestBet Comparison.pdf

Muruli, L.A., London, D.M., Misiko, M.T., Okusi, K., Sikana, P. and Palm, C. (1999) 'Strengthening research and development linkages for soil fertility: pathways of agricultural information dissemination', unpublished report to IDRC. Nairobi: TSBF & Institute of African Studies.

Nederlof, E.S. (2006) 'Research on agricultural research: towards a pathway for client-oriented research in West Africa', PhD thesis, Wageningen University, the Netherlands.

Nederlof, E.S. and Dangbégnon, C. (2007). 'Lessons for farmer-oriented research: experiences from a West African soil fertility management project', *Agriculture and Human Values*, 24:369–87.

Niemeijer, D. and Mazzucato, V. (2003) 'Moving beyond indigenous soil taxonomies: local theories of soils for sustainable development', *Geoderma*, 111: 403–24.

Okali, C., Sumberg, J. and Farrington, J. (1994) *Farmer Participatory Research: Rhetoric and Reality*. London: IT Publications.

Oniang'o, R.K. (2002) 'Making a difference in a rural community', paper presented at CODESRIA-IFS *Sustainable Agriculture Initiative Workshop*, 15–16 December 2002, Kampala, Uganda. www.codesria.org/IMG/pdf/Oniango.pdf

Orr, A. (2003) 'Integrated pest management for resource-poor African farmers: is the emperor naked?' *World Development*, 31(5): 831–45.

Otwoma, N.J. (2004) 'The role of indigenous knowledge in the management of soil fertility among smallholder farmers of Emuhaya division, Vihiga district 2001–2004', MA thesis, Institute of African Sciences (IES), University of Nairobi, Nairobi, Kenya.

Palm, C.A., Gachengo, C.N., Delve, R.J., Cadish, G. and Giller, K.E. (2001) 'Organic inputs for soil fertility management in tropical agroecosystems: application of an organic resource database', *Agriculture, Ecosystems and Environment*, 83: 27–42.

Ramisch, J.J. (2011) 'Experiments as "performances": interpreting farmers' soil fertility management practices in western Kenya', in Goldman, M., Nadasdy, P. and Turner. M.D. (eds) *Knowing Nature, Transforming Ecologies: Science, Power, and Practice*. Chicago, IL: University of Chicago Press, pp. 280–95.

Ramisch, J.J., Misiko, M.T., Ekise, I.E. and Mukalama, J.B. (2007) 'Strengthening "folk ecology": community-based learning for integrated soil fertility management, western Kenya', *International Journal of Agricultural Sustainability*, 4(2): 154–68.

Ramisch, J.J., Misiko, M.T, Mairura, F.S. and Otwoma, N.T. (2012) 'Whose land degradation counts? Contentious understandings of soil fertility management in Western Kenya', *Land Degradation and Development*, in press.

Republic of Kenya (2001) *The 1999 Population and Housing Census. Counting Our People for Development*, Vol. 1. Nairobi: CBS.

Rola, A.C., Quizon, J.B. and Jamias, S.B. (2002) 'Do farmer field school graduates retain what they learn? An investigation of Iloilo, Philippines', *Journal of International Agricultural and Extension Education*, 9(1): 65–76.

Semana, A.R. (2002) 'Agricultural extension services at crossroads: present dilemma and possible solutions for future in Uganda', paper presented at *CODESRIA–IFS Sustainable Agriculture Initiative Workshop*, 15–16 December 2002, Kampala, Uganda. www.codesria. org/IMG/pdf/Semana.pdf

Simpson, B.M. and Owens, M. (2002) 'Farmer field schools and the future of agricultural extension in Africa', *Journal of International Agricultural and Extension Education*, 9(2): 29–36.

Snapp, S.S., Kanyama-Phiri, G., Kamanga, B., Gilbert, R. and Wellard, K. (2002) 'Farmer and researcher partnerships in Malawi: developing soil fertility technologies for the near-term and far-term', *Experimental Agriculture*, 38: 411–31.

Sumberg, J. and Okali, C. (1997) *Farmers' Experiments: Creating Local Knowledge*. Boulder, CO: Lynne Rienner.

Swift, M.J., Heal, O.W. and Anderson, J.M. (1979) *Decomposition in Terrestrial Ecosystems*. Oxford: Blackwell Scientific Publications.

Tittonell, P., Vanlauwe, B., Leffelaar, P.A., Sheppard, K.D. and Giller, K.E. (2005) 'Exploring diversity in soil fertility management of smallholder farms in western Kenya: II. Within-farm variability in resource allocation, nutrient flows and soil fertility status', *Agriculture, Ecosystems and Environment*, 110: 166–84.

Thrupp, L. (1989) 'Legitimatizing local knowledge: "Scientized Packages" or empowerment for Third World people', in D. M. Warren, J. Slikkerveer and S. Titilola (eds), *Indigenous Knowledge Systems: Implications for Agriculture and International Development*, Studies in Technology and Social Change No. 11. Ames, IA: Iowa State University, Technology and Social Change Program, pp. 138–53.

Tungani, J.O., Mukwana, E. and Woomer, P.L. (2002) *MBILI is Number 1: A Handbook for Innovative Maize–Legume Intercropping*. Bungoma, Kenya: SACRED Africa.

Tripp, R., Wijeratne, M. and Piyadasa, V.H. (2005) 'What should we expect from farmer field schools? A Sri Lanka case study', *World Development*, 33: 1705–20.

TSBF–CIAT (2008) *The Folk Ecology Initiative*. www.youtube.com/watch?v=44hjmnrg6Vk

van Asten, P.J.A., Kaaria, S., Fermont, A.M. and Delve, R.J. (2008) 'Challenges and lessons when using farmer knowledge in agricultural research and development projects in Africa', *Experimental Agriculture*, 45: 1–14.

van den Berg, H. and Jiggins, J. (2007) 'Investing in farmers: the impacts of farmer field schools in relation to integrated pest management', *World Development*, 35(4): 663–86.

Youdeowei, A. (2003) 'Farmer field schools: science in action', interviewed by B. Dinham in *Pesticides News*, 61(September): 9–10. www.pan-uk.org/pestnews/Issue/pn61/pn61p9.htm

Witt, R., Waibel, H. and Pemsl, D.E. (n.d.) 'Diffusion of information among small-scale farmers in Senegal: the concept of Farmer Field Schools'. www.econstor.eu/bitstream/ 10419/19855/1/Witt.pdf

10

CONTESTING AGRONOMY THROUGH DISSENT

Experiences from India

C. Shambu Prasad, T.M. Thiyagarjan, O.P. Rupela, Amod Thakur and G.V. Ramanjaneyulu

Introduction

This chapter reflects on current agronomic controversies in India by exploring debates around two agroecological innovations – the System of Rice Intensification (SRI) and Non-Pesticidal Management (NPM). We present these innovations as sites of contestation and focus on the practices and contributions of a group that we refer to as 'dissenting agronomists' (Shambu Prasad 2009a, 2009b, 2011; Quartz 2010). Specifically, we reflect on our own experiences as agricultural scientists who have been active in research on and promotion of these innovations. We argue that important insights into the contribution of agronomic research to sustainability and development objectives can emerge from the study of dissenting agronomists. Of particular interest is their position at the boundaries of the discipline, which means frequent work and collaboration with farmers, civil society organisations, natural and social scientists, and networks outside formal research organisations. Further, we argue that the study of agricultural science 'at the margins', and the dissent that is integral to it, can add significant new insights to our understanding of dynamics of contestation within agronomy.

In the next part of this chapter, we explore the changing context of agricultural science in India through the recent contestation around Bt Brinjal. Following this, we describe the research pathways of four dissenting agronomists (who are also co-authors of this chapter) and their roles vis-à-vis the development and promotion of SRI and NPM. The chapter ends with a brief conclusion arguing that an understanding of dissent must be a central element of the contested agronomy research agenda.

The new context of agricultural science in India

2010 was a year of opening up of debates about Indian agriculture. The decision by the Minister of Environment and Forests, Jairam Ramesh, to declare a moratorium on further trials of Bt Brinjal (eggplant, *Solanum melongena*) after a series of widely attended and contested public meetings was unprecedented. The Indian scientific establishment was largely in favour of continuing with the field trials, a position supported (and funded) by private sector organisations and the government's Department of Biotechnology. On the other side were farmers' groups, civil society organisations, and a few sceptical scientists who orchestrated a public outcry over extending genetic engineering to food crops, successfully labelling Bt Brinjal a 'risk technology' and calling for the application of the precautionary principle. Explaining the rationale of a decision that he said was 'both responsive to science and responsible to society', Ramesh quoted extensively from the views of the various state governments. In an important subtext of relevance to this chapter, he also suggested that there could be other ways of reducing the use of pesticides while simultaneously meeting food security objectives. He specifically referred to the spread of NPM to over 600,000 farmers and 2 million acres in the state of Andhra Pradesh (Andhra Pradesh), but fell short of suggesting that this was a successful agroecological method of pest control.[1]

The decision was met with resistance from researchers, the genetic engineering lobby, and the Ministry of Agriculture and Ministry of Science and Technology. In response, the Department of Biotechnology introduced the Biotechnology Regulatory Authority (BRAI) Bill that would empower the government to fine or imprison people protesting against genetic engineering. The draft bill was critiqued for being unconstitutional and unethical (Bhargava 2011).

Following this, Ramesh urged the Indian science academies to undertake a comprehensive review of the Bt Brinjal question. In the event, the review panel refused to consider evidence provided by civil society groups and rejected an offer of dialogue. The report that carried the names of the top six academies was released in September 2010 and recommended limited release of Bt Brinjal. Citizens' groups pointed out that the report not only revealed conflicts of interest, but also breached accepted ethical standards by plagiarising substantial extracts from a newsletter supportive of genetic engineering. The report has since been criticised for not being a thorough 'scrutiny of science'[2] and for neither presenting new evidence nor providing a useful synthesis of existing evidence.

We are not interested in judging the merits or otherwise of genetic engineering in general, or of Bt Brinjal in particular. Rather, the Bt Brinjal case simply helps contextualise the present-day dynamics of agricultural research and technology promotion in India. On one hand, this context is characterised by a dominant view within the scientific establishment that favours pathways that are in line with national and international corporate interests, leaving little space for consideration of alternatives. For example, genetic engineering is projected as the only way to meet food security objectives, and there is resistance to any suggestion that society at large should have an opportunity to debate these questions openly. On the other hand, there is increasing push-back from civil society groups, who are demanding a say on key science and technology issues.

While the crisis in agriculture has received a fair amount of media attention, the response of the Indian agricultural establishment has not been sufficiently discussed or critiqued.

With one of the largest agricultural research systems in the world, Indian research suffers from stifling hierarchy, over-specialisation and isolation. India has over 40 specialised crop, horticulture and livestock research centres and directorates, which labour under a culture that discourages interdisciplinary research and engagement with actors outside the R&D system.[3] As a result there are few formal spaces for discussion of different models of research. It is ironic that, while the country has been divided into several agroecological zones, agroecology as a field has no presence or profile within the research establishment.

It is within this context that current research on SRI and NPM in India needs to be situated. Despite the over-specialisation and isolation of the Indian agricultural research establishment, the diverse contexts of its local operations allow for some surprises. In the Indian research system, plant breeders have always had pride of place, but the fact that plant breeding is not central to either SRI or NPM challenged the established hierarchy of knowledge and opened new spaces for other disciplines to take a leading role in their development. In what follows, we explore two examples where dissenting agronomists have gone out of their way to carry out unconventional research and, in so doing, engaged effectively with broader debates.

Research pathways

Dissenting agronomists

Two of the authors of this chapter, Thakur and Thiyagrajan (referred to as T.M.T. henceforth), have conducted research on SRI. T.M.T. was the first researcher from India to become involved with SRI, and one of the first internationally as well. His association with rice and SRI has been captured in his autobiographical essay 'My destiny, my profession' (Thiyagarajan 2010).[4] Thakur continues to work within an Indian Council of Agricultural Research (ICAR) centre, while T.M.T. is retired from Tamil Nadu Agricultural University (Tamil Nadu AU). Two of the other authors, Rupela and Ramanjaneyulu (referred to as Ramoo henceforth) have worked primarily with NPM, but have also had some involvement with SRI. Rupela is retired from ICRISAT (an India-based CGIAR centre) but remains active in promoting low-cost, bio-intensive agriculture relevant to smallholder farmers (referred to as organic farming henceforth). Along with others, he has been actively involved in shaping the NPM work in Andhra Pradesh. Ramoo previously worked for the ICAR and now leads a civil society organisation, the Centre for Sustainable Agriculture (CSA).

While Thakur, T.M.T., Rupela and Ramoo consider themselves to be agronomists, they came to agronomic research via different routes. Thakur was trained as a plant physiologist and did not do any work on rice before joining the Directorate of Water Development, an ICAR research centre at Bhubaneswar (Orissa). T.M.T. is a soil scientist but had only an indirect connection with agronomy in his MSc and PhD work; Rupela is a soil microbiologist; and Ramoo did his PhD on agricultural extension. Curiosity rather than disciplinary background shaped our later research interests: curiosity about fertiliser wastage in irrigated rice (T.M.T.); about fruit and plant growth (Thakur); about microorganisms and their interaction with fertilisers and pesticides (Rupela); and about the gap between research and farming during the Rural Agricultural Work Experience Programme (Ramoo). Except in the cases of Ramoo and T.M.T., the institutional contexts within which we worked did not encourage learning from farmers. We have all used unconventional modes of outreach to circumvent lack of interest in our work on the part of our colleagues within the research establishment.

The System of Rice Intensification

SRI is a methodology for increasing the productivity of irrigated rice by changing the management of the plants, soil, water and nutrients. SRI involves careful planting of young single seedlings (8–12 days old) at a wide spacing (25 cm or more), keeping the soil moist but well drained and well aerated and adding as much compost or other organic material to the soil as possible. Proponents claim that, together, these principles produce 'more with less' due to synergistic effects of plant–soil interactions, and that SRI can make a significant contribution to food security (Gujja and Thiyagarajan 2009). SRI is being promoted or is in use in over 40 countries, with reported benefits including increased yield (50–100 per cent or more), a reduction in seed requirements (up to 90 per cent) and water savings (50 per cent or more). Many SRI users also report a reduction in pests, diseases, grain shattering, unfilled grains and lodging. Promoters such as the SRI International Network and Resources Center suggest that SRI also delivers a whole range of environmental benefits, including reduced use of agricultural chemicals and water, and lower methane emissions.

Observing a serious water crisis in the state of Tamil Nadu, T.M.T. believed that the unconventional approach to water management that is central to SRI deserved to be researched. As Director of Soil and Crop Management, he was able to pursue this and proceeded to create a 'research ecosystem' around SRI. Specifically, he engaged MSc students, conceiving of their research as an integrated series of sub-projects on soil science, agronomy, crop physiology and microbiology, and actively linking them to the nascent international SRI community. T.M.T. was the only Indian scientist at the first international SRI conference in Sanya, China in 2002. He presented some initial findings at the annual meeting of rice scientists in his university in 2001, and followed up after the Sanya conference with large-scale adaptive research trials. SRI had begun to attract the attention of others, including policy-makers and senior research administrators, and by 2004 SRI was integrated into the policy of the Tamil Nadu state government. We estimate that approximately 50 researchers in India have worked on SRI, 20 of whom have worked on it consistently.

It is important to note that T.M.T. chose to work initially on creating a research ecosystem by linking with diverse actors – students, researchers in other disciplines, university administrators, policy-makers and farmers – rather than focus on journal publications alone. Email communications, policy notes and field visits by policy-makers were all used to create awareness and knowledge about SRI.

Through this approach, T.M.T. was ultimately successful in attracting funds for a series of adaptive research trials across the state (there were over 100 such trials in 2004).

Similarly to many others working on or interested in SRI, T.M.T. was one of the members of a growing international SRI network. T.M.T.'s colleague during a visit to Sri Lanka in 2002 was Dr Alapati Satyanarayana, then Director of Extension at the Acharya NG Ranga Agricultural University (ANGRAU) in the neighbouring state of Andhra Pradesh. This introduction to SRI debates led Satyanarayana to extend it to all of Andhra Pradesh's 23 districts in 2003, and gave rise to an extension-led research movement in the state. Satyanarayana contributed to the 'Rice Wars' controversy in 2004, and was one of the respondents to the debate in *Nature* (Shambu Prasad 2006, 2008). However, SRI has not taken off in Andhra Pradesh as it has in Tamil Nadu (Shambu Prasad 2009c). Part of the reason for this is continued resistance on the part of university researchers at ANGRAU, but there are also important ecological differences between the two states. There was a decline in research interest and publications on SRI from ANGRAU following Satyanarayana's retirement.

It was the Rice Wars controversy that attracted Thakur's attention. Thakur first heard of SRI in 2003, a few years after he completed his PhD at IARI. Although his doctoral thesis had nothing to do with rice science or agronomy (it was on the regulation of tomato fruit ripening and enhancement of shelf life), Thakur first became interested in rice while working at an engineering-oriented ICAR research centre in Bhubaneswar. The debates in *Science* (Surridge 2004) and *Rice Today* between Norman Uphoff (2004) and Thomas Sinclair (2004), and journal articles by Stoop et al (2002), Dobermann (2004) and Sheehy et al (2004), stirred his interest in SRI. He was keen to experiment with a practice that promised such impressive yield levels with few inputs. In January 2003, he performed a first pot experiment on SRI, and a year later initiated a field trial experiment on planting density. By 2005, trial results were showing the connections between planting density and the optimal environment for canopy growth and light interception. He pursued his research by experimenting with different varieties, water management systems and so forth.

It was not until 2008 that Thakur met with other SRI researchers. The occasion was a meeting of the SRI Learning Alliance at the Xavier Institute of Management, Bhubaneswar. In the absence of any coordinated research on SRI, it was not uncommon for papers presented at some national symposia to be repetitive, seeking essentially to prove the worth of SRI and its components. In contrast, Thakur's presentation was warmly received because he had worked systematically over several seasons, albeit in isolation. Thakur met Uphoff for the first time at Bhubaneswar, though they had already corresponded via email. Uphoff helped integrate Thakur into the international SRI community. Several of his subsequent publications contributed to the ongoing debates around SRI (Thakur 2010; Thakur et al 2010a, 2101b).

Some parts of the research community have been resistant to SRI because it challenges long-established tenets of rice science. Sinclair (2004) argued that SRI results in poor light interception because of low plant densities, and that the emphasis on organic nutrients to the exclusion of mineral fertiliser makes it difficult to supply sufficient nutrients to achieve high yields. He also argued that the physiology and physics of plant water use have been researched for more than 300 years, with the conclusion that 'ample water maximizes rice yields'. What constitutes 'ample' remains unspecified, but since he defended the inundation of rice paddies, the implication is that keeping them flooded is ideal. The practice of flooding may well be more productive than simple rainfed rice production; however, little is known about the physiology of rice when it is grown under conditions of low plant density and shallow irrigation with alternate wetting and drying.

This scepticism has been countered by a small group of Indian researchers. Detailed studies conducted by Thakur et al (2010a, 2010b) showed that alterations in management practices can induce multiple, significant and positive changes in phenotype from a given rice genotype. For example, the increase in yield with SRI when compared with recommended management practices reached 42 per cent, and was associated with various phenotypic changes such as longer panicles, more panicles, higher percentage of grain filling, increased productivity per plant, deeper and better distributed root systems, higher xylem exudation rates, etc. Increased water productivity to the extent of 96 per cent due to water-saving irrigation without detrimental effect on grain yield has been reported by Thiyagarajan et al (2002). Ceesay et al (2006) observed nearly three times higher grain yield with SRI (7.3 t ha^{-1}) compared with continuous flooding (2.5 t ha^{-1}). In Tamil Nadu, adaptive research trials (Rajendran et al 2005; Thiyagarajan et al 2005) have established that lower plant density can result in higher yields from several rice varieties. The merits of lower plant density have been known in Tamil Nadu for about a century: Madan and Smith (1928) state that 120,000 copies of a leaflet on 'single seedling method of paddy cultivation' were distributed in the Madras Presidency.

The fact that SRI was dismissed by scientists from the International Rice Research Institute (IRRI) (Sheehy et al 2004) made it 'untouchable' for many researchers in India. Nevertheless, the research ecosystem in India around SRI has grown in the past four to five years. After a lull in research following the retirement of T.M.T. and Alapati Satyanarayana, a second-generation research community is emerging through the work of a team at the Directorate of Water Development at Tamil Nadu AU and at the Directorate of Rice Research (DRR). Suprisingly, the opportunities for these researchers to meet and discuss SRI or agroecology have arisen largely through the intervention of actors outside the formal research establishment.

Non-Pesticidal Management

NPM can be seen as sitting between integrated pest management (IPM), which allows the use of pesticides (in principle as a last resort but in practice often more regularly), and organic farming, which shuns both inorganic fertilisers and pesticides. NPM seeks to shift crop pest management away from conventional chemical pesticides and towards safer biological methods and biopesticides. Preventative pest management is emphasised through the use of deep summer ploughing, bonfires and pheromone traps (Vijay

Kumar et al 2009). The research trajectory of NPM has been quite different from that of SRI. While the scientific controversy surrounding SRI pitted an international research centre and some of its scientists against a dispersed community of scientists and practitioners, for NPM, researchers from ICRISAT have been quietly collaborating with national scientists and civil society organisations.

Over the past decades, international agricultural research centres such as ICRISAT have seen their funding change from core to project-based. This change places the onus on scientists to obtain their own funding, but it also gives them some scope to shape the direction of research. Research that supports self-sufficiency of farmers and farming communities often receives less support than that which provides marketing opportunities for agri-input companies. Rupela's work on biopesticides at ICRISAT is an example of this.

Unlike some of his colleagues, Rupela had difficulty raising research funds. Since 1999, his interest was in articulating the science behind the products and processes of crop production used by organic farmers. He visited many organic farms and interacted with a large number of practitioners through workshops and meetings with groups like *Prayog Parivar*.[5] Rupela was convinced that many of the practices used by organic farmers were scientifically sound, even though few researchers within the mainstream system took them seriously. The Honey Bee grassroots innovation network was a source of inspiration for him, and the large numbers of innovations it has identified helped firm up his resolve. He embarked on a ten-year study on organic farming. A small grant of Rs 100,000 ($2200) to study the microbiology of some bio-products developed by the Society for Research and Initiatives for Sustainable Technologies and Institutions (SRISTI), based on farmers' innovations, helped convince the ICRISAT management that there was a market for his approach. This enabled him to explore further funding opportunities, with the outcome that he worked as a consultant for several bio-products companies under the Biopesticides Research Consortium (BRC).

Rupela had to live with a dilemma. The outputs of the work he was doing under the BRC, while potentially leading to quality products, would make farmers even more dependent on markets. He was, however, also able to pursue research on the bio-pesticidal properties of cattle dung and urine. The consortium helped shield him from comments by peers about doing research on low-status objects like *gobar* (cow dung) and *peshab* (urine). He also had difficulty in attracting funds that would allow him to validate these practices using modern molecular biology tools. Scientists and farmers alike were more attracted to new products than to traditional ones. ICRISAT management was hoping its researchers would identify a super-functioning microorganism, rather than be told that cow dung, in combination with other things, could promote nitrogen fixing, provide P-solubilisers, promote plant growth and retard disease-causing fungi.

In addition to the work with the BRC, Rupela also conducted training programmes on organic farming to raise funds and ensure greater visibility. He ran four such five-day programmes from 2005 to 2007, each attracting 10–20 participants. The participants were from ICAR, state agricultural departments, central agencies and NGOs. It was important that the term 'organic' farming was avoided in any of the brochures or presentations. Indeed it was successfully camouflaged as 'low-cost bio-intensive farming'.

The research atmosphere at ICRISAT was more supportive of Rupela's approach than in the national agricultural research centres, where hierarchies are stronger. One of his strategies was to use MSc student projects to address some of the research questions (at least 20 between 1999 and 2007). A list of research questions was developed along with planning for long-term experiments. These questions were continually revised through interaction with visitors to the experiments and farm visits. Some of this work has been published (Rupela et al 2003; Sriveni et al 2004; Hameeda et al 2006); however, much remains unpublished because the primary objective was to answer as many questions as possible before Rupela retired.

The difficulty that Rupela had was not so much in getting the work published, but the criticism of peers and seniors, who at times scoffed at the work the team was doing (e.g. looking at the microbiology of cow dung, urine and related products while everyone else was moving towards biotechnology and molecular biology). At times, even getting students was difficult because they were willing to accept a studentship only if the assigned topic involved hands-on use of molecular biology tools. Faced with this negativity, he used daily meetings of research staff to maintain the level of morale, and specifically to emphasise that through their work they were helping smallholder farmers in poor countries.

Based largely on the collaboration between ICRISAT, national researchers and civil society organisations, NPM went to scale through civil society organisations such as the Centre for World Solidarity (CWS) and later the concerted efforts of CSA. From 2003, CSA worked with its partners to establish 'pesticide-free villages' in Andhra Pradesh and then worked through a strategic partnership with the Society for Elimination of Rural Poverty (SERP) to upscale NPM to over 2 million acres. While NPM has been recognised by policy-makers, including Jairam Ramesh (mentioned above), it has been less controversial than SRI. Only recently was NPM officially recognised by the Andhra Pradesh Agriculture Department, despite thousands of farmers practising it. This paradox of a system that was 'upscaled' and accepted by a million farmers but not 'mainstreamed' was discussed at a workshop in March 2010. Discussions highlighted the difficulty, even inability, of the agricultural system to accept innovations that emerge outside the formal sector, especially when they came from farmers and civil society.

Conclusion

This chapter highlights the role of dissenting agronomists in the development of two agroecological innovations. These dissenters have demonstrated that it is in working across disciplinary boundaries and engaging with broad networks that agronomy and farming practice can be reshaped. We have also shown that proactive engagement by agronomists with civil society organisations and social scientists can help rework some of the axioms of agronomic research, making it more relevant to current discussions on the increasing ecological footprint of agriculture and the need to have a small-farmer focus. Rather than being mere 'extension agents' of a one-way transfer of knowledge, they have enabled creative dissenters to better articulate their own research questions, facilitate knowledge transfers within the innovation system, and even challenge researchers with newer ideas that could lead to important insights.

The examples of SRI and NPM demonstrate that, along with the broad-brush of neoliberalism and the participation and environmental agendas (see Chapter 1 in this volume), an understanding of the dynamics of contestation within agronomy requires that detailed attention be given to knowledge conflicts and dialogues that take place on farmers' fields in India and elsewhere. Thus researchers interested in political agronomy should seek scientific controversies, but not as journalists in search of the latest scoop. Rather, they should draw from science studies and focus on the everyday practice of agronomists, some of the most interesting of which take place at the very periphery of the discipline.

Notes

1 Centre for Environment Education (CEE) and Ministry of Environment and Forests, National Consultations on Bt Brinjal, Nehru Foundation for Development, Ahmedabad, 2010.
2 Shiv Visvanathan (2010) 'Scrutiny of science', *The New Indian Express*, 8 October, http://expressbuzz.com/opinion/columnists/scrutiny-of-science/213594.html. The Report has since been rejected, with the Scientific Advisor to the Prime Minister also embarrassed by the whole plagiarism issue, suggesting that it does not augur well for science. See Pallava Bagla (2010) 'Plagiarized report presents new hurdle to GM eggplant in India', http://news.sciencemag.org/scienceinsider/2010/09/plagiarized-report-presents-new.html.
3 www.icar.org.in/node/325
4 We thank Sabarmatee for sharing with us the English translation of Willem Stoops' address to the Dutch Social Science Association titled 'From soil scientist to agronomist to agricultural systems researcher'. This served as an inspiration for T.M.T. to write his own story, 'My destiny, my profession'.
5 For more on Prayog Parivar see www.prayogparivar.net

References

Bhargava, P. (2011) 'Unconstitutional, unethical, unscientific', *The Hindu*. Opinion page, December 28.

Ceesay, M., Reid, W.S., Fernandes, E.C.M. and Uphoff, N.T. (2006) 'The effects of repeated soil wetting and drying on lowland rice yield with System of Rice Intensification (SRI) methods', *International Journal of Agricultural Sustainability*, 4: 5–14.

Dobermann, A. (2004) 'Critical assessment of the system of rice intensification', *Agricultural Systems*, 79: 261–81.

Gujja, B. and Thiyagarajan, T.M. (2009) *New Hope for Indian Food Security? The System of Rice Intensification*, IIED Gatekeeper Series. London, UK: International Institute for Environment and Development.

Hameeda, B., Rupela, O.P., Wani, S.P. and Reddy, G. (2006) 'Indices to assess quality, productivity and sustainable health of soils receiving low-cost biological and/or conventional inputs', *International Journal of Soil Science*, 1(3): 196–206.

Madan, J.A. and Smith, F.W.H. (1928) *Royal Commission on Agriculture in India*. Bombay: Government Central Press.

Quartz, J. (2010) 'Creative dissent with technoscience in India: the case of non-pesticidal management (NPM) in Andhra Pradesh', *International Journal of Technology and Development Studies*, 1(1): 55–92.

Rajendran, R., Ravi, V., Ramanathan, S., Chandrasekaran, B., Jayaraj, T. and Balasubramanian, V. (2005), 'Evaluation of selected crop management components for enhancing rice productivity and profitability in Tamil Nadu, India', in Thiyagarajan, T.M., Hengsdijk, H.

and Bindraban, P.S. (eds) *Transitions in Agriculture for Enhancing Water Productivity*, Proceedings of an International Symposium held in Killikulam, Tamil Nadu, India, 23–25 September 2003. Wageningen: Tamil Nadu AU, Coimbatore and Plant Research International.

Rupela, O.P., Gopalakrishnan, S., Krajewski, M. and Sriveni, M. (2003) 'A novel method for the identification and enumeration of microorganisms with potential for suppressing fungal plant pathogens', *Biology and Fertility of Soils*, 39(2): 131–34.

Shambu Prasad, C. (2006) *SRI in India: Innovation History and Institutional Challenges*. WWF International–ICRISAT Dialogue Project and Xavier Institute of Management, Patancheru.

——(2008) 'Learning alliances: emerging trends in knowledge intensive agriculture', paper presented at *Workshop on Rethinking Impact: Understanding the Complexity of Poverty and Change*, Cali, Colombia, March 26–28.

——(2009a) 'Encounters, dialogues and learning alliances: the System of Rice Intensification in India', in Scoones, I. and Thompson, J. (eds) *Farmers First Revisited: Innovation for Agricultural Research and Development*. London: Earthscan, pp. 82–87.

——(2009b) 'Conversations on knowledge and democracy: fables from SRI', seminar issue of *Knowledge in Question*, no. 597 (May).

——(2009c). 'Can the big learn from the small? Insights on policy dialogue and innovation capacity in SRI in India', paper presented at the *Innovation Asia Pacific Symposium*, Kathmandu, Prolinnova and Practical Action, 4–7 May.

——(2011) 'Creative dissent: linking vulnerability, democracy and knowledge in India', in Hommels, A., Mesman, J. and Bijker, W.E. (eds) *The Vulnerability of Technological Cultures. New Directions in Research and Governance*. Cambridge, MA: MIT Press.

Sheehy, J.E., Peng, S., Dobermann, A., Mitchell, P.L., Ferrera, A., Yang, J., Zoue, Y., Zhong, X. and Huang, J. (2004) 'Fantastic yields in the system of rice intensification: fact or fallacy?', *Field Crops Research*, 88: 1–8.

Sinclair, T.R. (2004) 'Agronomic UFOs waste valuable scientific resources', *Rice Today*, July–September. Los Baños: IRRI.

Sriveni, M., Rupela, O.P., Gopalakrishnan, S. and Krajewski, M (2004) 'Spore-forming bacteria, a major group among potential antagonists isolated from natural sources such as termitaria soil and composts used by organic farmers', *Indian Journal of Microbiology*, 44(2): 95–100.

Stoop, W.A., Uphoff, N. and Kassam, A.H. (2002) 'A review of agricultural research issues raised by the system of rice intensification (SRI) from Madagascar: opportunities for improving farming systems for resource-poor farmers', *Agricultural Systems*, 71: 249–74.

Surridge, C. (2004) 'Feast or famine?', *Nature*, 428(6981): 360–61.

Thakur, A.K. (2010) 'Critiquing SRI criticism: beyond skepticism with empiricism', *Current Science*, 98(10): 1294–99.

Thakur, A.K., Rath, S., Roychowdhury, S. and Uphoff, N. (2010a) 'Comparative performance of rice with system of rice intensification (SRI) and conventional management using different plant spacings', *Journal of Agronomy and Crop Science*, 196(2): 146–58.

Thakur, A.K., Uphoff, N. and Antony, E. (2010b) 'An assessment of physiological effects of system of rice intensification (SRI) practices compared to recommended rice cultivation practices in India', *Experimental Agriculture*, 46(1): 77–98.

Thiyagarajan, T. M. (2010) 'My destiny, my profession', unpublished essay written for the conference on *Contested Agronomy* at the Institute of Development Studies, Sussex, 18–19 November 2010.

Thiyagarajan, T.M., Senthilkumar, K., Priyadarshini, R., Sundarsingh, J., Muthusankaranarayanan, A., Hengsdijk, H. and Bindraban, P.S. (2005) 'Evaluation of water saving irrigation and weeder use on the growth and yield of rice', in Thiyagarajan, T.M., Hengsdijk, H. and Bindraban, P.S. (eds) *Transitions in Agriculture for Enhancing Water Productivity*, Proceedings of an International Symposium held in Killikulam, Tamil Nadu, India, 23–25 September 2003. Wageningen: Tamil Nadu AU, Coimbatore and Plant Research International.

Thiyagarajan, T.M., Velu, V., Ramasamy, S., Durgadevi, D., Govindarajan, K., Priyadarshini, R., Sudhalakshmi, C., Senthilkumar, K., Nisha, P.T, Gayathry, G., Hengsdijk, H. and

Bindraban, P.S. (2002) 'Effects of SRI practices on hybrid rice performance in Tamil Nadu, India', in Bouman, B.A.M., Hengsdijk, H., Hardy, B., Bindraban, P.S., Tuong, T.P. and Ladha, J.K. (eds) *Water-wise Rice Production*. Los Baños: IRRI.

Uphoff, N. (2004) 'System of rice intensification responds to 21st century needs', *Rice Today*, July–September. Los Baños: IRRI.

Vijay Kumar, T., Raidu, D.V., Killi, J., Pillai, M., Shah, P., Vijasekhar, K. and Lakhey, S. (2009) *Ecologically Sound, Economically Viable: Community Managed Sustainable Agriculture in Andhra Pradesh, India*. Washington, DC: World Bank.

11

SUCCESS-MAKING AND SUCCESS STORIES

Agronomic research in the spotlight[1]

James Sumberg, Robin Irving, Elisabeth Adams and John Thompson

Introduction

> But the question is whether Africa has the technologies that can do this [allow the 300 million Africans living on less than a dollar a day to produce food, generate incomes, employment and higher savings]. The answer is a resounding yes. The International Food Policy Research Institute (IFPRI) in its book *Successes in African Agriculture* says Africa has developed technologies with transformative potential for turning around the fight against hunger.[2]

Over the past decade or so there has been much interest in the gathering, analysis and telling of 'success stories' about agriculture and agricultural development in sub-Saharan Africa (SSA) (see special issue of *International Journal of Agricultural Sustainability* 2011, 9(1); also Tiffen et al 1994; Snrech 1995; Dijkstra 1997; Roper 1999; Wiggins 2000; Uphoff 2002; Gabre-Madhin and Haggblade 2004; Mortimore 2005; Wiggins 2005; Baffes and Baghdadli 2007; Reij and Smaling 2008; Jacovelli 2009; Spielman and Pandya-Lorch 2009b; Haggblade and Hazell 2010; Pretty et al 2011).[3] The websites and publicity materials of development actors ranging from international funders to local NGOs feature hundreds of agricultural success stories.

At one level the interest in success stories can be understood as part of the larger 'development fight-back', an effort to change negative public perceptions of Africa and of development assistance more broadly. The focus on success stories also links directly to ongoing academic and policy debates around aid effectiveness (Bourguignon and Sundberg 2007) and impact evaluation (Ravallion 2009), as well as the role and importance of development narratives within policy processes (Roe 1994; Keeley and Scoones 2003). At another level, success stories are also one of the ways that research and development organisations justify their existence and seek to secure larger budget allocations in an increasingly competitive funding environment.

It is important to note that the recent interest in success stories about African agriculture coincides with the apparent movement of agriculture up the public policy agenda (de Janvry and Sadoulet 2010).

Wiggins (2005) provides an analysis of the lessons that can be gleaned from success stories about African agriculture, stories generated either through the synthesis of published case studies (Turner et al 1993; Snrech 1995; Wiggins 1995; Wiggins 2000) or through the nomination of individual cases (Gabre-Madhin and Haggblade 2004). The focus of Wiggins' analysis is on what the stories say about the factors required to achieve successful agricultural development: for example, the need to reduce transport costs; the need for institutional innovation in agricultural supply chains; and the need for a better understanding of markets and market failures. On the other hand, he says little about the stories themselves.

In this chapter, our focus is on the stories as opposed to the underlying research results, technology, change, 'progress' or 'success' that they describe and (in some cases) attempt to explain. We are not setting out to evaluate the validity of particular success claims, but rather to understand why and how such claims are constructed and promoted. Ultimately we seek to throw light on the dynamic between success stories and agronomic research.

The act of styling a project, programme or experience a 'success' and communicating this through a story draws attention to two closely related sets of questions: What is success, and how and by whom was it defined? Who is telling the story, to whom, how and why? Addressing these questions creates the basis for an analysis of the politics around development success stories. By exploring the proposition that these 'good news stories' must be read as innately political, it is not our intention to be churlish or reinforce the stereotype of inward-looking, complexifying, success-denying academics. Rather, we want to use the burgeoning interest in success stories about agriculture in SSA to open up a more nuanced consideration of how the results of agronomic research are used within public policy processes, and the implications of these dynamics for agricultural research, agricultural development and rural livelihoods.

Two common sayings draw attention to the politics of success. The first, '*Nothing succeeds like success*', suggests that success reproduces itself, or in other words, that it is possible (and obviously desirable) to enter into a virtuous circle of success. If this is so, then there should be a strong motivation for claiming success and by doing so, placing oneself within the virtuous circle. The second saying, '*Success has many parents but failure is an orphan*', highlights the idea that given such a strong motivation, the competition to be associated with success is keen. With so much at stake, it should not be surprising that parental claims to particular successes can be strongly contested.

The argument we make is that in the realm of African agriculture (and more broadly within development), success stories are becoming an increasingly important instrument in the competition for policy attention and financial resources. We also argue that these success stories are becoming integral to policy processes: they legitimise new kinds of 'evidence', and because of their story format, that evidence can be particularly potent. As a result, success stories are playing an important role in the tactical dynamics within agricultural policy processes, allowing actors to breathe new life into their advocacy for particular policy positions. Again we want to emphasise that we are in no way disputing the proposition that agronomic research has delivered significant and tangible benefits to (some) farmers in (some parts of) SSA, as well as to consumers, food processors, national economies and so on.

The remainder of this chapter is organised in four sections. The next section explores the meanings of success. Then we present a simple theoretical framework for understanding the dynamics of 'success making'. Following this, we examine these dynamics primarily through the success stories generated by the Millions Fed project. The final section discusses some implications of this analysis for agronomic research in Africa.

Defining success

Success is the achievement of a good or desirable outcome, and a successful project, technology or policy is one that contributes to that outcome. For most people involved in agricultural development, reductions in the incidence of hunger and poverty are good and desirable outcomes. Similarly, most would consider growth of the agricultural economy, increased rural incomes and productivity gains as desirable outcomes. Along these lines, in his consideration of agricultural success stories from SSA, Wiggins (2005) defined success as periods of sustained agricultural growth. Similarly, for the Millions Fed project, Spielman and Pandya-Lorch (2009b) measured success in terms of feeding additional people and eliminating hunger.[4]

However, for some observers of rural development, the notion of success is open to interpretation, manipulation and contestation. The work of David Mosse (2004a, 2004b) probably best exemplifies this approach, with success being actively produced, constructed and reconstructed by, and to meet the evolving needs of, individuals, implementing organisations, local officials and funders. Mosse's analysis of his 10 years of engagement with the Indo-British Rainfed Farming Project led him to a definition of success that is unlikely to be to everyone's taste: to 'conceal ideological differences, to allow compromise and the enrolment of different interests, to build coalitions, to distribute agency and to multiply criteria of success within project systems' (Mosse 2004b).

But are these two approaches to success really so far apart? We don't have to be card-carrying post-modernists or social constructivists to accept the proposition that in any particular situation there will likely be some ambiguity and contestation around the meaning of success. An acknowledgment of social difference and a nuanced, multi-dimensional understanding of poverty demand an equally nuanced, multi-dimensional understanding of success; and there are legitimate differences of opinion regarding the weight that should be given to the different dimensions. Thus there will be winners and losers associated with every development intervention, no matter how strong or well articulated its claims to success. The differential impacts of 'successful' technical change within agriculture are an important theme of feminist and gendered analyses of agriculture in SSA (Stamp 1989; World Bank et al 2009).

It is also important to remember that in the world of agricultural development it is appropriate to see success as both emergent and contingent, which means that claims of success must be re-evaluated in the light of changing circumstances. For example, while the 'maize revolution' in Zimbabwe in the early 1990s was repeatedly declared a success (Eicher and Rukuni 1994; Eicher 1995), seen from the vantage point of 2011, following a decade of political and economic chaos, the meaning and significance of this particular success must surely be re-examined. Sara Berry (1993) reminds us that in rural SSA, 'no condition is permanent', to which we must add 'even success'.

Finally, any consideration of success must also take failure into account. Here we suggest that, from a development perspective, 'learning' should be one of the 'good and desirable' outcomes associated with every policy, initiative or project. It is undoubtedly true that successful learning does not require broader project success: a project that fails to deliver on any of its main objectives may nevertheless provide invaluable learning (and other unanticipated benefits). Fenichel and Smith (1992) refer to these as 'successful failures'. For example, in his analysis of the disastrous Niger Agricultural Project in Nigeria, Baldwin (1957) clearly and systematically highlighted the importance (for future projects) of recognising and making full use of the detailed agricultural and environmental knowledge of local people. If this 'learning' had fallen on fertile ground at the time (in fact it took another 25 years to germinate), the cost of this 'failed' project would have been repaid many times over. Does a single-minded focus on the demonstration and celebration of success, which incentivises a dynamic of 'success making' (and the burying of all that cannot easily be construed as success), significantly reduce the opportunity to learn and benefit from 'successful failures'?[5]

Success making

In this section, we introduce a simple theoretical framework for understanding the process and dynamics of 'success making'. Drawing from securitisation theory in the field of international relations (Taureck 2006), we suggest that success making is first and foremost a speech act: simply by proclaiming 'success' something is being done. In other words, labelling something a success is a critical first step in the construction of a success story. Success making requires a 'success maker', an actor who is motivated and able to proclaim a particular project, programme, innovation, technology, policy or organisation a success. By proclaiming something a success, the success maker initiates a process that in time may shelter the claim from normal scrutiny and critical evaluation (although in some cases this may backfire and instead draw increased attention to it). As outlined here, success has no objective meaning, and claims of success do not arise through an objective process of evaluating results, outcomes or impacts. Rather, success is what the success maker says it is, what he or she can make stick. Success stories are an integral element of success making.

We hypothesise that the main driver of the recent spate of success making is the increasing pressure on development actors at all levels to demonstrate results, effectiveness, impacts, value-added and/or 'value for money' in order to justify their existence and continued financial support. We also hypothesise that there are two further conditions that lend themselves to high levels of success making. First, when the desired outcomes are complex and/or expected to emerge over the long term (e.g. 'sustainable rural livelihoods'; 'sustainable farming systems'; 'climate-resilient cropping systems'; or 'empowerment') and it is therefore difficult to identify meaningful and measurable outcome indicators. Second, when an organisational imperative is such that it swings the communications balance towards simple, compelling messages at the expense of nuanced or critical analysis.

Not all attempts at success making yield the desired result, which in the first instance is the widespread recognition of the particular project, technology or programme as a success. We hypothesise that attempts at success making are more likely to gain traction in cases where the proclaimed success is framed in a way that does not challenge mainstream thinking and sits comfortably within a dominant narrative; and where the success story is told in a simplistic way and promoted using a range of easily accessible media.

Like researchers all over the world, individuals and organisations involved in agricultural research have long sought to create an air of expectation around particular lines of research. The agronomic literature from SSA is full of claims that particular technologies, often still at the experimental stage, are 'promising' or have 'potential': examples include alley cropping (Kang et al 1981); black sigatoka-resistant plantain (Vuylsteke et al 1993); fodder legumes (Tarawali 1994); organic matter technologies for soil management (Snapp et al 1998; Fischler et al 1999); agricultural biotechnology (Wambugu 1999); conservation agriculture (Fowler and Rockstrom 2001); and vegetable soybeans (Chadha and Oluoch 2004). The incentives to present research findings in the best possible light are clearly long-standing, yet claims such as these can be seen as a first, tentative step in a process of success making.

Orr et al (2008) used the case of NERICA rice to explore some of the dynamics of success making identified above. The name NERICA was derived from the phrase 'New Rice for Africa': selected following a process of inter-specific hybridisation, these varieties have received much media attention and are now being heavily promoted in rice growing areas of SSA. In tracing the origin of claims made about the agronomic characteristics, performance, spread and impacts of the NERICA varieties, Orr et al showed that the making of success claims began very early in the technology development process, so that most of the initial claims were based on data that were at best preliminary and limited. Through repetition (by WARDA)[6] and propagation (by WARDA's funders, partners, development-oriented news sites, etc) these early claims became deeply embedded in both narratives about NERICA and the World Wide Web. Orr et al concluded that, even as a more nuanced picture of the performance characteristics and potential of these varieties began to emerge, the continuation of this dynamic suited WARDA, as the simple story line, accompanying publicity and international accolades[7] helped buttress the organisation's precarious financial position. Perhaps not surprisingly, these conclusions were contested by WARDA (Wopereis et al 2008).

Over the past decade, interest in the potential for 'scaling up' and achieving 'impact at scale' – despite the acknowledged importance of location specificity and Wiggins' conclusion that developments in African agriculture have generally been 'a cumulative effect of a series of quite small improvements for any given crop or locality' (Wiggins

2005: 18) – have changed the game for all development actors. Specifically, the need for ever more impressive success stories, combined with new communications opportunities, has super-charged the dynamics around, and the implications of, success making.

Writing success

Success stories about African agriculture fall into two broad categories. In the first are stories that are told primarily for non-specialists, but also speak to policy makers. These include some outputs from the recent Millions Fed project (Spielman and Pandya-Lorch 2009a) as well as the hundreds of stories that appear in the publicity materials and websites of bi- and multi-lateral funding agencies, research institutions, continent-wide initiatives, NGOs and agri-business companies.[8] Some common features of this genre of success story include simplified language; general descriptions and overviews often formatted as summaries or highlights; the use of compelling images; and a dissemination approach that draws on a marketing 'push strategy' (Hair et al 2009: 413), where demand for information is created through broad promotion and accessibility.

The second category includes success stories that are primarily for professional and academic audiences, and where the policy messages are more explicit (Tiffen et al 1994; Dijkstra 1997; Uphoff 2002; Gabre-Madhin and Haggblade 2004; Mortimore 2005; Baffes and Baghdadli 2007; Reij and Smaling 2008; Spielman and Pandya-Lorch 2009b; Haggblade and Hazell 2010). The (largely) internally generated results demonstrating high returns to investment in CGIAR research could also be seen as falling within this category (e.g. Plucknett 1991; Collinson and Tollens 1994; Maredia and Eicher 1995; Maredia and Byerlee 2000; Zeddies et al 2001; Alene et al 2009; Alene 2010; Nalley et al 2010). Some common features of these success stories include language that is acceptable and popular within particular academic and professional communities; an emphasis on the application of an established or emerging theoretical or conceptual framework; dissemination through a means or media that is respected within the community (a peer-reviewed journal or professional publication) and that often has restricted accessibility; and a dissemination approach that builds on a marketing 'pull strategy' (Hair et al 2009: 413) where the audience is more engaged in a process of seeking out new information. Related to this second category is a small body of work aimed at academic and professional audiences that explores failure (e.g. Baldwin 1957; Hogendorn and Scott 1981; Webb 1991; Gibbon 1992; Filipovich 2001; Orr and Ritchie 2004; Zoomers 2005).

An important recent initiative to identify and disseminate success stories about agriculture was the Millions Fed project. Millions Fed was designed to 'assess the evidence on what works in agriculture' (Spielman and Pandya-Lorch 2009b: vii) in an effort to leverage initiatives to address issues of hunger and malnutrition. The project was initiated and funded by the Bill & Melinda Gates Foundation (BMGF), which approached the International Food Policy Research Institute (IFPRI) to 'examine successes in agricultural development and draw out the lessons they offer'

(Spielman and Pandya-Lorch 2009b: vii). A few years earlier, BMGF funded a similar project – Millions Saved: Proven Successes in Global Health (Levine 2004, 2007) – in partnership with the Center for Global Development.

Drawing on the work of Gabre-Madhin and Haggblade (2004) and Levine (2004, 2007), Spielman and Pandya-Lorch (2009b: 154) developed a methodology for the Millions Fed project with the objective of selecting 20 case studies representative of 'relatively large-scale and long-term success ... backed by strong evidence of positive impact'. This involved a global 'call for nominations' that drew on case submissions, suggestions of experts and desk research. With over 250 nominations, the project team sorted the cases according to two qualifying criteria (that the intervention had been conducted in at least one developing country; and that the intervention related to agricultural development directly) and three primary evaluative criteria (relevance to improving food security among vulnerable groups; a scale appropriate at least to the national level; and implementation within the past 50 years). Additional evaluative criteria relating to proven impact and sustainability were also considered, but in a more informal manner to allow consideration of non-traditional evidence. A final set was compiled of 20 stories (five relating exclusively to SSA) – each drawing on a synthesis of multiple sources including first-hand accounts and impact assessments – and an overview of general lessons learned, including what worked and why.

A strategic communications package was produced by IFPRI to disseminate the stories. A primary output was the book titled *Millions Fed: Proven Successes in Agricultural Development* (Spielman and Pandya-Lorch 2009b), which features an opening overview chapter, 20 chapters profiling the individual success stories, and several appendices relating to methodology and references. This 184-page publication is glossy, colourful and attractive, containing many photographic images. However, some of the stories have enough data and technical detail to put them beyond a general readership.[9] Thus this book straddles the two categories of success stories identified above: some parts appear to be primarily for non-specialists, but others would present a challenge to this group. It is available only in English.

A smaller booklet version, *Highlights from Millions Fed*, was also produced (Spielman and Pandya-Lorch 2009a), in addition to an 11-minute video.[10] In the booklet, the success stories are presented in relatively little detail and are grouped under six headings, including 'Intensifying staple food production', 'Integrating people and the environment' and 'Expanding the role of markets'. The booklet then addresses two questions – 'Why did it work?' and 'What can we learn?' – and ends with a section titled 'Looking ahead'. In an appendix titled 'Case studies', a brief summary of each success story is presented; the summaries for the three stories having a link to agronomic research in SSA are reproduced in Box 11.1. In terms of the level of technical detail and overall presentation, it is fair to conclude that *Highlights from Millions Fed* and the accompanying video are meant primarily for consumption by non-specialists. They nevertheless promote more or less explicit policy messages. The 24-page booklet is available in English, Spanish, simplified Chinese, French and Hindi.

The Millions Fed outputs were presented at 'book launch events' in Nairobi, Dhaka, Seattle, Addis Ababa and Washington, in which audiences were provided opportunities for questions and dialogue relating to the project and agricultural development more generally (IFPRI 2009). Additional communications outputs of the project include online content within IFPRI's website, and various media and public relations tools. In August 2010, the *Millions Fed* book was awarded the Quality of Communications Award by the Agricultural and Applied Economics Association (IFPRI 2010).

Box 11.1 Case studies from *Highlights from Millions Fed* with a link to agronomic research in SSA (source: Spielman and Pandya-Lorch 2009a: 18–19).

Breeding an 'Amaizing' crop: improved maize in Kenya, Malawi, Zambia, and Zimbabwe

Melinda Smale and T.S. Jayne
Key Period: 1965–90
Geographic region: Kenya, Malawi, Zambia, Zimbabwe
The intervention: Sustained investments in innovative breeding programs, dedicated scientists, and supportive public policies drove the development and spread of more productive maize that translated into better livelihoods for millions of farm households. By expanding access to modern (improved) maize seeds among smallholder farmers, yields multiplied several-fold and contributed significantly to improving food production and food security in the region. While the fiscal burdens of state-led marketing and credit policies rendered the growth unsustainable, by 2000–2005, maize, most of it modern maize, covered more than three-quarters of the land under cereal cultivation in the four countries.

Resisting viruses and bugs: cassava in sub-Saharan Africa

Felix Nweke
Key period: 1971–89
Geographic region: Sub-Saharan Africa
The intervention: Two major control programs were designed to combat serious threats to cassava production in Sub-Saharan Africa – the cassava mosaic disease and the cassava mealybug. These programs played a critical role in raising cassava yields beginning in the 1970s, turning cassava into a cash crop that is now spreading throughout Africa. In the early 1970s, the introduction of bio-control strategies to destroy mealybug infestations reduced yield losses by 2.5 tons per hectare. In the late 1970s, the introduction of improved, disease-resistant varieties controlled cassava mosaic disease while contributing to yield increases of 40 per cent. These two programs played a particularly critical role in countries such as Nigeria and Ghana, and have contributed to improvements in food security for at least 29 million people.

> **Re-greening the Sahel: farmer-led innovation in Burkina Faso and Niger**
>
> Chris Reij, Gray Tappan, and Melinda Smale
> **Key period:** 1980–present
> **Geographic region:** Burkina Faso and Niger
> **The intervention:** The rediscovery and diffusion of traditional agroforestry, water, and soil management practices in Burkina Faso and Niger has transformed large swathes of the region's arid landscape into productive agricultural land. In Burkina Faso's Central Plateau, the rehabilitation of between 200,000 and 300,000 hectares translated into roughly 80,000 tons of additional food per year, enough to sustain about half a million people in the region. In southern Niger, farmer investments in agriculture are estimated to have transformed approximately 5 million hectares of land, improving food security for at least 2.5 million people.

Reading success

First reading

The seven chapters of the *Millions Fed* book focusing on SSA, while reflecting some diversity in their internal organisation (as reflected in the non-uniformity of sub-headings), are distinctly structured in a chronological narrative scenario format that features discussion of a problem, the solution and the successful results (Roe 1994). Although less explicit than in the opening chapter, the individual chapters also contain a call to action, which is most often embedded within the solution or results section of the narrative. The *Millions Fed* booklet features the same headings and sub-headings as the opening chapter of the book, with the exception of a section in the book titled 'Caveats', which offers several qualifications relating to the successes outlined.

Key vocabulary within the titles of the success story chapters reflects a strong military or battle reference. Title words include *fighting*, *enemy*, *unlocking*, *conquering*, *resisting* and *navigating*. The use of words such as these can serve as signifiers reflecting a cultural construction that links military references to crisis, mobilisation and a call to unified action (Eisenburg 1984).

The covers of both the book and booklet feature two horizontal bands of images. The top band is made up of six close-up images of people's faces. The subjects of these six images are diverse in terms of gender, age, ethnicity and dress. As argued by Deacon et al. (1999), the informal composition of images like these – reflected in the different image angles and backgrounds – could be seen to suggest familiarity. The subject of each image makes direct eye contact with the camera, which from a Western cultural perspective signals equality of status and personal connection (Deacon et al 1999: 194). The bottom band of the cover features images of food items that have been blurred through image enhancement. These cover images, as iconic signs that resemble what they represent, help to anchor the issues of people and food as key themes of the book and the booklet.

Women feature in a high proportion of the images in the opening chapter of the book, as well as in those in the seven chapters relating directly to SSA. Of the 40 images in total, 23 feature people as their primary subjects.[11] Of these images, 13 depict only women, seven feature only men, and three depict men and women together. The preference for images featuring women is even more evident in the booklet, where nine of the ten internal images that feature people have women as the subject.[12] This could reflect an acceptance of the dominant narrative which suggests that women are particularly vulnerable to poverty, hunger and malnutrition; play a significant role in smallholder and subsistence farming; yet have generally been neglected by agricultural research and development (World Bank 2007a). At the same time, the high proportion of images depicting women in *Millions Fed* might prompt a reader to conclude that women are the key benefactors of the successes outlined.

In the 17 images in which people's facial features are identifiable, they are all either smiling or looking content or focused. Within the field of social psychology, these types of facial expression tend to be considered symbolic of happiness, enthusiasm and progress (Rashotte 2002). In all but one of the SSA success story chapters, there is at least one image, often prominent, that depicts action or movement.[13] It is also of interest that the majority of the images depicting people (23 in total) tend to focus on an individual or apparent household group (15) rather than larger or mixed groups (eight). It could be argued that these images are in line with a policy narrative that emphasises the significance of individuals, particularly women, taking action individually or in small family groups to increase their agricultural productivity.

In summary, the African success stories in *Millions Fed* are based on a linear or process model of communication (Fiske 1990); are closely aligned with dominant narratives about agriculture in SSA and how the challenges it faces should be addressed; and use photographic images to try to create a personal, if not emotional, link to the reader. The main message in these stories is that while African agriculture faces many problems, rigorous analysis of the evidence shows that these challenges can be successfully overcome through investment in the right kinds of research and development activities.

Second reading

As noted above, Millions Fed built directly on work by Gabre-Madhin and Haggblade (2004), in which experts were surveyed in order to identify 'emerging successes' in African agriculture. This study was published in the highly respected *World Development* journal, and earlier as an IFPRI discussion paper (Gabre-Madhin and Haggblade 2003) – both very much oriented toward academic and professional audiences. There are also crossovers between Millions Fed and the 2010 monograph *Successes in African Agriculture: Lessons for the Future*, edited by Steve Haggblade and Peter Hazell (2010), which is also aimed at professional and academic readers.

There are several important linkages and commonalities between these efforts to identify and publicise success stories. First, the World Bank and IFPRI were central to all three, and individuals working for or closely associated with these organisations played major roles in project conception and management, the associated research, writing case studies, and editing and producing the collected stories. Second, all put considerable emphasis on using 'evidence' and 'rigorous analysis' to identify 'what works' and 'lessons' that will lead to 'sound agricultural investments' and ultimately poverty and hunger reduction. Finally, one is struck by the degree to which a limited number of examples – maize breeding, cassava pest control, soil fertility management and small-holder cotton production – are fashioned and refashioned as success by the different studies (Table 11.1). On the other hand, some other examples, such as adaptive on-farm breeding of bananas and increased rice production in Mali, have not been re-used to the same degree. Did they not stand up to close scrutiny and rigorous analysis, or were they deemed less amenable to the simple messaging inherent in the success story format?

In the earlier presentation of the success making framework, a number of hypotheses about the factors associated with this process were identified. Here we return to these and ask: What is driving the dynamic of success making that we argue is discernible in efforts such as *Millions Fed* and *Successes in African Agriculture*, and why do the different actors contribute to and engage with this dynamic in the ways they do?

Historically, the World Bank has been a major funder of agricultural research and development activities in SSA, both through national governments and via the CGIAR. While the priority given to agriculture has declined over the past decade, there is some indication that agriculture is moving up the policy and funding agenda (de Janvry and Sadoulet 2010). However, some World Bank activities in agriculture have been heavily critiqued (e.g. Harrigan 2003; Fortin 2005), and the Bank's own evaluations of its agricultural investments in SSA make sobering reading (World Bank 2007b, 2010). Given this record and the difficulties of reducing poverty and food insecurity in SSA, the Bank must be under ever-increasing pressure to demonstrate positive impact from its strategy of investing in agricultural growth via market reform and liberalisation, technology development and infrastructure. With the exception of the 'Re-greening the Sahel' story, with its focus on farmer innovation, food security and adaptation, the success stories are framed by and support the narrative that underpins this strategy: if you allow the market to work and provide access to modern technology, the farmers themselves can deal with the poverty problem.

IFPRI, through the CGIAR, is both funded by the World Bank and closely associated with much of the Bank's thinking about agricultural development in SSA. The CGIAR is also under pressure to demonstrate the value of the 'global public goods' it produces, and to produce these more cost-effectively. The pressure for more coordinated action and greater impact, particularly in SSA, was one factor driving the latest in a series of exercises to reorganise the CGIAR international agricultural research system (CGIAR 2009).

In the space of just a few years, the BMGF has become an important and influential funder of agricultural development in SSA, primarily through the Alliance for a

TABLE 11.1 Recycling of a small number of success stories

Example	Successes in African Agriculture (Gabre-Madhin and Haggblade 2004)	Millions Fed (Spielman and Pandya-Lorch 2009a, 2009b)	Successes in African Agriculture (Haggblade and Hazell 2010)
Maize breeding	Maize breeding	Breeding an 'Amaizing' crop: improved maize in Kenya, Malawi, Zambia, and Zimbabwe	'Seeds of success' in retrospect: hybrid maize in Eastern and Southern Africa
Cassava pest control	Combatting mosaic virus and pests in cassava	Resisting viruses and bugs: cassava in sub-Saharan Africa	Cassava transformation in West and southern Africa
Soil fertility	Soil fertility enhancement	Re-greening the Sahel: farmer-led innovation in Burkina Faso and Niger	Sustainable soil fertility management systems
Growth of cotton sector	Rapid growth of cotton production and exports in West Africa	Navigating through reforms: cotton reforms in Burkina Faso	Mali's White Revolution: smallholder cotton, 1960–2006
Growth of smallholder dairying	Smallholder income gains from dairying in Kenya	Dairying in Kenya [included as a Box on p.123]	Smallholder dairying in eastern Africa
Fertiliser market reforms	Policy reforms	Unlocking the market: fertiliser and maize in Kenya	
Control of livestock disease	Control of the devastating rinderpest disease for livestock	Conquering the cattle plague: the global effort to eradicate rinderpest	
Growth of horticultural exports	Expansion of horticulture and flower exports		Are horticultural exports a replicable success story? Evidence from Kenya and Côte d'Ivoire
Banana breeding	Adaptive on-farm breeding of bananas in the Central Highlands		
Growth of rice sector	Increased rice production in Mali		

Green Revolution in Africa (AGRA) initiative (Toenniessen et al 2008). The approach taken by BMGF and AGRA, based essentially around technology development and promotion, and greater market engagement by family farmers, fits well with that espoused by the Comprehensive Africa Agriculture Development Programme (CAADP) and the World Bank, and is underpinned by research from the CGIAR. BMGF makes clear its belief that coordinated, strategic investment can pay handsome dividends – or, in their terms, can be transformative – even over the relatively short term. The identification and dissemination of success stories that can demonstrate these transformative effects (to governments, other donors and development actors) is an important part of this strategy.

Finally, the dynamic of success making depends on the fact that individuals and organisations that are actually involved in agricultural research and development on the ground are strongly incentivised to have one of 'their' technologies or projects named and recognised as a success. The validation by recognised international organisations such as IFPRI through the 'rigorous analysis' of 'evidence' would be a public relations coup for most organisations. If handled properly, such an endorsement should increase the influence of the organisation and help secure additional financial resources. The potential benefits of being associated with a success story must explain why so many successes were identified in the early stages of Millions Fed (some 250, of which an unknown number were 'nominated').

Discussion and conclusions

We began this chapter by noting the growing interest in success stories around agriculture in SSA. We then proposed a framework for analysing the dynamic of success making, and used this framework to 'read' success stories from the recent Millions Fed project relating to agronomic research.

If, indeed, the motivation for and dynamic around success making are as we suggest above, it raises important questions for those involved in the funding, management and implementation of agronomic research, and for those who use the results of such research. For example, with pressure to demonstrate impact being felt by development actors at all levels, and with success making being an increasingly important (and understandable) response, we can well imagine that in relation to agronomic research there could be important effects on the following.

- **The choice of research areas, problems and questions** (e.g. *away from* perennial crops, complex cropping systems and technologies likely to exhibit a high degree of site specificity; and *toward* major crops, commercial crops, simple systems and technologies with high spatial transferability).
- **The choice of research methods** (e.g. *away from* multi-year, multi-site, multi-treatment, multi-disciplinary, appropriately participatory studies; and *toward* short-term, single-site, simplistic studies amenable to 'rigorous' impact evaluation).
- **The choice of how results are analysed and communicated** (e.g. *away from* a focus on understanding variability, heterogeneity, interactions, contingent outcomes,

site and year effects and 'failure'; and *toward* a focus on averages, main effects and inferred impacts with future scaling-up).

This initial exploration of the dynamics of success making also raises important and perhaps uncomfortable questions about the new generation of funders of agricultural research and development in SSA. The framings and narratives employed by some of these new funders and initiatives (including AGRA) foreground notions of rapid, technology-led transformation, effectiveness, payment by results, public–private partnerships and public engagement. But in so doing, are they in effect setting the bar for agronomic research at an unrealistic height? Are they simply adding more fuel to the fire that already has the success making pot at rapid boil; and if so, will this not force research organisations into even more aggressive success making? In this respect, it is important to note that the Millions Fed success stories relating to SSA are built on agricultural research that was conceived and undertaken before the success making imperative became so strong. Would this same long-term research, with its focus on incremental improvements and uncertain 'impact pathways', be funded if it was proposed for the first time today?

We also find ourselves wondering whether the dynamic of success making has the potential to crowd out any possibility of learning from 'unsuccessful' agronomic research (to allow, or even celebrate, 'successful failures'). With a deeply ingrained disciplinary aversion to 'negative results' and a growing premium on success, the temptation to 'big-up' some results while burying research that cannot easily be construed as successful will undoubtedly grow. Acknowledging and finding a way around this trap will be critical if agronomic research is to remain both a useful and a learning-based enterprise.

It was not our purpose to evaluate or contest the success stories put forward by Millions Fed. We do, however, note that around each of the three stories most closely related to agronomic research in SSA – maize breeding, cassava pest control and soil management – there is a considerable body of scholarship. Given that these literatures address agronomic, social and economic concerns, it should not be surprising that they present mixed and often contradictory pictures. In other words, except perhaps for the cassava pest control example, the research literature does not generally point to the kind of unequivocal success alluded to in the success stories, particularly those aimed at non-professional audiences. Analysis (or even simple recognition) of the ambiguities, of the winners and losers associated with agricultural change, goes against the grain in success making. Nevertheless, it must surely remain a central concern of agronomic and rural development research.

Finally, it will be important to analyse the life cycles of the emerging cohort of success stories, and specifically to ask how they will play out on the ground over time. Perhaps even more critical will be careful analyses of if and how these stories are used to influence policy processes around agriculture and rural development, and development assistance more broadly. Do the success stories become 'evidence' in their own right? Do the 'lessons' that are so carefully woven into these stories become central to ongoing contestation and negotiation around agricultural research policy and practice; and how do they ultimately affect the narratives that drive the politics of these processes?

Notes

1 Parts of this chapter draw on Irving, R. (2010) 'Narrating success: an analysis of the process and politics of success stories in African agricultural development', MA dissertation, Institute of Development Studies, University of Sussex, Brighton.

2 *A Green Revolution for Africa: Fulfilling the Borlaug Dream*, Keynote speech delivered by Dr Akinwumi A. Adesina, Vice President, Alliance for a Green Revolution in Africa (AGRA), *Feeding the Future Borlaug Symposium 2010*, 13–14 July, Addis Ababa, Ethiopia (www.agra-alliance.org/content/news/detail/1172)

3 For a variant – termed 'progress stories' – see www.developmentprogress.org. The interest in development success stories is not limited to African agriculture, but can also be seen in relation to health (Levine 2004, 2007).

4 Operationally this becomes less elegant, with potential successes being judged against criteria relating to importance, scale, time and duration, proven impact and sustainability (Spielman and Pandya-Lorch 2009b: Annex B. Methodology).

5 In this regard the *Failure Report* published annually by the NGO Engineers Without Borders Canada is an interesting initiative: www.ewb.ca/en/whoweare/accountable/failure.html.

6 WARDA (now the Africa Rice Centre or AfricaRice) is the CGIAR-supported research institute where work on the NERICA varieties was initiated.

7 Monty Jones, who was instrumental in the development of NERICA rice, was awarded the World Food Prize in 2004; WARDA received the King Baudouin Award in 2000 for the NERICA work.

8 For example, **DFID** (currently www.dfid.gov.uk/Media-Room/Press/?tab=2; past http://webarchive.nationalarchives.gov.uk/+/www.dfid.gov.uk/aboutdfid/dfidsuccesses.asp); **USAID** (www.usaid.gov/stories/archiveafr.html); **BMGF** (www.gatesfoundation.org/agriculturaldevelopment/Pages/default.aspx); **ICRISAT** (www.icrisat.org/icrisat-impacts.htm); **Africa Bio** (www.africabio.com/pages/farmers-biotech-success.php); **AGRA** (www.agra-alliance.org/section/people/stories); **FARMAfrica** (www.farmafrica.org.uk/cms.php?page=3; www.youtube.com/profile?user=FarmAfrica#p/u/12/zUZYTCAOQHk); **Pioneer** (www.pioneer.com/web/site/portal/menuitem.07de136cde40c7ff21332133d10093a0/)

9 The chapter on maize breeding, for example, contains a full-page box labelled 'The techniques and technologies of breeding better maize' that distinguishes between single-cross hybrids, double-cross hybrids, three-way hybrids, top-cross hybrids and varietal hybrids.

10 IFPRI video: *Millions Fed: Proven Successes in Agricultural Development* (www.youtube.com/watch?v=xHZqtIWi-l8); on 23 August 2010 *YouTube* reported that since 7 November 2009, the *Millions Fed* video had been viewed 2953 times.

11 Two images (pp. 5 and 14) were excluded from this count as the gender of the image subject was not identifiable.

12 One image (p. 13) was excluded from this count as the gender of the image subject was not identifiable.

13 It is interesting to note that none of the three images in the chapter entitled 'Re-greening the Sahel: farmer-led innovation in Burkina Faso and Niger' depicts either people or action (two depict *zai* planting pits and one is a landscape shot).

References

Alene, A.D. (2010) 'Productivity growth and the effects of R&D in African agriculture', *Agricultural Economics*, 41: 233–38.

Alene, A.D., Menkir, A., Ajala, S.O., Badu-Apraku, B., Olanrewaju, A.S., Manyong, V.M. and Ndiaye, A. (2009) 'The economic and poverty impacts of maize research in West and Central Africa', *Agricultural Economics*, 40(5): 535–50.

Baffes, J. and Baghdadli, P. (2007) *The Cotton Sector in West and Central Africa: A Success Story with Challenges Ahead*. World Bank Working Paper No. 108. Washington, DC: World Bank.

Baldwin, K.D.S. (1957) *The Niger Agricultural Project: An Experiment in African Development*. Oxford: Blackwell.

Berry, S. (1993) *No Condition is Permanent: Social Dynamics of Agrarian Change in Sub-Saharan Africa*, Madison, WI: University of Wisconsin Press.

Bourguignon, F. and Sundberg, M. (2007) 'Aid effectiveness – opening the black box', *American Economic Review*, 97(2): 316–21.

CGIAR (2009) *CGIAR Joint Declaration*. Washington, DC: Consultative Group for International Agricultural Research.

Chadha, M.L. and Oluoch, M.O. (2004) 'Vegetable soybean research and development in Africa', in Moscardi, F., Hoffmann-Campo, C.B., Saraiva, O.F., Galerani, P.R., Krzyzanowski, F.C. and Carrão-Panizzi, M.C. (eds) *Proceedings VII World Soybean Research Conference, IV International Soybean Processing and Utilization Conference, III Congresso Brasileiro de Soja (Brazilian Soybean Congress)*, Foz do Iguassu, PR, Brazil, 29 February–5 March, 2004, pp. 921–28.

Collinson, M.P. and Tollens, E. (1994) 'The impact of the International Agricultural Centers – measurement, quantification and interpretation', *Experimental Agriculture*, 30(4): 395–419.

Deacon, D., Pickering, M., Golding, P. and Murdock, G. (1999) *Researching Communications: A Practical Guide to Methods in Media and Cultural Analysis*. New York: Oxford University Press.

Dijkstra, T. (1997) 'Commercial horticulture by African smallholders: a success story from the highlands of Kenya', *Scandinavian Journal of Development Alternatives*, 16(1): 49–74.

Eicher, C.K. (1995) 'Zimbabwe maize-based Green Revolution: preconditions for replication', *World Development*, 23(5): 805–18.

Eicher, C.K. and Rukuni, M. (1994) 'Zimbabwe's agricultural revolution: lessons for southern Africa', in Rukuni, M. and Eicher, C.K. (eds), *Zimbabwe's Agricultural Revolution*. Harare: University of Zimbabwe Publications.

Eisenburg, E. (1984) 'Ambiguity as strategy in organizational communication', *Communication Monographs*, 51(3): 227–42.

Fenichel, A. and Smith, B. (1992) 'A successful failure: integrated rural development in Zambia', *World Development*, 20(9): 1313–23.

Filipovich, J. (2001) 'Destined to fail: forced settlement at the Office du Niger, 1926–45', *Journal of African History*, 42(2): 239–60.

Fischler, M., Wortmann, C.S. and Feil, B. (1999) 'Crotalaria (*C. ochroleuca* G. Don.) as a green manure in maize-bean cropping systems in Uganda', *Field Crops Research*, 61(2): 97–107.

Fiske, J. (1990) *Introduction to Communication Studies* (2nd edn). London: Routledge.

Fortin, E. (2005) 'Reforming land rights: The World Bank and the globalization of agriculture', *Social & Legal Studies*, 14(2): 147–77.

Fowler, R. and Rockstrom, J. (2001) 'Conservation tillage for sustainable agriculture – an agrarian revolution gathers momentum in Africa', *Soil & Tillage Research*, 61(1–2): 93–107.

Gabre-Madhin, E.Z. and Haggblade, S. (2003) *Successes in African Agriculture: Results of an Expert Survey*. MSSD Discussion Paper No. 53. Washington, DC: IFPRI.

——(2004) 'Successes in African agriculture: results of an expert survey', *World Development*, 32(5): 745–66.

Gibbon, P. (1992) 'A failed agenda? African agriculture under structural adjustment with special reference to Kenya and Ghana', *Journal of Peasant Studies*, 20(1): 5096.

Haggblade, S. and Hazell, P. (eds) (2010) *Successes in African Agriculture: Lessons for the Future*. Baltimore, MD: Johns Hopkins University Press.

Hair, J.F., Lamb, C. and McDaniel, C. (2009) *Essentials of Marketing* (6th edn). Mason: South-Western College Publishing.

Harrigan, J. (2003) 'U-turns and full circles: two decades of agricultural reform in Malawi 1981–2000', *World Development*, 31(5): 847–63.

Hogendorn, J.S. and Scott, K.M. (1981) 'The East African Groundnut Scheme: lessons of a large-scale agricultural failure', *African Economic History*, 10: 81–115.

IFPRI (2009) *Our Work: Project Portfolio – Millions Fed Proven Successes in Agricultural Development*. Washington, DC: IFPRI. www.ifpri.org/book-5826/ourwork/programs/2020-vision-food-agriculture-and-environment/millions-fed-intiative

——(2010) *AAEA Honours 'Millions Fed': IFPRI Book Receives Quality of Communications Award*. Washington, DC: IFPRI. www.ifpri.org/blog/aaea-honors-millions-fed

Jacovelli, P.A. (2009) 'Uganda's Sawlog Production Grant Scheme: a success story from Africa', *International Forestry Review*, 11(1): 119–25.

de Janvry, A. and Sadoulet, E. (2010) 'Agriculture for development in Africa: business-as-usual or new departures?', *Journal of African Economies*, 19(Suppl. 2): 7–39.

Kang, B.T., Wilson, G.F. and Sipkens, L. (1981) 'Alley cropping maize (*Zea mays* L.) and Leucaena (*Leucaena leucocephala* Lam.) in southern Nigeria', *Plant and Soil*, 63(2): 165–79.

Keeley, J. and Scoones, I. (2003) *Understanding Environmental Policy Processes: Cases from Africa*. London: Earthscan.

Levine, R. (2004) *Millions Saved: Proven Successes in Global Health*. Washington, DC: Center for Global Development.

——(2007) *Case Studies in Global Health: Millions Saved*. Sudbury, MA: Jones & Bartlett Learning.

Maredia, M.K. and Byerlee, D. (2000) 'Efficiency of research investments in the presence of international spillovers: wheat research in developing countries', *Agricultural Economics*, 22(1): 1–16.

Maredia, M.K. and Eicher, C.K. (1995) 'The economics of wheat research in developing countries: the 100,000,000 dollar puzzle', *World Development*, 23(3): 401–12.

Mortimore, M. (2005) 'Dryland development: success stories from West Africa', *Environment*, 47(1): 8–21.

Mosse, D. (2004a) *Cultivating Development: An Ethnography of Aid Policy and Practice*. London: Pluto Press.

——(2004b) 'Is good policy unimplementable? Reflections on the ethnography of aid policy and practice', *Development and Change*, 35(4): 639–71.

Nalley, L.L., Barkley, A.P. and Featherstone, A.M. (2010) 'The genetic and economic impact of the CIMMYT wheat breeding program on local producers in the Yaqui Valley, Sonora, Mexico', *Agricultural Economics*, 41(5): 453–62.

Orr, A. and Ritchie, J.M. (2004) 'Learning from failure: smallholder farming systems and IPM in Malawi', *Agricultural Systems*, 79(1): 31–54.

Orr, S., Sumberg, J., Erenstein, O. and Oswald, A. (2008) 'Funding international agricultural research and the need to be noticed: a case study of NERICA rice', *Outlook on Agriculture*, 37(3): 159–68.

Plucknett, D.L. (1991) *Saving Lives Through Agricultural Research*. Washington, DC: CGIAR.

Pretty, J., Toulmin, C. and Williams, S. (2011) 'Sustainable intensification in African agriculture', *International Journal of Agricultural Sustainability*, 9(1): 5–24.

Rashotte, L. (2002) 'What does that smile mean? The meaning of nonverbal behaviors in social interaction', *Social Psychology Quarterly*, 65(1): 92–102.

Ravallion, M. (2009) 'Evaluation in the practice of development', *World Bank Research Observer*, 24(1): 29–53.

Reij, C.P. and Smaling, E.M.A. (2008) 'Analyzing successes in agriculture and land management in Sub-Saharan Africa: is macro-level gloom obscuring positive micro-level change?', *Land Use Policy*, 25(3): 410–20.

Roe, E. (1994) *Narrative Policy Analysis: Theory and Practice*. Durham, NC: Duke University Press.

Roper, J. (1999) 'Agroforestry research in Africa – a success story for Canada's foreign aid program', *Forestry Chronicle*, 75(6): 916–916.

Snapp, S.S., Mafongoya, P. L. and Waddington, S. (1998) 'Organic matter technologies for integrated nutrient management in smallholder cropping systems of southern Africa', *Agriculture Ecosystems & Environment*, 71(1/3): 185–200.

Snrech, S. (1995) 'Les transformations de l'agriculture ouest-africaine: evolutions 1960–90. Défis pour l'avenir. Implications pour les pays saheliens', mimeo (Sah/(95)451). Paris: Club du Sahel.

Spielman, D.J. and Pandya-Lorch, R. (2009a) *Highlights from Millions Fed: Proven Successes in Agricultural Development*. Washington, DC: IFPRI.

Spielman, D.J. and Pandya-Lorch, R. (eds) (2009b) *Millions Fed: Proven Successes in Agricultural Development*. Washington, DC: IFPRI.

Stamp, P. (1989) *Technology, Gender, and Power in Africa*. Ottawa: IDRC.

Tarawali, S.A. (1994) 'Evaluating selected forage legumes for livestock and crop production in the subhumid zone of Nigeria', *Journal of Agricultural Science*, 123: 55–60.

Taureck, R. (2006) 'Securitization theory and securitization studies', *Journal of International Relations and Development*, 9: 53–61.

Tiffen, M., Mortimore, M. and Gichuki, F. (1994) *More People, Less Erosion: Environmental recovery in Kenya*. Chichester: John Wiley & Sons.

Toenniessen, G., Adesina, A. and DeVries, J. (2008) 'Building an Alliance for a Green Revolution in Africa', in Kaler, S. and Rennert, O. (eds), *Reducing the Impact of Poverty on Health and Human Development: Scientific Approaches*. Oxford: Blackwell Publishing.

Turner II, B.L., Hyden, G. and Kates, R.W. (eds) (1993) *Population Growth and Agricultural Change in Africa*. Gainesville, FL: University Press of Florida.

Uphoff, N. (2002) *Agroecological Innovations: Increasing Food Production with Participatory Development*. London: Earthscan.

Vuylsteke, D.R., Swennen, R.L. and Ortiz, R. (1993) 'Development and performance of Black Sigatoka-resistant tetraploid hybrids of plantain (*Musa* spp, AAB group)', *Euphytica*, 65(1): 33–42.

Wambugu, F. (1999) 'Why Africa needs agricultural biotech', *Nature*, 400(6739): 15–16.

Webb, P. (1991) 'When projects collapse: irrigation failures in The Gambia from a household perspective', *Journal of International Development*, 3(4): 339–53.

Wiggins, S. (1995) 'Change in African farming systems between the mid-1970s and the mid-1980s', *Journal of International Development*, 7: 807–48.

——(2000) 'Interpreting changes from the 1970s to the 1990s in African agriculture through village studies', *World Development*, 28(4): 631–62.

——(2005) 'Success stories from African agriculture: what are the key elements of success?', *IDS Bulletin*, 36(2): 17–22.

Wopereis, M.C.S., Diagne, A., Rodenburg, J., Sie, M. and Sornado, E.A. (2008) 'Why NERICA is a successful innovation for African farmers: a response to Orr et al from the Africa Rice Center', *Outlook on Agriculture*, 37(3): 169–76.

World Bank (2007a) *Agriculture for Development: World Development Report 2008*. Washington, DC: World Bank.

——(2007b) *World Bank Assistance to Agriculture in Sub-Saharan Africa: An IEG Review*. Washington, DC: World Bank.

——(2010) *Evaluative Lessons from World Bank Group Experience: Growth and Productivity in Agriculture and Agribusiness (Conference Edition)*. Washington, DC: World Bank.

World Bank, FAO and IFAD (2009) *Gender in Agriculture Sourcebook*. Washington, DC: World Bank, Food and Agriculture Organization and International Fund for Agricultural Development.

Zeddies, J., Schaab, R.P., Neuenschwander, P. and Herren, H.R. (2001) 'Economics of biological control of cassava mealybug in Africa', *Agricultural Economics*, 24(2): 209–19.

Zoomers, A. (2005) 'Three decades of rural development projects in Asia, Latin America, and Africa – learning from successes and failures', *International Development Planning Review*, 27(3): 271–96.

12

NULLIUS IN VERBA

Contestation, pathways and political agronomy

John Thompson and James Sumberg

Introduction

This book brings together a collection of case studies highlighting contestation around everyday agronomic research in developing country contexts. In the opening chapter, we assert that the analysis of this contestation – which we term 'political agronomy' – is important because it can reveal the dynamics between the epistemic communities involved in and with agronomic research. These dynamics are becoming increasing discordant and conflicted, which has important implications for the methods, legitimacy and saliency of agronomic research. We build on these insights in this concluding chapter to argue that a 'pathways approach' – with a focus on directionality, distribution and diversity within the innovation processes supported by agronomic research – may be particularly valuable for political agronomy analysis.

Facing up to the politics of agronomy

For most of the twentieth century, agronomy was seen as a technical discipline that focused on the important but largely practical matter of improving crop production. In this context, politics was limited mainly to interactions between the state, which set agricultural policy priorities and funded research; the national research organisations and universities, where agronomists undertook their research; and farming communities. The rise of the neoliberal agenda and emergence of environmental and participation movements from the 1970s onwards served to undermine that comfortable relationship and the unity of purpose on which it was built (see Chapter 1). New actors and interests entered the scene, both from the private sector and from civil society, and began to challenge the 'normal science' of agronomy, question long-established norms and practices, and reorient research priorities. Moreover, these debates have spilled out of peer-reviewed plant and soil science journals onto the internet and other public forums. Some agronomists have been taken aback by these disputes, some of which have been fractious, polarised, and dismissive of their knowledge and expertise. They have also been surprised by the fact that these contestations have introduced normative agendas about values, interests and power into seemingly technical discussions, whereas normative arguments in agronomic research have traditionally been restricted to questions of methods and objectives (e.g. increased productivity).

Some agronomists have responded robustly to these epistemological, ontological and normative challenges, branding those who express concerns about the introduction of new agricultural technologies or agronomic practices as 'naysayers' or 'luddites'; defining arguments in favour of environmental precaution as 'illegitimate' and 'pseudoscience'; and questioning suggestions that agronomy is subject to moral choices about where investments in research are directed and where they are not (Scoones and Thompson 2011; Stirling 2011). Unfortunately, in this way they reject not only what may be irrational, but also entirely reasonable social scepticism concerning potential risks, costs and benefits associated with the everyday practice of agronomic science.

It is ironic that recent debates around agro-ecology, the System of Rice Intensification, Bt cotton, conservation agriculture, drought-tolerant maize for Africa, crop biofortification (e.g. Golden Rice) and NERICA rice have become so emotive. Agronomic science, like science writ large, does not have a monopoly on social rationality. Although imperfectly realised, the principal distinctions between formal science and, say, politics, religion or journalism are arguably social practices of organised scepticism. Experimentation, critical respect for evidence, peer review and open publication help promote reasoned argument. But rational scepticism is important outside as well as inside the social practices of science: hence the motto of Britain's Royal Society, 'nullius in verba' ('take nobody's word for it'), taken from the *Epistles* of Horace, '*Nullius addictus iurare in verba magistri*' ('not in bond to any master' or 'not bound to swear allegiance or subservience to any master') (Sutton 1994; Hunter 1995). Implicit in this motto is a distrust of authority and the conviction that knowledge should be sought through careful observation and not connected to any single school of thought. In other words, take nothing on expert opinion alone – even from learned agronomists.

In open and democratic societies, where all groups – including poor farmers and consumers – have a right to be heard, the setting of priorities for agronomic research and directions for agricultural development result from the interplay of contending visions, interests and values. Agricultural innovations are partly shaped by social and political factors, not simply determined by unfolding technical knowledge (Sumberg 2005; Vanloqueren and Baret 2009). Economic, institutional and political pressures help to push agronomic science in particular directions along particular innovation pathways. The internal dynamics of agronomic science and its associated disciplines are not immune to the politics of knowledge, driven by principle and perspective, but also personality, prejudice and the pursuit of privilege, prestige, profit and power. Critically, intrinsic scientific uncertainties in agronomy underscore the importance of debate on priorities and directions. Closing down debate around agricultural policy and agronomic research can foster cynicism, doubt, polarisation and citizens' resistance to agricultural technologies. The potential of agronomic research as a progressive force is therefore supported – not hindered – by greater tolerance for scepticism and contestation. But this new world of contested agronomy takes some getting used to.

Why is it important for agronomists to take contestation seriously, indeed, to welcome it? It is because the world's agri-food systems are facing increasingly dynamic, uncertain and complex ecological, social and technological challenges (Ingram et al 2010; HLPE 2011). They are also being expected to produce, process and distribute more food, fibre and ecosystem services, and agronomic science is called upon to deliver innovations to support this at an ever-faster rate (Foresight 2011). But it is no longer adequate for research agronomists to deliver these new technologies, practices and processes effectively and efficiently – they must also be mindful of sustainability and equity goals. This means embracing a diversity of perspectives and approaches, acknowledging trade-offs and tensions between them, and engaging with a host of different actors, each with their own interests and agendas. It also means acknowledging the political economy of food and agriculture and how this is both changing and changed by the way food is produced, transformed, consumed and researched across the planet.

A pathways approach to political agronomy

The term 'pathways' is used to refer to the particular directions in which interacting social, technological and environmental systems co-evolve over time (Leach et al 2010). A 'pathways approach' recognises that the social, technological and environmental dimensions of an agri-food system change in interactive and dynamic ways. These interactions can be complex, uncertain and result in non-linear effects, and can create multiple potential pathways, some threatening poor people's livelihoods, others creating new opportunities for sustainability and social justice. A pathways approach challenges conventions that treat technical innovation, social and economic development, and environmental change as separate domains. Within these conventions, interactions, local specificities and contested values are seldom made explicit (and consequently the research framed by them can lead to policy recommendations that prove technically ineffective, politically infeasible, or have adverse impacts on poor people, or the environment, or both) (Smith and Stirling 2010; Smith et al 2010). In contrast, a pathways approach recognises that there are numerous possible pathways and outcomes, which different groups may prioritise differently. What actually happens in practice will depend on the social, economic and institutional arrangements, policy processes and governance regimes that prevail in particular contexts. It is the interaction of potential pathways with these factors that affects whether or not sustainable and pro-poor outcomes are achieved. A pathways approach can be explicitly normative by focusing, for example, on reductions in poverty, improved access to land, water and other productive assets, and enhanced social injustice.

Specific framings and narratives are used by particular actors to promote favoured responses. Shaped by powerful institutions and interests, some of these favoured responses become dominant: these are the motorways that channel the bulk of agricultural research and development efforts. Other, alternative framings, narratives and responses remain as byways and side routes, or simply disappear. To one degree or another, all pathways – dominant (the motorways) and alternative (the side routes) – address the challenges of dynamics, incomplete knowledge and the different aspects of risk, including uncertainty, ambiguity and ignorance (Leach et al 2010).

There are four main reasons why a pathways approach is useful for understanding agronomy in its new age of contestation. First, dynamics, by which we mean the internal feedback loops and time delays that affect the behaviour of complex systems, have often been ignored by agricultural research. The result has been analyses, technologies and recommendations that are underpinned by linear and equilibrium views of the world. By way of contrast, a pathways approach recognises the centrality of dynamics within and between components of an agri-food system, and most importantly the impacts of these dynamics on innovation processes, and vice versa.

Second, governments, businesses and others are increasingly preoccupied with risk, and with the insecurities associated with real and perceived threats, such as climate change and growing water scarcity (Ingram et al 2010). However, much agronomic research in the developing world works with a very partial notion of risk. It concentrates, for example, on risks that can be reliably calculated, controlled and managed, and so discounts other risks for which understandings of possible outcomes are more intractable. Some of these risks involve uncertainty, where the possible outcomes are known but there is no basis for assigning probabilities. Others involve ambiguity, where there is disagreement over the nature of the outcomes, or different groups prioritise concerns that are incommensurable. Finally, some social, technological and ecological dynamics involve ignorance, where 'we don't know what we don't know' (Wynne 1992, 2002), and the possibility of surprise, which cannot be discounted (Stirling 2009, 2011). Whereas conventional approaches to agronomic research are steeped in the use of probability and statistical inference, they are inadequate in situations where other kinds of incomplete knowledge can occur, as is increasingly found in attempts to predict future changes in global agri-food systems (cf. Foresight 2011). To complicate matters further, risk-based scientific advice to policy-makers is also usually presented in aggregated and consensual form: there is always pressure on expert committees or consultative processes, such as the International Assessment of Agricultural Knowledge, Science and Technology for Development (IAASTD) and the Global Conference on Agricultural Research for Development (GCARD), to reach a 'consensus' opinion (Scoones 2009; GFAR 2010). This raises profound questions over what is most useful for policy. Is it a picture asserting an apparent agreement, even where one does not exist? Or would it be more helpful to set out a measured range of contrasting perspectives, explaining underlying reasons for different interpretations of the evidence? Whatever the political pressures for the former, surely the latter is more consistent both with scientific rigour and democratic accountability (Stirling 2010). Thus a wider appreciation of the dimensions of risk and uncertainty is essential if we are to avoid the dangers of creating illusory, control-based approaches to change within agri-food systems.

Third, underlying conventional approaches to agricultural research are often wider assumptions about what constitutes 'development' and 'sustainability'. Specifically, the existence of an objective view of a problem and a singular path to 'progress' are often assumed (Thompson and Scoones 2009). However, different people and groups can have radically different views of both the nature of a problem and the most desirable responses. They bring diverse kinds of knowledge and experiences to bear, often combining informal and more experiential ways of knowing in contrast to the disciplines and procedures associated with formal science (Stirling 2010). Rather than singular notions of progress, it is increasingly clear that there is a multiplicity of possible (and often contested) goals. By paying attention to these divergent views – and the framings and narratives that underpin them – a pathways approach creates opportunities to advance debates about sustainability and connect them more firmly with questions of social justice.

Fourth, while concepts like integration, sustainability and resilience have come into the agricultural mainstream, to some degree casual rhetorical usage has been allowed to mask a lack of real commitment to change. In addition, the notions of integration, sustainability and resilience are being co-opted into managerial and bureaucratic attempts to solve problems that are actually far more complex and political than publicly acknowledged. This has led some to suggest abandoning these terms altogether. However, a pathways approach seeks to recast these as more explicitly normative concepts. Rather than treat them in a general, colloquial sense – implying the combining of parts or components so that they work together or form a whole (integration); the maintenance of unspecified features of systems over time (sustainability); or the ability to maintain form and function (resilience) – a pathways approach is concerned with their specific political implications. Thus, from a pathways perspective, integration relates to a context in which more and less powerful actors negotiate and renegotiate roles and rights to resources to achieve sustainable and equitable agricultural development. The fact that contestation can be expected around each of these makes it essential to recognise the central roles of public deliberation and negotiation.

In short, a pathways approach is a response to the pervasive tendency – supported by professional, institutional and political pressures – for powerful actors and institutions to try to 'close down' around particular 'framings' and commit to pathways that emphasise stability and control. This tendency can, in turn, obscure alternatives that may work better for poor people in particular situations and places. In contrast, addressing the full implications of dynamics and incomplete knowledge requires an 'opening up' to methods and practices that involve flexibility, diversity, adaptation, learning and reflexivity, and an alternative politics of integration and sustainability that highlights and supports the alternative pathways (Millstone et al 2009).

Pathways, systems and political agronomy

As discussed above, competing framings and narratives concerning the challenges facing agriculture and preferred response pathways are promoted by different actors in specific contexts. While any explanation of why some of these framings, narratives and pathways come to dominate while others remain marginal will necessarily be multifaceted, governance – politics shaped by power relations and institutional interests – must be a central consideration. This is at the heart of political agronomy analysis.

To understand the politics around agronomic research and agricultural change, it is useful to recognise three key dimensions of innovation – directionality, distribution and diversity – or the '3-Ds' (STEPS Centre 2010; Stirling 2011). With our interest in political agronomy, we might consider these in relation to four closely related 'systems': the cropping system, the farming system, the innovation system, and the agri-food system. Each of these systems can be characterised as 'socio-technical' or 'socio-ecological', in that they encompass social, institutional and political economic elements on the one hand, and technical and agro-ecological elements on the other – and in some important ways they articulate around agronomic research and practice (Smith and Stirling 2010).

The notion of directionality is important because innovation in agricultural science and technology often exhibits characteristics of path-dependency and lock-in. However, such innovation trajectories are not simple or necessarily linear (e.g. from less to more technologically advanced agricultural practices). Instead, drivers of, and constraints on, the directionality of innovation typically arise from historical, social, institutional and political economy factors. Once directionality is established, however, positive feedback can serve to reinforce the particular innovation pathway taken, as shown in the analysis of maize innovation pathways in Africa (Thompson et al 2010; McCann 2011) and research on biofortification of rice in the Consultative Group on International Agricultural Research (see Chapter 5 in this volume). This is evidence not of inevitability, but of the 'crowding out' of potential alternatives. Likewise, locking-in occurs in the prioritising of certain areas of scientific enquiry over others. The paths taken are far from inevitable: deliberately or blindly, the direction of change is inherently a matter of social choice (STEPS Centre 2010). Thus it is both the promise and the fear of path-dependence and lock-in, reinforced by positive feedback, that puts much of the heat into contemporary debates about the introduction and regulation of GM crops (Glover 2009; van Zwanenberg et al 2011).

Directionality matters in part because it helps to shape the distribution of the various benefits, costs and risks associated with innovation. The fact that descriptors such as 'scale-neutral' and 'pro-poor' are commonly used to refer to agricultural innovations indicates that, to some degree, distributional effects are already within the realm of agronomic research. On the other hand, debates over conservation agriculture (Chapters 2 and 3) and SRI (Chapters 8 and 10) illustrate the level of contestation over distributional issues. Again, the example of GM crops is particularly poignant, as it has been used by some observers to highlight concerns about the changing distribution of autonomy and power among farmers, biotechnology companies, the state and consumers (Scoones 2005; Glover 2009; van Zwanenberg et al 2010).

Finally, it is crucial to focus attention on whether the prevailing forms and levels of diversity (e.g. in crop gene pools, agronomic practices and the resulting landscapes) are increasing or diminishing. In a world of even more momentum toward globalisation, harmonisation and standardisation, diversity can easily be seen as retrograde. However, there are strong arguments for the role of diversity in assuring the resilience and robustness of agri-food systems (Stirling 2007). Only by nurturing a diversity of innovation pathways in agri-food systems can agronomic research contribute to greater food security for the least advantaged and cultivate more sustainable and equitable food futures.

The argument we make here is that by addressing directionality, distribution and diversity, a pathways approach can bring important social, technological and ecological factors – and political actors and interests – into sharp relief. Thus a pathways approach to political agronomy forces us to ask not only, 'Yes or no?', 'How much?', 'How fast?' and 'Who leads?', but also, 'Which way?', 'What else?', 'Who says?' and 'Why?' In so doing, it can help shed new light on contestation around agricultural change in the developing world and the role of agronomic research within it.

References

Foresight (2011) *The Future of Food and Farming: Challenges and Choices for Global Sustainability, Final Project Report.* London: Government Office for Science.

GFAR (2010) *The GFAR RoadMap: Transforming Agricultural Research for Development (AR4D) Systems for Global Impact.* Rome: Global Forum for Agricultural Research.

Glover, D. (2009) *Undying Promise: Agricultural Biotechnology's Pro-Poor Narrative, Ten Years On,* STEPS Working Paper 15. Brighton: STEPS Centre.

HLPE (2011) *Price Volatility and Food Security,* report by the High Level Panel of Experts on Food Security and Nutrition of the Committee on World Food Security. Rome: Food and Agriculture Organization.

Hunter, M. (1995) *Establishing the New Science: The Experience of the Early Royal Society.* Woodbridge, UK: The Boydell Press.

Ingram, J., Ericksen, P. and Liverman, D. (eds) (2010) *Food Security and Global Environmental Change.* London: Earthscan.

Leach, M., Scoones, I. and Stirling, I. (2010) *Dynamic Sustainabilities: Technology, Environment, Social Justic.* London: Earthscan.

McCann, J. (2011) 'The political ecology of cereal seed development in Africa: a history of selection', *IDS Bulletin*, 42(4): 24–35.

Millstone, E., Thompson, J. and Brooks, S. (2009) *Reforming the Global Food and Agriculture System: Towards a Questioning Agenda for the New Manifesto,* STEPS Working Paper 26. Brighton: STEPS Centre.

Scoones, I. (2009) 'The politics of global assessments: the case of the International Assessment of Agricultural Knowledge, Science and Technology for Development (IAASTD)', *Journal of Peasant Studies*, 36(3): 547–71.

——(2005) *Science, Agriculture and the Politics of Policy. The Case of Biotechnology in India.* Hyderabad: Orient Longman.

Scoones, I. and Thompson, J. (2011) 'The politics of seed in Africa's Green Revolution: alternative narratives and competing pathways', *IDS Bulletin*, 42(4): 1–23.

Smith, A., and Stirling, A. (2010) 'The politics of social-ecological resilience and sustainable socio-technical transitions', *Ecology and Society* 15(1): 11. www.ecologyandsociety.org/vol15/iss1/art11

Smith, A., Voss, J.P. and Grin, J. (2010) 'Innovation studies and sustainability transitions: the allure of the multi-level perspective, and its challenges', *Research Policy*, 39: 435–48.

Stirling, A. (2011) 'Pluralising progress: from integrative transitions to transformative diversity', *Environmental Innovation and Societal Transitions*, 1: 82–88.

——(2010) 'Keep it complex', *Nature*, 468 (7327): 1029–31.

——(2009) *Direction, Distribution, Diversity! Pluralising Progress in Innovation, Sustainability and Development*, STEPS Working Paper 32. Brighton: STEPS Centre.

——(2007) 'A general framework for analysing diversity in science, technology and society', *Interface, Journal of the Royal Society*, 4(15): 707–19.

STEPS Centre (2010) *Innovation, Sustainability, Development: A New Manifesto*. Brighton: STEPS Centre.

Sumberg, J. (2005) 'Systems of innovation theory and the changing architecture of agricultural research in Africa', *Food Policy*, 30(1): 21–41.

Sutton, C. (1994) '"Nullius in verba" and "nihil in verbis": public understanding of the role of language in science', *British Journal for the History of Science*, 27(1): 55–64.

Thompson, J., Brooks, S., Morgan, M., Millstone, E., Odame, H., Karin, F. and Adwera, A. (2010) *Maize Security ≠ Food Security? Breaking the "Lock In" to the Dominant Maize Pathway*, STEPS Maize Briefing Paper 4. Brighton: STEPS Centre.

Thompson, J. and Scoones, I. (2009) 'Addressing the dynamics of agri-food systems: an emerging agenda for social science research', *Environmental Science & Policy*, 12(4): 386–97.

Vanloqueren, G. and Baret, P.V. (2009) 'How agricultural research systems shape a technological regime that develops genetic engineering but locks out agroecological innovations', *Research Policy*, 38(6): 971–83.

Wynne, B. (1992) 'Uncertainty and environmental learning: reconceiving science and policy in the preventive paradigm', *Global Environmental Change*, 2(2): 111–27.

——(2002) 'Risk and environment as legitimatory discourses of technology: reflexivity inside out?', *Current Sociology*, 50(3): 459–77.

van Zwanenberg, P., Ely, A. and Smith, A. (eds) (2011) *Regulating Technology: International Harmonization and Local Realities*. London: Earthscan.

INDEX

Page numbers in *italics* denote a table/illustration

For Product Safety Concerns and Information please contact our EU
representative GPSR@taylorandfrancis.com
Taylor & Francis Verlag GmbH, Kaufingerstraße 24, 80331 München, Germany

www.ingramcontent.com/pod-product-compliance
Ingram Content Group UK Ltd.
Pitfield, Milton Keynes, MK11 3LW, UK
UKHW020959180425
457613UK00019B/743